By David Venable

In the Kitchen with David:
QVC's Resident Foodie Presents
Comfort Foods That Take You Home

In the Kitchen with David:
QVC's Resident Foodie Presents
Back Around the Table

QVC's Resident Foodie Presents

Back Around the Table

David Venable

Foreword by Ree Drummond

Ballantine Books
New York

Published in the United States by Ballantine
Books, an imprint of Random House,
a division of Random House LLC, a Penguin
Random House Company, New York.

BALLANTINE and the HOUSE colophon are
registered trademarks of Random House LLC.

Some of the recipes in this work were originally
featured on *In the Kitchen with David* on QVC.

A trade edition of this work has been simultaneously
published in slightly different form by Ballantine Books,
an imprint of Random House, a division of Random
House LLC, a Penguin Random House Company,
New York.

Photographs by Ben Fink Photography, Inc.

ISBN 978-0-8041-7687-3

Printed in the United States of America on acid-free paper

www.ballantinebooks.com

9 8 7 6 5 4 3 2 1

First QVC Edition

Book design by Peter Browne & Joe Pascavage

For courageous and creative home cooks everywhere, who inspire comfort in the kitchen

Contents

Foreword

I first met David when I appeared on his Sunday QVC show, *In the Kitchen with David,* several years ago. A first time cookbook author, I was there to highlight my new book, and I was so nervous that I'd barely slept the night before. Fortunately, my intimidation and trepidation disappeared the moment David walked into the green room to introduce himself. He hugged me and said "Welcome!" I could see in his eyes that he meant it. At that very moment, a friendship was born!

David's warmth and larger-than-life enthusiasm are absolutely contagious, and in his presence, one can't help but feel special and loved. This generosity of spirit most certainly carries over to all aspects of his life, not the least of which is his cooking. Whether he's throwing an elegant dinner party, hosting a couple of friends for Sunday brunch, or just whipping up a simple supper on a weeknight, there's kindness and care behind the food David cooks. In a way, I guess you could say David Venable's food is his ministry! And in that sense, I am a faithful follower.

David's new cookbook, *Back Around the Table,* absolutely knocks my socks off and makes me want to stop everything I'm doing and spend a month in the kitchen cooking and baking every single recipe. As I read through the book for the first time, I thought, *Well, he's done it. He's pretty much touched on every single food I love . . . and then some.*

The recipes in the book are out of this world, and the way they're organized is perfectly illustrative of David's life in the kitchen. The first chapter, "Mix & Mingle," contains the most irresistible party foods—it makes me wish I lived closer to David so I could be one of his regular guests. The Buffalo Chicken Dip, Garlic-Curry Hummus and Sweet Potato Chips, and Mac 'n' Cheese Bites are enough to make anyone drool, but the Chicken

Cheesesteak Egg Rolls? I've never heard of anything so divine. (David, I'll do your dishes if you invite me to your next shindig!) David's brunch recipes are equally irresistible: Eggs Benedict Bread Pudding (wow), Strawberry–Cream Cheese Stuffed French Toast (double wow), and—one I must try immediately— Breakfast Poppers with Grits and Bacon.

I repeat: I want to be a guest at David's house!

For weeknight meals, David shares his delicious and utterly doable versions of Beef Bourguignon, French Onion Soup (with Asiago croutons, no less), along with side dishes and salads that will instantly become part of your recipe rotation. To give light eaters more scrumptious options, his "Light & Bright" section is full of luscious classics, lightened up. The Better-Than-Ever Tuna Casserole is at the top of my list.

Along the way, David provides helpful sidebar tips on topics most of us need help with: the difference among pancetta, prosciutto, and bacon; how to shop for different quantities of cheese; and how to use a pressure cooker, to name a few. He also shares the stories behind the food he makes, what the recipes mean to him, and what memories are tied to certain dishes. David's passion for each dish is evident. To put it succinctly: This cookbook makes you want to cook—no two ways about it!

I've saved the best for last: the desserts in this book. Don't get me started! From Coconut Cream Pie to Cherry Strudel, Mimi's Blackberry Cobbler to Black Bottom Cupcakes, the cookbook ends on a beautifully sweet note. I would expect nothing less from my fellow lover of all things sweet!

For those of you who know David, this cookbook will show you more of what you've grown to love about his food. For those of you who haven't yet been bitten by the David bug, this cookbook will show you everything you need to know. It will reignite your excitement about cooking and encourage you to start making more and more memories around your table.

Love,
Ree Drummond, The Pioneer Woman

Introduction

Isn't it great to reconnect with family and friends? It seems that no matter how much time goes by, we always pick up where we left off. For me, getting back together always centers around food. When I was growing up, some of my fondest memories of family happened around our dinner table. Laughter, tears, arguments, and celebrations all took place when there was great food on the table. As I look back, the table was where we grew stronger as individuals and certainly as a family. And I'd like to think that the food had something to do with it.

My first cookbook, *Comfort Foods That Take You Home,* was a celebration of the classic comfort foods that I've loved all my life. I am so grateful and humbled by the response to that book—it was simply overwhelming.

Comfort Foods That Take You Home resonated with so many people because comfort food is truly universal. Readers and *In the Kitchen with David* viewers alike responded that the recipes and stories rekindled their own memories of home-cooked dishes. Hearing from people all over the country made me realize that comfort food doesn't live in one region. Comfort food is what we remember. It's the food we want to come home to and eat again and again.

Back Around the Table shows how to transform the recipes we love into new and exciting dishes without losing any of their comfort. For instance, I offer my all-time, go-to comfort food mac 'n' cheese as three different possibilities, yet all three remain true to the gooey, cheesy, noodle-y dish I adore. Mac 'n' Cheese Bites are cocktail party treats. Five-Cheese, Fifteen-Minute Stovetop Mac 'n' Cheese is for those weeknights when getting dinner on the table can be a challenge. Lighter Baked Macaroni 'n' Cheese has all the great flavors of the classic casserole but with fewer calories and less fat.

I like to think that each chapter can stand on its own as a mini cookbook. For example, I understand the needs of busy families and have written two chapters that will help get satisfying meals on the table, especially when time and energy are limited. One is devoted to set-and-forget slow cooking, so you can go about your day while the slow cooker does the work. The other chapter is dedicated to using a pressure cooker, so you can get comfort food meals on the table in less than an hour. I even include a chapter with delicious recipes that you can make and eat while watching your waistline.

Everyone's idea of comfort is very personal. It's tied to memories, objects, and, of course, food. Being wrapped up in a warm blanket in front of a crackling fire makes that warm bowl of soup all the more special. We all have a cozy sweatshirt, a soft easy chair, or a memorable dish that makes us feel . . . well . . . comfortable!

With all this in mind, it is clear to me that there are still more comfort food stories to tell. *Back Around the Table* explores new approaches to classic comfort foods, such as transforming Italian wedding soup into a casserole, or combining the flavors of French onion soup into dumplings. This is the kind of comfort food that makes us happy to gather around the table. And stay for a while.

Mix & Mingle

I love to entertain at home, but work, family, and all the other stuff of life sometimes make it difficult to put together a three-course meal for company. So I often invite a group of people over for small bites and cocktails instead. A cocktail party with appetizers lets your guests meet and mingle with new people.

Hosting cocktail parties allows me to spend more time with my guests, because I don't have to always be jumping up and down, clearing plates, and serving the next course. I make sure to include a variety of appetizers. For an all-appetizers party, I allow for five or six hors d'oeuvres per person, plus a dip or two. For a dinner party, I offer two or three appetizers before sitting down to the meal. At an elegant evening, I might offer French Onion Soup Dumplings, Bacon Cheese Straws, and Smoked Salmon Crostini with Avocado Cream accompanied by flutes of sparkling wine. If vegetarians are coming, I make sure to include Garlic-Curry Hummus and Sweet Potato Chips or Spinach-Feta Cups. A holiday party means more people of all ages and more food. Mini Crab Cakes with Old Bay Mayonnaise; my take on my mom's Sausage Party Bites; some Warm Bacon-Cheese Dip; and super creamy, super cheesy Mac 'n' Cheese Bites offer something for everyone. Many of these recipes—Potato Pierogies and Chicken Cheesesteak Egg Rolls, for example—can be made ahead and frozen. That way you'll always have small bites of comfort at the ready for a fun and festive gathering.

Buffalo Chicken Dip `FAN FAVORITE`

Buffalo chicken wings are a favorite of mine, especially when dining out. Once I see them on a menu, I usually go no further. Making them at home is more of a commitment than I usually have time for. Honestly, I'd rather be with my guests than frying wings in the kitchen. So, whether it's movie night, game day, or party time, serve this warm, make-ahead dip that includes all the quintessential flavors of Buffalo chicken wings in one bowl. Surround it with an assortment of dippers, including celery and carrot sticks, broccoli florets, and tortilla, pita, or bagel chips. This dip is so good, I could lick the bowl. And I do. When no one is looking.

Makes 6 cups

3 8-ounce packages cream cheese, softened

¾ cup bottled ranch dressing

¾ cup bottled blue cheese dressing

1 cup Buffalo wing sauce

2 store-bought rotisserie chickens, skin and bones removed and discarded, finely shredded

3 cups (12 ounces) shredded Monterey Jack

Tortilla chips and carrot and celery sticks

Preheat the oven to 375°F.

Put the cream cheese, ranch dressing, blue cheese dressing, and wing sauce in a bowl. Whisk until creamy. Fold in the shredded chicken and 1½ cups of the shredded cheese.

Spread the mixture into a 3½-quart baking dish, cover, and bake for 20 minutes.

Remove the dip from the oven and sprinkle the remaining 1½ cups cheese on top. Bake, uncovered, for an additional 15 minutes, or until hot and bubbly. Let the dip cool for 10 minutes, then serve with tortilla chips, carrot sticks, and/or celery sticks.

Warm Bacon–Cheese Dip

To me, cheese and bacon are two of God's most perfect foods, so I'm always looking for new ways to combine them. When you serve this rich, comforting dip in a hollowed-out bread bowl, the presentation alone says, "Party time!" I like the mix of cheeses suggested below, but if you have a favorite blend, go for it. This dip lends itself well to most kinds of cheeses. For the bread bowl, I recommend a sourdough loaf, but any sturdy bread, like pumpernickel or rye, will work, too. It does take one hour for the dip to get hot all the way through, but trust me; it's definitely worth the wait.

Makes 3½ to 4 cups

1 pound bacon slices, softened

1 cup chopped Vidalia onions

1 8-inch round sourdough loaf

1 8-ounce package cream cheese, at room temperature

1 cup sour cream

⅓ cup mayonnaise

1 cup (4 ounces) shredded Monterey Jack

¾ cup (3 ounces) shredded yellow Cheddar

3 tablespoons Worcestershire sauce

1 scallion, thinly sliced, for garnish

Line a baking sheet with aluminum foil. Arrange the bacon in a single layer on the prepared baking sheet. Put the baking sheet in the cold oven. Turn on the oven to 400°F. Bake until the bacon is crispy, 10 to 15 minutes. Remove the bacon from the pan and drain on paper towels. Save 2 to 3 tablespoons bacon drippings to sauté the onions. Reduce the oven temperature to 375°F. Once the bacon is cool, chop it into small pieces. Reserve ¼ cup chopped bacon to garnish the dip.

While the bacon is cooking, use a serrated knife to slice off the top quarter of the bread. Pull out most of the soft interior, leaving a 1-inch thickness on the inside. Cut the interior bread into cubes, place in a single layer on a baking sheet, and lightly toast in the oven for 8 to 10 minutes.

Heat the reserved bacon drippings in a skillet over low heat. Add the onions and cook, stirring occasionally, until caramelized, 25 to 30 minutes. Remove from the heat and drain off any excess oil.

While the onions are cooking, whisk together the cream cheese, sour cream, mayonnaise, ¾ cup of the Monterey Jack, ½ cup of the Cheddar, and the

Worcestershire sauce in a bowl until smooth. Add the chopped bacon and the onions to the cream cheese mixture, stirring well. Spoon the dip into the hollowed-out bread. Wrap the bread with aluminum foil, place it on a baking sheet, and bake for 45 minutes. Remove the foil from the bread bowl and sprinkle the top with the remaining ¼ cup Monterey Jack, the remaining ¼ cup Cheddar, the reserved ¼ cup chopped bacon, and the scallion. Bake for about 15 minutes, or until hot and bubbly. Serve with the toasted bread cubes.

Garlic-Curry Hummus and Sweet Potato Chips FAN FAVORITE

This recipe combines flavors and textures from two different regions of the world. I add some Indian-inspired cumin and curry powder to the Middle Eastern hummus combination of chickpeas and tahini. Instead of pita, I make sweet potato chips to balance the dip's zestiness. Another option is to arrange a platter of zucchini coins, baby squash, cherry tomatoes, asparagus, bell peppers, snap peas, and green beans with a bowl of the hummus in the center.

Makes 3 cups

Hummus

2 15-ounce cans chickpeas, drained and rinsed

½ cup tahini

½ cup extra-virgin olive oil

½ cup fresh lemon juice

2 garlic cloves

1½ teaspoons kosher salt

1 teaspoon ground cumin

1 teaspoon curry powder

¼ teaspoon cayenne

¼ cup chopped fresh cilantro (optional)

Sweet Potato Chips

Vegetable oil spray

3 sweet potatoes, peeled and thinly sliced

Kosher salt and freshly ground black pepper

To make the hummus, combine the chickpeas, tahini, olive oil, lemon juice, garlic, salt, cumin, curry powder, cayenne, and cilantro (if using) in a food processor. Purée until smooth and transfer to a serving dish.

To make the chips, preheat the oven to 350°F. Line a baking sheet with parchment paper and lightly spray with vegetable oil spray.

Arrange the sweet potatoes in a single layer on the baking sheet. Spray the potatoes with the vegetable oil spray and sprinkle with salt and black pepper. Bake for about 10 minutes, or until crisp. Serve the chips with the hummus.

Bacon Cheese Straws

Down South, cheese straws were served at every cocktail party and wedding reception I attended. I decided that it's time to dress up these bites and, trust me, if there's a way to get bacon and cheese into something, I will do it. Cheese straws are traditionally made by pushing dough through a cookie press with a star tip. Who has time for that? I use frozen puff pastry to save time and press the filling into the dough. Once the straws are filled and cut, freeze them for about one hour before baking.

Makes 18 to 24

Vegetable oil spray

1 pound sliced apple wood–smoked bacon

1 8-ounce package cream cheese, at room temperature

1¼ cups (5 ounces) shredded mozzarella

½ cup (2 ounces) grated Parmigiano-Reggiano

½ teaspoon garlic powder

¼ teaspoon freshly ground black pepper

1 large egg

1 teaspoon whole milk

All-purpose flour, for rolling out puff pastry

1 package (2 sheets) frozen puff pastry, thawed according to package directions

Line a baking sheet with aluminum foil. Line another baking sheet with parchment paper. Spray the parchment paper with vegetable oil spray.

Arrange the bacon on the foil-lined baking sheet—no overlapping. Put the baking sheet in the cold oven. Turn on the oven to 400°F. Partially cook the bacon for 8 to 10 minutes. Drain the bacon on paper towels, but reserve the bacon fat. Let cool and chop the bacon into tiny bits.

Using a fork, mix together the cream cheese, mozzarella, Parmesan, bacon bits, garlic powder, and pepper in a bowl. Whisk together the egg and milk in a small bowl.

On a floured cutting board, roll out the puff pastry sheets to a ¹⁄₁₆-inch thickness. Brush the puff pastry with the bacon fat. Spread the bacon-cheese mixture over half of the pastry. Fold the other side over the top of the bacon-cheese mixture. Using a rolling pin, roll the two sides together so the cheese-bacon mixture is incorporated into the puff pastry. Cut into ½-inch strips.

Starting at one end, twist each cheese straw several times and place it flat on the parchment-lined baking sheet. Repeat with the remaining straws. Press both ends of each straw onto the baking sheet to keep it from untwisting as it bakes. Brush each straw lightly with the egg wash. Place the baking sheet in the freezer for 1 hour. Don't skip this step. Freezing the cheese straws ensures that they will hold their shape and won't untwist. It is best that the cheese straws are baked from frozen.

Preheat the oven to 400°F. Bake for 13 to 16 minutes, until the cheese straws puff and turn a light golden brown. Remove from the oven and let cool for about 5 minutes before serving.

Spinach-Feta Cups FAN FAVORITE

Hosting a cocktail party with lots of hors d'oeuvres is one of my favorite ways to entertain. I move the chairs away from the dining table and put out platters and bowls with all kinds of finger foods and dips. Since I usually don't have time to make intricate hors d'oeuvres, I serve small bites that can be made ahead or put together in minutes. Spanakopita, a Greek savory pie with a filling of spinach, feta, and herbs wrapped in phyllo dough, was my inspiration for these hors d'oeuvres. But instead of fussing with layers of phyllo, I spoon a spinach-feta filling—it can be made a day or two ahead—into frozen mini phyllo cups and bake them for twenty minutes.

Makes 30

30 frozen mini fluted phyllo shells

1 tablespoon extra-virgin olive oil

½ large onion, chopped

1 garlic clove, minced

3 scallions, thinly sliced

1 10-ounce package frozen chopped spinach, thawed and squeezed dry

¼ cup ricotta cheese

1 large egg, beaten

2 tablespoons chopped fresh parsley

1 tablespoon chopped fresh dill

½ teaspoon kosher salt

½ teaspoon freshly ground black pepper

Generous pinch of ground nutmeg

1 cup (4 ounces) crumbled feta cheese

Preheat the oven to 350°F.

Arrange the mini phyllo shells ½ inch apart on 2 baking sheets. Heat the olive oil in a skillet over medium heat. Add the onion and garlic and cook until the onion is translucent, 5 to 6 minutes. Add the scallions and toss to combine. Remove the pan from the heat.

Put the spinach, ricotta, egg, parsley, dill, salt, pepper, nutmeg, and cooked onion mixture in a large bowl. Using a rubber spatula, mix well. Fold in the feta.

Fill each mini shell with a generous tablespoon of the spinach mixture. Bake for about 20 minutes, or until they are hot and cooked through. Serve warm.

Mac 'n' Cheese Bites

If I've said it once, I've said it a million times: When it comes to mac 'n' cheese, I'm the kid who never grew up. I could eat it three times a day, especially when it's bite size. My favorite cheese combination here includes a mix of Fontina, Cheddar, and Gouda, but go ahead and substitute your favorites. These bites will disappear in no time at your next party.

Makes 36

Vegetable oil spray

1 tablespoon plus 2 teaspoons kosher salt

8 ounces elbow macaroni

1 tablespoon unsalted butter

1 tablespoon plus ½ cup all-purpose flour

1 cup whole milk, warmed, plus 2 tablespoons

1 cup (4 ounces) shredded chipotle Gouda

2½ cups (10 ounces) shredded yellow sharp Cheddar

¾ cup sour cream

6 ounces cooked ham, cut into small dice

1 cup (4 ounces) shredded Italian Fontina

½ teaspoon white pepper

½ teaspoon freshly ground black pepper

3 large eggs

1½ cups panko bread crumbs

Canola oil, for frying

Spray a 9 x 13-inch baking dish with vegetable oil spray.

Bring a large pot of water to a boil. Add 1 tablespoon of the salt and the macaroni and cook until tender but still al dente. Drain the macaroni in a colander.

Make a roux by melting the butter in a large saucepan over medium heat. Whisk in 1 tablespoon of the flour and cook, whisking constantly, for 2 minutes. Whisk in the warm milk and continue stirring until the sauce thickens slightly. Add the Gouda and 1 cup of the Cheddar and stir until melted.

Pour the cooked macaroni, cheese sauce, sour cream, ham, 1½ cups Cheddar, the Fontina, 1 teaspoon salt, and the white pepper into a large bowl and mix well. Taste for seasoning. Pour the macaroni and cheese into the prepared dish. Cover with plastic wrap, press down, and refrigerate for at least 2 to 3 hours or overnight, until the macaroni is chilled, firm, and set.

Mix the remaining ½ cup flour, 1 teaspoon salt, and the black pepper together in a shallow bowl. In another shallow bowl, whisk the eggs and the remaining 2 tablespoons milk together. Put the bread crumbs in a third shallow bowl. Remove the chilled macaroni and cheese from the refrigerator and slice into 36 pieces. Roll each piece into a 1- to 1½-inch ball, about the size of a golf ball.

Dredge each ball in the flour mixture, dip into the beaten egg mixture, and then dredge in the bread crumbs, making sure to coat completely during each step. Refrigerate the bites while heating the canola oil for deep-frying. (The mac 'n' cheese bites can be wrapped and frozen for 1 month.)

Heat the oil in a deep fryer to 350°F. Or clip a deep-frying thermometer to the side of a heavy deep pot. Add 2 inches of oil and heat on medium-high until the temperature reads 350°F. Using a slotted spoon, add 8 to 10 balls to the hot oil and fry until golden brown, about 3 minutes, turning them halfway through cooking. (Cook the bites in batches or the oil won't stay hot and they will be soggy rather than crisp.) Using a slotted spoon, remove the fried bites to paper towels. Fry the remaining bites. Serve immediately.

Roux Versus Slurry

There are several ways to thicken sauces, soups, and gravies. Sometimes I use a roux, other times I prefer a slurry. So, what's the difference between them?

The first step in cooking many dishes like the Mac 'n' Cheese Bites (page 13) or Lighter Baked Macaroni 'n' Cheese (page 212) is to *start* with a roux. A roux is equal parts of flour and fat (butter, bacon drippings, or oil) that is slowly cooked in a pan until smooth and thick. Hot liquid (juice, milk, or broth) is whisked into the roux in stages and simmered until the sauce is thick and the raw flour taste is undetectable.

A slurry, sometimes called a whitewash, is added to hot ingredients at the *end* of cooking a dish. To make a slurry, whisk together equal amounts of a thickener such as flour or cornstarch with cold broth or another liquid in a bowl until dissolved. Whisk the slurry into the hot liquid or food and cook until thickened. If you add flour or cornstarch directly to a hot mixture, it will clump. Always dissolve either thickener in cold liquid. When mixing a slurry, be sure to whisk it well so there are no lumps. For example, slurries are used as a quick thickener in Honey Dijon Chicken (page 92) and Mimi's Blackberry Cobbler (page 255).

Potato Pierogies with Sour Cream–Chive Sauce

When I was a TV news anchor and reporter at WTAJ in Altoona, Pennsylvania, I was assigned to cover the Cambria City Ethnic Festival. Lucky me! It was the first time I ate a pierogi, and I didn't stop with just one. I was determined to learn to make these pillowy pockets of dough filled with mashed potatoes, onions, chives, and cheese and served with some tangy sour cream. Since this recipe makes a lot of pierogies, freeze them on a baking sheet, put them in plastic bags, and reheat as many as you need at a time in the oven when guests come over.

Makes 50 to 60

Filling

1½ pounds Yukon gold potatoes, peeled and cut into quarters

2 tablespoons plus ½ teaspoon kosher salt

¼ cup sour cream

⅓ cup half-and-half, warmed

3 tablespoons unsalted butter, melted

¼ teaspoon white pepper

1 cup (4 ounces) shredded white sharp Cheddar

2 tablespoons minced fresh chives

Dough

4 cups all-purpose flour, plus more for kneading

2 teaspoons kosher salt

1 cup sour cream

2 large eggs

2 large egg yolks

2 tablespoons (¼ stick) unsalted butter, melted

1 teaspoon canola oil

Pierogies

2 tablespoons kosher salt

2 tablespoons canola oil

4 medium white onions, cut in half and thinly sliced

4 to 8 tablespoons (½ to 1 stick) unsalted butter

2 cups sour cream

¼ cup minced chives

To make the filling, fill a large pot half full with water. Add the potatoes and 2 tablespoons of the salt and bring to a boil. Reduce the heat and simmer the potatoes until they can be pierced with a fork, 20 to 25 minutes. Drain the potatoes and put in the bowl of a standing mixer. Add the sour cream, half-and-half, melted butter, the remaining ½ teaspoon salt, and the white pepper and blend on medium speed until the potatoes are mashed and smooth. Using a rubber spatula, fold in the cheese and chives. Cover and refrigerate while making the dough.

To make the dough, mix together the flour and salt in a bowl and make a well in the center. Whisk together the sour cream, eggs, egg yolks, butter, and canola oil in another bowl. Pour the sour cream mixture into the flour mixture and, using a fork, blend until well combined and the dough holds together. Flour a work surface and turn the dough out onto it. Using your hands, knead the dough until a ball forms and all the ingredients are just blended. Do not overknead or the dough will become tough. Divide the dough into 2 balls and cover with a towel. Let the dough rest in a cool spot, but not the refrigerator, for 20 minutes.

To make the pierogies, take ½ tablespoon of the potato mixture and shape into a 1-inch ball. Set the ball on a baking sheet and repeat until the mixture is used up.

Roll out 1 ball of dough on a floured work surface to a ⅛-inch thickness. Using a 3-inch biscuit cutter, cut out as many circles as possible. Place 1 potato ball in the center of each circle. Fill a dish with water and, using your finger, rub the edges of each circle with water. Fold the dough over the potato ball to form a half moon. Pinch the edges of the dough together. Repeat with the remaining circles. Place the pierogies on a tray lined with parchment paper and cover them with a towel to prevent them from drying out. Repeat with the remaining dough and potato balls. Cover and refrigerate for 30 minutes. (The pierogies can be frozen on a baking sheet, then transferred to plastic bags for 1 month.)

Bring a large pot of water and the salt to a boil. Lower 5 or 6 pierogies into the boiling water. Boil for 4 to 5 minutes, stirring occasionally with a wooden spoon to prevent them from sticking together. Using a slotted spoon, transfer the pierogies to a colander and drain thoroughly. Bring the water back to a boil and repeat until all the pierogies have been boiled.

Heat the canola oil over medium-high heat in a large skillet. Add the onions and sauté until translucent, 5 to 6 minutes. Using a slotted spoon, remove the onions to a bowl. Melt 2 tablespoons of the butter in the same skillet. In 2 or 3 batches, add the pierogies to the pan and lightly brown on both sides. Add more butter as necessary when browning the remaining pierogies. Return the onions and pierogies to the skillet and toss lightly for 1 to 2 minutes. Mix the sour cream and chives together in a bowl. Serve the pierogies with the onions and the chive sauce.

French Onion Soup Dumplings `FAN FAVORITE`

Inspired by some French onion soup dumplings I devoured at a trendy restaurant on New York City's Lower East Side, I couldn't wait to get home and make my own version. These have all the classic hallmarks of this warming soup—caramelized onions, melted cheese, and all the right seasonings—tucked into bite-size, juicy pouches made with wonton wrappers. The dumplings are fried, then browned in the oven with a sprinkle of Gruyère for that traditional touch.

Makes 50

3 large egg yolks

3 large eggs

2 cups panko bread crumbs

2 tablespoons extra-virgin olive oil

½ red onion, thinly sliced

½ white onion, thinly sliced

1 8-ounce package cream cheese, cubed and at room temperature

1 1.4-ounce envelope French onion soup mix

¼ teaspoon kosher salt

¼ teaspoon freshly ground black pepper

Canola oil, for frying

1 package (50) wonton wrappers

2 cups (8 ounces) shredded Gruyère

½ bunch of fresh chives, finely chopped

Place the egg yolks in a shallow bowl and beat lightly. Place the whole eggs in another bowl and beat lightly. Put the bread crumbs in another bowl.

Pour the olive oil into a skillet over low heat. Add the red and white onions to the skillet and cook, stirring frequently, until caramelized, 25 to 30 minutes. Add the cream cheese, onion soup mix, ⅛ teaspoon of the salt, and ⅛ teaspoon of the pepper to the skillet, stirring until the mixture is smooth and creamy, about 3 minutes. Pour the mixture into a bowl and let it sit at room temperature for 1 hour.

Once the mixture has cooled, clip a deep-frying thermometer to the side of a heavy deep pot. Add 2 inches canola oil to the pot and slowly heat the oil to 350°F.

While the oil is heating, lay several wonton wrappers out on a flat surface. Using a pastry brush, coat one side of a wonton wrapper with some egg yolk. Place 1 to 1½ teaspoons cheese mixture in the middle of the wonton. Bring all four corners of the wonton up. Gently press the edges together to seal the pouch. Repeat with the remaining wontons, working in batches until all the cheese mixture is used. *(Uncooked dumplings can be frozen on a baking sheet, then transferred to plastic bags for 1 month.)*

Beat the whole eggs again until frothy. Dip each dumpling into the beaten eggs and then dip into the bread crumbs, making sure to coat evenly. Using a slotted spoon, lower 5 dumplings into the hot oil and cook for 1 minute, or until golden brown. Remove the dumplings from the oil and place them on paper towels to drain. Season each batch with the remaining salt and pepper. Transfer them to an aluminum foil–lined baking sheet.

While the dumplings are cooking, preheat the broiler. Top each dumpling with a pinch of Gruyère. Place the dumplings under the broiler until the cheese starts to melt, about 1 minute. Remove the dumplings from the oven and garnish each with a pinch of chopped chives before serving.

Onions: The Savory and the Sweet

Onions, believe it or not, are naturally sweet. All they need is some heat and a little fat to coax out their natural sugars. So many recipes call for onions to be soft, translucent, or caramelized. Those same recipes give different directions and amounts of time to get the desired results. So, armed with pounds of onions, I went into my kitchen and timed how long it took me to cook onions to different stages. The results: It all depends on the kind of skillet used (the wider the better), the type of fat used (butter, oil, or bacon fat), and the level of heat (the lower the heat the better).

My go-to cooking onions are the yellow, also called Spanish. Try red, sweet (Vidalia and Walla Walla), or white onions. Slice, dice, or mince the onions to the same size, so they cook evenly.

Soft Onions
Cook the onions in a skillet with some fat over low heat for 4 to 5 minutes.

Translucent Onions
Cook the onions in a skillet with some fat over low heat for 5 to 6 minutes. They will turn from bright, opaque white to a paler white.

Caramelized Onions
Cook the onions in a skillet with some fat over low heat. Toss the onions to coat. As they cook, the onions will give up a lot of water that will soon evaporate. Cook the onions, tossing frequently, until they are meltingly tender and a deep, even brown, 25 to 30 minutes. If the onions start to burn, reduce the heat even more. Burned onions taste like … burned onions. Don't add any sugar—that's cheating and unnecessary. *Keep a container of caramelized onions in the refrigerator up to 5 days or in the freezer for 1 month to use in omelets, casseroles, and soups and on sandwiches or pizzas.*

Chicken Cheesesteak Egg Rolls FAN FAVORITE

You can't walk down South Street without being drawn in by the aromas of this local Philadelphia favorite. Since I live and work in the shadow of Philadelphia, I want to give a shout-out to the classic cheesesteak with these reinvented chicken egg rolls. If your guests have an appetite like mine, be sure to double the recipe.

Makes 8

2 teaspoons canola oil, plus more for frying

⅓ cup finely chopped onion

⅓ cup finely chopped red or green bell pepper, or a combination

1 9-ounce package Steak-umm Chicken Breast Sandwich Steaks

¼ teaspoon kosher salt

¼ teaspoon freshly ground black pepper

6 ounces Velveeta, cut into ⅛-inch cubes

8 egg roll wrappers

Heat 1 teaspoon of the canola oil in a skillet over medium heat. Add the onion and bell pepper and sauté until soft, 4 to 5 minutes. Transfer the vegetables to a bowl.

Add the remaining 1 teaspoon oil to the skillet and raise the heat to medium-high. Add the chicken to the skillet. Season with the salt and pepper. Cook the chicken until brown, 5 to 7 minutes. Stir, breaking up the chicken into smaller pieces. Transfer the cooked chicken to the bowl of onion and bell pepper. Toss to evenly distribute and then refrigerate until cool. When the ingredients are cool, stir in the Velveeta.

Preheat the oven to 350°F. Clip a deep-frying thermometer to the side of a heavy deep pot. Add 2 inches canola oil to the pot and slowly heat the oil to 350°F.

To assemble the egg rolls, position 1 wrapper on a work surface like a diamond. Place 2½ tablespoons filling close to the corner nearest you and spread it up toward the middle. Using a pastry brush, brush the edges with a little water. Fold the corner closest to you up over the mixture, fold the left and right corners toward the center, and continue to roll. Brush the final corner with water to help seal the egg roll. *(The egg rolls can be frozen for up to 1 month before frying.)*

Using a slotted spoon, lower 4 egg rolls into the hot oil and cook until golden brown, 3 to 5 minutes, turning them halfway while frying. Transfer the cooked egg rolls to a paper towel–lined plate to drain. Fry the remaining egg rolls and serve hot.

Coconut Shrimp with Spicy Mango Dipping Sauce

When it comes to the perfect seafood appetizer, nothing disappears faster at a party than a pile of coconut shrimp. Grown-ups love the shrimp's hint of spice, kids love their sweetness, and everyone loves their crunch. For a tropical treat, pair these with Mango Mojitos (page 67) for the adults and mango juice with a splash of sparkling water for the young ones.

Makes 48

Dipping Sauce

2 mangos, peeled and diced

½ cup mango chutney

½ cup coconut milk

3 tablespoons sweet Thai chili sauce

1 small jalapeño, seeded and finely chopped

Shrimp

2 pounds jumbo (21/25 count) shrimp, tails on, peeled and deveined

½ cup all-purpose flour

¼ teaspoon cayenne

½ teaspoon kosher salt

3 large egg whites

¾ cup coconut milk

1 7-ounce package sweetened flaked coconut

⅔ cup panko bread crumbs

Canola oil, for frying

To make the dipping sauce, combine the mangos, chutney, coconut milk, chili sauce, and jalapeño in a blender. Blend on medium speed until combined well. Pour into a bowl.

To make the shrimp, rinse and drain the shrimp in a colander and dry them thoroughly on paper towels. Line a baking sheet with parchment or wax paper. Combine the flour, cayenne, and salt in a shallow bowl. Whisk together the egg whites and coconut milk in a second shallow bowl. Combine the coconut flakes and bread crumbs in a third shallow bowl.

Holding a shrimp by the tail, dredge it in the flour mixture, shaking off any excess flour. Dip the shrimp into the egg mixture to coat thoroughly, allowing any excess to drip off. Dredge the shrimp in the coconut mixture, being sure to coat completely. Place the shrimp on the prepared baking sheet. Repeat with the remaining shrimp. Cover with plastic wrap and refrigerate the shrimp for 20 minutes.

Clip a deep-frying thermometer to the side of a heavy deep pot. Add 3 inches canola oil to the pot and slowly heat the oil to 350°F. Using a slotted spoon, add 5 or 6 shrimp to the hot oil and fry until golden brown, 2 to 3 minutes, turning them halfway through cooking. Using a slotted spoon, remove the cooked shrimp to a wire rack or paper towels. Between batches, use the slotted spoon to remove any excess coconut from the oil and discard. Serve hot with the dipping sauce.

Mini Crab Cakes with Old Bay Mayonnaise

Baltimore's Inner Harbor is known for its cultural attractions, nightlife, and, most of all, restaurants. As you wander around, you can't help but notice the smell of fresh seafood, especially Maryland crab cakes. All crab cakes start with the lump meat of blue crabs pulled from the waters of the Chesapeake Bay. From there, everyone has his or her own idea of what belongs—or doesn't—in Maryland-style crab cakes. My bite-size version is paired with a dipping sauce of homemade mayonnaise and Old Bay Seasoning, an essential ingredient in this Maryland tradition.

Makes 30 to 32

Crab Cakes

Vegetable oil spray

½ cup mayonnaise

1 large egg, lightly beaten

Zest and juice of 1 lemon

½ teaspoon kosher salt

¼ teaspoon white pepper

¼ cup panko bread crumbs

1½ teaspoons Old Bay Seasoning

2 tablespoons finely chopped red onion

2 tablespoons finely chopped fresh parsley

2 tablespoons finely chopped jarred roasted red bell peppers

1 pound lump crabmeat, picked over for shells

Old Bay Mayonnaise

3 large egg yolks

1 tablespoon plus 1 teaspoon Old Bay Seasoning

1 tablespoon white wine vinegar

1 tablespoon water

1½ cups canola oil

2 teaspoons fresh lemon juice

To make the crab cakes, preheat the oven to 375°F. Line a baking sheet with parchment paper. Spray the parchment paper with vegetable oil spray.

Put the mayonnaise, egg, lemon zest, lemon juice, salt, white pepper, bread crumbs, Old Bay, red onion, parsley, and bell peppers in a bowl and mix. Using a spatula, carefully fold the crabmeat into the mayonnaise mixture, taking care not to break up the crabmeat too much. Do not overmix. Using your hands, form the crab mixture into 30 to 32 cakes. Arrange the crab cakes on the prepared baking sheet.

(The crab cakes can be wrapped well in plastic wrap and aluminum foil and frozen for up to 1 month.) Bake the crab cakes for 10 to 12 minutes, until lightly brown. (If frozen, bake for 12 to 15 minutes.)

To make the mayonnaise, put the egg yolks, Old Bay, vinegar, and water into a blender. Blend well to combine. With the blender running, gradually add the canola oil in a steady stream and blend until the oil is incorporated and the mayonnaise becomes thick. Transfer the mayonnaise to a bowl and whisk in the lemon juice. *(Cover and refrigerate the mayonnaise for up to 3 days.)* Serve the hot crab cakes with the mayonnaise on the side.

Beef and Bean Tostados

Boy, do I love Mexican food. It's spicy, satisfying, and oh so comforting. Who knew there could be so many ways to combine corn, beans, and chiles with cheese and beef? Tostados are lightly toasted or fried tortillas that make a great base for all kinds of toppings. I make mine with beef sautéed with onions and a bit of chipotle pepper as well as some refried beans. The filling can be made ahead and reheated—just add a little water to thin out the filling—while the tortillas are cooking. Offer bowls of shredded lettuce and cheese, chopped tomatoes, red onion, sour cream, and some lime wedges. For parties, cut the tostados into quarters, or serve them whole as a first course or entrée.

Makes 8

Beef

2 tablespoons canola oil

1 cup finely chopped Spanish onion

1½ pounds 80% lean ground beef

1 canned chipotle pepper in adobo sauce, chopped

1 teaspoon kosher salt

Tostados

½ cup canola oil, or more

8 4- to 6-inch corn tortillas

About 1 teaspoon kosher salt

Refried Beans

2 tablespoons bacon fat or canola oil

½ cup finely chopped Spanish onion

2 garlic cloves, minced

1 canned chipotle pepper in adobo sauce, chopped

2 15-ounce cans pinto beans, rinsed and drained

1 teaspoon kosher salt

1 cup water

Toppings

¼ head of iceberg lettuce, shredded

1 cup finely diced fresh plum tomatoes

1 cup (4 ounces) shredded pepper Jack

½ cup sour cream

¼ cup coarsely chopped fresh cilantro

¼ cup finely minced red onion

1 lime, cut into wedges

Tabasco chipotle pepper sauce

Preheat the oven to 200°F. Line a baking sheet or a large platter with paper towels.

　　To make the beef, heat the canola oil in a skillet over medium-high heat. Add the onion and sauté until soft, 4 to 5 minutes. Add the beef and cook until brown, stirring occasionally, 8 to 10 minutes. Drain most of the oil, leaving the beef and 1 to 2 tablespoons of fat in the skillet. Add the chipotle pepper and salt to the skillet and cook for 2 to 3 minutes over medium heat. Cover the pan until ready to serve.

To make the tostados, heat the canola oil in another skillet over medium heat. Using tongs, place a tortilla in the oil and cook until lightly brown, about 30 seconds on each side. Put the cooked tortilla on a paper towel–lined baking sheet and sprinkle with a bit of salt. Repeat with the remaining tortillas, adding oil as necessary. Keep the tostados warm in the preheated oven while preparing the refried beans. Discard any remaining oil.

To make the refried beans, heat the bacon fat in a skillet. Add the onion and sauté until translucent, 5 to 6 minutes. Add the garlic and sauté until fragrant, about 1 minute. Add the chipotle pepper and cook for an additional minute until fragrant. Add the beans, salt, and water. Using a potato masher or the back of a fork, quickly mash some of the beans, keeping some of them whole. Continue cooking until the beans are heated through, all the water has been absorbed, and the beans have a smooth consistency, 4 to 5 minutes.

To serve, spread ½ cup refried beans on each warm tortilla. Top each with ½ cup beef mixture, ⅛ cup shredded lettuce, ⅛ cup tomatoes, ⅛ cup shredded cheese, 1 tablespoon sour cream, and a sprinkling of cilantro and red onion for garnish. Serve the tostados with lime wedges and hot sauce.

Smoked Salmon Crostini with Avocado Cream

Sometimes I feel like hosting a party that's a little more on the elegant side, a bit more formal. That calls for an appetizer that's a little fancy, but not difficult—silky smoked salmon on toasts topped with a simple avocado cream. Arrange the crostini on your best crystal or silver platter and pour Prosecco-Pomegranate Cocktails (page 66) to accompany them. Now, where did I put my tuxedo?

Makes 12

Crostini

1 baguette, sliced into 12 ½-inch pieces

Extra-virgin olive oil

Kosher salt and freshly ground black pepper

Avocado Cream

2 ripe avocados

½ cup mascarpone

2 tablespoons sour cream

2 tablespoons finely chopped red onion

1 tablespoon finely chopped fresh cilantro

Juice of 1 lime

¼ teaspoon kosher salt

Freshly ground black pepper

4 ounces sliced smoked salmon, in 12 pieces

Turn on the oven to broil.

To make the crostini, arrange the bread slices in a single layer on a baking sheet. Brush each slice with olive oil and sprinkle on a little salt and pepper. Broil the bread slices until they are light golden brown and crunchy, about 2 minutes. Remove the crostini from the oven and let cool.

To make the avocado cream, halve the avocados, remove the pits, and scoop out the flesh into a food processor. Add the mascarpone, sour cream, 1½ tablespoons of the red onion, the cilantro, and lime juice to the food processor and blend until creamy. Season with the salt and pepper. Spread 1 tablespoon avocado cream on each slice of toasted bread. Top each with a piece of folded smoked salmon. Sprinkle the remaining ½ tablespoon chopped red onion on the crostini before serving.

Sausage Party Bites with Mustard Sauce

I fondly remember helping Mom make these spicy sausage bites for our Christmas parties. My job was to roll and arrange the small balls on baking sheets before they went into the oven. Made with hot pork sausage, these bites have a bit of kick. I tweaked Mom's recipe and added a few herbs and spices and added a mustard dipping sauce for the perfect finishing touch.

Makes 50 to 60

Sausage Bites

1 tablespoon canola oil

½ cup finely minced onion

2½ cups Bisquick

1 pound hot pork sausage, casings removed

2½ cups (10 ounces) shredded white extra-sharp Cheddar

2 large eggs, beaten

2 tablespoons (¼ stick) unsalted butter, melted

2 teaspoons ground sage

1 teaspoon paprika

1 teaspoon kosher salt

Mustard Sauce

1 cup whole grain Dijon mustard

1 cup mayonnaise

1 tablespoon heavy cream

¼ cup minced fresh parsley

1 teaspoon paprika

1 tablespoon honey (optional)

Preheat the oven to 350°F. Line 2 baking sheets with parchment paper.

To make the sausage balls, heat the canola oil in a skillet over medium heat. Add the onion and cook until translucent, 5 to 6 minutes. Put the cooked onion, Bisquick, sausage, Cheddar, eggs, butter, sage, paprika, and salt in a bowl. Using your hands, mix well until the ingredients are combined. Shape the mixture into 1-inch balls. *(The balls can be frozen on baking sheets, then transferred to plastic bags for 1 month.)* Arrange the balls 1 inch apart on the prepared baking sheets. Bake for 15 to 20 minutes, until the balls are slightly puffed and cooked through.

To make the sauce, whisk together the mustard, mayonnaise, cream, parsley, and paprika. For a sweeter sauce, stir in the honey. *(The sauce can be made and refrigerated several hours in advance.)*

Brunch & Beyond

I work just about every Saturday and Sunday, so when I do get a rare weekend off, I like to go out, or even better, invite people over for brunch. Making brunch for friends and family allows me to be creative with comforting breakfast fare. Instead of ordinary French toast dipped in eggs and fried, I make sandwiches by spreading bread with cream cheese, strawberry jam, and fresh strawberries before cooking them on the griddle. For even more strawberry goodness, I drizzle each piece with some homemade strawberry syrup. While buttermilk pancakes are fine, separating the eggs and using ricotta cheese makes Blueberry-Lemon Ricotta Pancakes almost light and airy enough to float away. Thread bacon slices onto skewers and bake them for a unique presentation. Eggs Benedict Bread Pudding and the Brunch Panini can be put together the night before your guests are due. All you have to do in the morning is pop them into the oven and turn on the coffeemaker.

If you want to greet your guests with a nibble as soon as they arrive, offer them Piña Colada Muffins or fresh-from-the-fryer Breakfast Poppers with Grits and Bacon with a glass of juice or a Bloody Mary.

I also love breakfast for dinner, especially when I want something light like a Western Omelet or a Spaghetti Frittata with a salad and some Italian bread.

Blueberry-Lemon Ricotta Pancakes with Blueberry Syrup

When we went on family vacations, my mom liked to hit the road early, usually before the sun came up. After a few hours of driving, we often stopped at a Howard Johnson's restaurant for breakfast. HoJo's was a popular chain that dotted America's highways before fast-food places came into existence. I can still remember the first time I ordered a stack of their blueberry pancakes. Here's a light, fluffy take on those traditional flapjacks with the addition of ricotta and lemon, topped with a generous pour of homemade blueberry syrup.

Makes 8 to 10

Syrup

2 cups blueberries

¼ cup water

½ cup honey

¼ cup corn syrup

2 teaspoons pure vanilla extract

Pancakes

1½ cups buttermilk

1½ cups whole milk ricotta cheese

Zest and juice of 1 lemon

3 large eggs, separated

2 teaspoons pure vanilla extract

1¾ cups all-purpose flour, sifted

3 tablespoons sugar

1 teaspoon baking powder

½ teaspoon baking soda

½ teaspoon kosher salt

½ teaspoon cream of tartar

8 tablespoons (1 stick) unsalted butter

2 cups blueberries

To make the syrup, combine the blueberries, water, honey, corn syrup, and vanilla in a saucepan over medium-high heat. Stir constantly until the mixture comes to a boil. Reduce the heat and simmer for 15 to 20 minutes, stirring frequently, while making the pancakes.

Preheat the oven to 200°F.

To make the pancakes, whisk together the buttermilk, ricotta, lemon zest, lemon juice, 3 egg yolks, and vanilla in a bowl. In another bowl, whisk together the flour, sugar, baking powder, baking soda, and salt. Make a well in the center of the flour mixture and pour in the buttermilk mixture. Mix together until just combined. Do not overmix.

Put the egg whites and the cream of tartar in the bowl of an electric mixer with a whisk attachment and beat until soft peaks form. Using a spatula, gently fold the egg whites into the batter until no streaks remain. Let the mixture sit for 10 minutes.

Melt 1 tablespoon of the butter in a nonstick skillet or a griddle over medium heat. Using a ⅓-cup measure, pour the pancake batter into the pan. Scatter 8 to 10 blueberries on the top of each pancake. Cook until bubbles form on the tops of the pancakes, then flip and cook until the undersides are lightly brown and cooked through, 2 to 3 more minutes. Repeat with the remaining butter and batter. Keep the finished pancakes warm in the oven until they're all made and ready to serve with the warm blueberry syrup.

Vanilla

Heavenly vanilla comes from the specific vanilla orchid grown in Tahiti, Mexico, Madagascar, and other hot, humid, tropical climates. Once cured, vanilla pods—or beans—are sold whole, as a powder, or combined with alcohol to make extract. Like chocolate, wine, or any number of other foods, vanilla pods are graded from high to low quality.

There are two things to spend money on when baking—chocolate and vanilla. My favorite vanilla is Madagascar Bourbon Pure Vanilla. It has a rich, complex aroma and sweet flavor. If I use any other vanilla in my recipes, I'm always disappointed in the results. You can find this particular vanilla in many supermarkets and online. It keeps indefinitely.

What's interesting is that Madagascar Bourbon has nothing to do with Kentucky bourbon at all! This vanilla is grown on the island of Réunion, once known as Bourbon, off the coast of Madagascar.

To make your own vanilla extract, put 2 split beans and the seeds in a small bottle. Fill the bottle with vodka and let it sit for several weeks before using.

When shopping, be sure to read the label and buy pure vanilla extract, not imitation vanilla, which is made with synthetic flavoring and bears little resemblance to the real thing.

Hash Brown Breakfast Pizza FAN FAVORITE

While some folks like cold pizza for breakfast, I prefer mine piping hot. Here's a version that's guaranteed to get you going in the morning. This one starts with a crust made from frozen hash brown potatoes. I like an "everything" breakfast pizza—bacon, scrambled eggs, Cheddar, red bell pepper, and scallions.

Makes 6 servings

Vegetable oil spray

Crust

3 cups frozen hash brown potatoes, thawed

⅓ cup minced onion

1 large egg, beaten

2 tablespoons all-purpose flour

1 teaspoon kosher salt

¼ teaspoon freshly ground black pepper

⅛ teaspoon paprika

Topping

5 large eggs

3 tablespoons whole milk

½ teaspoon kosher salt

⅛ teaspoon freshly ground black pepper

2 uncooked bacon strips, chopped

⅓ cup diced red bell pepper

1½ cups (6 ounces) shredded Cheddar

4 links breakfast sausage, cooked and sliced into ¼-inch rounds

¼ cup sliced scallions

Preheat the oven to 375°F. Spray a 9-inch round cake pan with vegetable oil spray.

To make the crust, combine the potatoes, onion, egg, flour, salt, pepper, and paprika in a mixing bowl. Toss until the potatoes are evenly coated, then spread them in the prepared pan. Bake for 30 minutes, or until golden brown.

To make the topping, whisk together the eggs, milk, salt, and pepper in a mixing bowl.

Cook the bacon in a small nonstick skillet over medium-high heat until crisp. With a slotted spoon, remove the bacon from the fat and drain on paper towels. Remove all but 1 tablespoon bacon fat from the pan. Add the bell pepper and cook for about 5 minutes, or until softened. Pour in the egg mixture and cook until nearly set.

Top the crust with ¾ cup of the Cheddar, followed by the egg-pepper mixture, bacon, and sausage. Sprinkle on the remaining ¾ cup cheese and the scallions. Bake for 15 minutes, until the cheese is bubbly. Let cool for 3 to 5 minutes.

Dutch Baby with Apple Butter

The first time I tasted a Dutch baby was when Bob Warden, a frequent guest on *In the Kitchen with David,* prepared one during a cookware demonstration. When the billowing pancake came out of the oven, it looked like one big popover. One taste just wasn't enough. When we were off camera, I helped myself to a few more bites. I couldn't wait to try making a Dutch baby at home. Make sure everyone is at the table, so they can all *ooh* and *aah* as soon as the Dutch baby comes out of the oven. Bread flour, instead of all-purpose, results in an even puffier pancake. Oh, and I decided to add a Southern spin by serving it with a dollop of sweet apple butter.

Makes 4 to 6 servings

1 cup bread flour or all-purpose flour, sifted

1 cup whole milk, at room temperature or warmed slightly

4 large eggs, at room temperature

2 teaspoons sugar

2 teaspoons pure vanilla extract

½ teaspoon kosher salt

½ teaspoon ground cinnamon

⅛ teaspoon ground nutmeg

5 tablespoons unsalted butter, at room temperature

1 cup apple butter

Confectioners' sugar and lemon slices

Place a 10- to 12-inch cast-iron skillet in the oven and preheat the oven to 425°F.

Put the flour, milk, eggs, sugar, vanilla, salt, cinnamon, and nutmeg in a blender. Blend at medium-high speed until the batter is smooth and creamy, about 30 seconds.

Using oven mitts, remove the hot skillet from the oven and put the butter into the skillet to melt. *(Be careful; the pan will be very hot, so hold it away from you.)* Tilt the hot skillet back and forth to evenly coat the bottom and sides. Quickly pour the batter into the skillet and place the skillet in the oven. Bake for 20 to 25 minutes, until the batter is puffed and lightly brown. Don't open the oven or the Dutch Baby will deflate.

Carefully remove the skillet from the oven and place it on a trivet on the table. The pancake will begin to deflate as soon as it comes out of the oven, so cut it into 4 to 6 pieces as quickly as possible. Serve with a dollop of apple butter, a dusting of confectioners' sugar, and lemon slices.

Eggs Benedict Bread Pudding

Eggs Benedict has long been a classic brunch dish, but making it at home can be a bit complicated. You have to poach all those eggs, make the hollandaise sauce, and plate each dish like an assembly line so everyone gets their hot food at the same time. Instead of trying to serve individual portions, I thought, Why not combine the basic elements into a bread pudding? This one-dish version preserves the essence of the original recipe, but it's easy to put together the night before, or at least six hours in advance. The addition of a cup of fresh fruit is now all you need for an unforgettable brunch.

Makes 6 to 8 servings

1 to 2 tablespoons unsalted butter, at room temperature

Bread Pudding

6 English muffins, separated and cut into quarters

1 pound Canadian bacon, cubed

8 medium asparagus spears. trimmed and cut into ½-inch pieces

2 tablespoons minced fresh chives

1 0.9-ounce package Knorr Hollandaise Sauce Mix

1½ cups whole milk

12 large eggs

1½ cups half-and-half

1 teaspoon kosher salt

¾ teaspoon white pepper

Hollandaise Sauce

¾ cup (1½ sticks) unsalted butter, cubed

3 large egg yolks

1½ teaspoons fresh lemon juice

½ teaspoon kosher salt

Pinch of white pepper

Pinch of cayenne

Preheat the oven to 375°F. Lightly butter the bottom and sides of a 9 x 13-inch baking dish with the softened butter.

To make the bread pudding, arrange the English muffin pieces on a baking sheet. Bake for 10 to 12 minutes, until toasted and crunchy.

Heat a large skillet over medium heat. Add the Canadian bacon and cook until light brown. Add the asparagus pieces and cook, turning frequently, for 4 minutes. Add the toasted English muffin pieces to the bacon-asparagus mixture and toss well. Pour the mixture into the prepared baking dish. Sprinkle the chives over the top.

Put the hollandaise sauce mix and milk into a large bowl and whisk well. Add the eggs, half-and-half, salt, and white pepper and whisk until well blended. Pour the egg mixture over the ingredients in the baking dish. Cover and refrigerate for at least 6 hours or overnight.

Preheat the oven to 375°F.

Remove the casserole from the refrigerator and let it come to room temperature for 30 minutes. Cover the casserole with aluminum foil and bake for 50 minutes. Remove the foil and bake for an additional 15 to 20 minutes, until a toothpick inserted into the center comes out clean. Make the hollandaise sauce while the casserole is baking.

To make the hollandaise sauce, melt the butter in a microwave-safe bowl in the microwave or in a saucepan on the stovetop until frothy, but not boiling. Put the egg yolks, lemon juice, salt, white pepper, and cayenne in a blender. Blend to combine. With the blender running, gradually add the melted butter. The sauce will thicken. Taste and add a little more lemon juice, salt, or white pepper as needed. To keep the hollandaise sauce warm if the casserole is still baking, place the blender container in a pan of hot water. If the sauce becomes too thick, stir in 1 tablespoon hot water to thin it out.

Cut the bread pudding into wedges and serve with a generous pour of hollandaise sauce.

Spiced Bacon Skewers

These easy-to-make skewers are like bacon lollipops. Use them in Cobb salads, with breakfast eggs, or with a bowl of hot tomato soup. Everything *is* better with bacon.

Makes 6 to 8 servings

Vegetable oil spray

1 cup (packed) light brown sugar

½ cup granulated sugar

½ teaspoon cayenne

¾ teaspoon ground cinnamon

¾ teaspoon ground nutmeg

½ teaspoon ground cloves

1 pound apple wood–smoked, thick-cut bacon, excess fat trimmed from the short ends

Preheat the oven to 375°F. Line a baking sheet with aluminum foil or parchment paper. Spray a wire rack with vegetable oil spray and place the rack on top of the baking sheet. You will need fifteen to twenty 8-inch metal or wooden skewers (if using wooden skewers, soak them in water for 30 minutes).

Put the brown sugar, granulated sugar, cayenne, cinnamon, nutmeg, and cloves in a resealable plastic bag. Shake the bag well to mix the ingredients.

Thread 1 bacon slice onto each skewer like ribbon candy. Don't push the bacon together too closely or the skewers won't cook evenly. Dip each bacon skewer into the plastic bag with the sugar mixture, making sure to coat both sides well. Lay each skewer on the prepared wire rack. Sprinkle the skewers with any remaining sugar mixture. Bake for 25 to 30 minutes, until the bacon is brown and crisp, turning the skewers after 12 to 15 minutes. Serve hot.

Bringing Home the Bacon, Pancetta, and Prosciutto

Bacon is the pig's sides that have been cured in salt or in a brine, and then smoked over wood. I use hickory- or apple wood–smoked bacon in my recipes.

Pancetta is air-dried pork belly that has been cured with salt, pepper, and sometimes other spices, but not smoked. Pancetta must be cooked before eating. Long rolls of pancetta are found at supermarket or Italian deli counters where you can purchase as many slices as you need and then chop or dice at home.

Prosciutto is Italian ham that has been salt-cured and air-dried. The thinner the better when sliced, prosciutto is best eaten as an appetizer. Add prosciutto to cooked dishes at the last minute so it doesn't become tough.

Spaghetti Frittata

A frittata, an open-faced Italian omelet, is the best way I know of to use up last night's leftover vegetables, cheese, and even spaghetti. With that in mind, I always make extra pasta so I can put together a spaghetti frittata in minutes for brunch, lunch, or dinner the next day. Cut it into wedges and serve it hot from the oven or at room temperature. I'm always happy to find a slice of frittata in my refrigerator when I'm looking for a quick snack.

Makes 6 to 8 servings

3 tablespoons extra-virgin olive oil

½ pound pancetta, cut into ½-inch cubes

2 tablespoons (¼ stick) unsalted butter

1 small onion, diced

2 garlic cloves, minced

12 ounces (about 2 cups) cold cooked spaghetti

8 large eggs

3 large egg whites

3 tablespoons grated Parmigiano-Reggiano

3 tablespoons whole milk

½ teaspoon kosher salt

¼ teaspoon freshly ground black pepper

2 plum tomatoes, seeded and diced

6 to 8 fresh basil leaves, thinly sliced

1 cup (4 ounces) shredded cheese, such as Italian Fontina, mozzarella, or provolone, or a mixture

Preheat the broiler.

Heat 2 tablespoons of the olive oil in a large ovenproof skillet over medium-high heat. Add the pancetta and sauté until lightly brown and crispy, 3 to 4 minutes. Using a slotted spoon, transfer the pancetta to a bowl, leaving the fat and oil in the pan. Add the remaining 1 tablespoon olive oil and the butter to the skillet. Add the onion to the skillet and sauté until translucent, 5 to 6 minutes. Add half of the garlic and sauté until fragrant, about 1 minute. Using the slotted spoon, transfer the onion-garlic mixture to the bowl with the pancetta. Add the remaining garlic to the pan and sauté for 1 minute. Add the spaghetti and, using tongs, toss to warm and mix with the oil, onion, garlic, and butter, 3 to 4 minutes.

While the spaghetti is warming, whisk together the eggs, egg whites, Parmesan, milk, salt, and pepper in a bowl. Stir in the tomatoes, basil, and the pancetta mixture.

Pour the egg mixture over the spaghetti. Gently stir the spaghetti to make sure all the ingredients are blended. Jiggle the skillet a bit to level out the ingredients, or use a spatula to smooth out the frittata. Reduce the heat to medium and cook the frittata for 10 to 12 minutes, until the eggs are almost set and firm. Run a rubber spatula around the edge of the pan every few minutes to make sure everything is cooking evenly and not sticking to the pan. The spaghetti on the bottom will begin to brown. If it's browning too quickly, lower the heat.

Sprinkle the shredded cheese on top of the frittata, then transfer the skillet to the oven. Broil until the cheese is melted and the top is light brown. Remove from the oven and let the frittata sit for 2 to 3 minutes before cutting it into wedges.

Eggs in the Hole

Looking for a way to add some fun to breakfast? Sometimes the simplest preparations give us the most comfort, like an egg fried in bread with a cut-out hole. There are many names for this dish—toad in the hole, frog in the hole, egg in a nest, one-eyed jacks, or Popeyes. I add cheese, bacon, and scallions to this classic, which is traditionally just made with eggs and bread. Seconds anyone?

Makes 4 servings

4 tablespoons (½ stick) unsalted butter, at room temperature

4 ¾-inch-thick slices sourdough or other bread

4 extra-large eggs

Kosher salt and freshly ground black pepper

1 cup (4 ounces) shredded white sharp Cheddar

8 slices bacon, cooked and crumbled

1 to 2 scallions, chopped (optional)

Butter both sides of the bread. Using a 2-inch biscuit cutter, cut out a hole in each slice of bread. Reserve the bread circles.

Heat a large skillet over medium heat. (Prepare the eggs in two batches or use 2 skillets.) Put 2 pieces of bread into the pan and cook until lightly brown, about 2 minutes. Turn the bread over. Crack 1 egg into each hole, taking care not to break the yolk. Sprinkle with salt and pepper. Cook for about 1 minute, until the egg is almost set. Sprinkle ¼ cup of the cheese, one quarter of the bacon bits, and 1 tablespoon of the scallions (if using) over each slice of bread, but not over the yolks. To help melt the cheese, add 1 tablespoon water to the pan, cover with a lid, and cook for 1 to 2 more minutes, until the eggs are cooked to the desired doneness. If there is room, add the bread circles to the pan and toast them. They're perfect for dipping into the yolks.

Western Omelets

I've always considered going out for brunch to be a treat! As soon as I see a Western omelet on a menu, I'm sold. A Western—sometimes called a Denver—is an omelet with a filling of confetti-like pieces of tomatoes, onions, bell peppers, and ham. When I make these omelets at home, I also whip up a zippy Southwestern-style salsa to serve alongside. If you prefer a Western sandwich, just slide the omelet and some salsa between two slices of toasted sourdough bread for a hearty breakfast sandwich.

Makes 2 servings

Salsa

Makes 2½ cups; use leftovers for another purpose

1½ cups diced plum tomatoes, seeded (4 or 5)

¼ cup finely chopped red onion

¼ cup finely chopped yellow bell pepper

¼ cup finely chopped green bell pepper

1 jalapeño, seeded and finely chopped

3 teaspoons minced fresh cilantro

Juice of 1 to 2 limes

1 teaspoon kosher salt

¼ teaspoon freshly ground black pepper

Omelets

2 tablespoons canola oil

½ cup cubed cooked ham

¼ cup finely chopped red bell pepper

¼ cup finely chopped green bell pepper

½ cup chopped white onion

6 large eggs

2 tablespoons whole milk

Kosher salt and freshly ground black pepper

2 tablespoons (¼ stick) unsalted butter

1 cup (4 ounces) shredded yellow sharp Cheddar

To make the salsa, combine the tomatoes, red onion, yellow bell pepper, green bell pepper, jalapeño, cilantro, lime juice, salt, and black pepper in a bowl. Mix well.

To make the omelet, heat the canola oil in a skillet over medium-high heat. Add the cubed ham and cook, stirring, for about 1 minute or so. Add the red bell pepper, green bell pepper, and white onion and continue to cook until the onion is translucent, 5 to 6 minutes. While the vegetables are cooking, whisk together the eggs and milk in a bowl for a full minute to aerate them for a fluffy, light omelet. Season with salt and pepper.

Melt 1 tablespoon of the butter in a skillet over medium-high heat. Pour half of the egg mixture into the skillet. Once the eggs start to cook, gently move them around with a rubber spatula so they don't brown. When the eggs begin to set, but are still a little wet, after 1 minute, place half of the ham-and-vegetable mixture in a line on one side of the omelet. Top the vegetables with ½ cup of the cheese. Fold the omelet over the vegetables and cheese. Put 1 or 2 tablespoons water into the pan. (The steam from the water will help melt the cheese and seal the omelet.) Turn the heat down to medium, cover the pan, and continue cooking for 2 to 3 minutes to finish the omelet. Slide the omelet onto a serving plate. Serve with salsa. To make the second omelet, wipe the pan with a paper towel and repeat with the remaining ingredients.

Brunch Panini with Apple-Cranberry Chutney

In Italy, panini are small sandwiches made on bread or rolls that haven't been presliced. On this side of the ocean, the word "panini" refers to sandwiches that are pressed and grilled and served warm. Why settle for turkey or ham when you can have them both and some creamy, savory Brie? To give the panini an extra-special touch and a bit of sweetness, I like to spread some apple-cranberry chutney or Apple, Pear, and Fig Chutney (page 130) on the sandwiches.

Makes 4 servings

Chutney

Makes 2½ to 3 cups

2 tablespoons extra-virgin olive oil

1 medium white onion, finely chopped

3 Granny Smith apples, peeled, cored, and coarsely chopped

1 Gala apple, peeled, cored, and coarsely chopped

1½ cups dried cranberries

½ cup fresh orange juice

2 tablespoons (packed) light brown sugar

1 tablespoon chopped fresh parsley

½ teaspoon kosher salt

¼ teaspoon ground nutmeg

Pinch of freshly ground black pepper

½ cup water

Panini

8 ½-inch slices sourdough bread

¼ cup whole grain Dijon mustard

8 to 10 thin slices smoked turkey

8 to 10 thin slices smoked ham

12 ounces Brie or 1 small round of Brie, thinly sliced

Extra-virgin olive oil

0o make the chutney, heat 1 tablespoon of the olive oil in a saucepan over low heat. Add the onion and cook until translucent, 5 to 6 minutes. Add the Granny Smith apples, Gala apple, cranberries, orange juice, brown sugar, parsley, salt, nutmeg, and pepper and continue cooking over low heat for 1 hour, stirring occasionally. Add the water and cook for an additional 15 minutes, or until the apples and cranberries are soft and spreadable. *(The chutney can be made 1 week ahead and refrigerated.)*

To make the panini, spread 2 tablespoons chutney on each of 4 slices of bread and 1 tablespoon of the mustard on each of the 4 other slices of bread. Top each of the 4 bread slices with chutney with 2 slices turkey, 2 slices ham, and 3 slices Brie. Top the sandwiches with the remaining 4 bread slices.

Heat a nonstick skillet to medium-high heat. Lightly brush the outsides of the sandwiches with olive oil. Place the sandwiches in the hot skillet and weigh them down with a heavy skillet or a pot lid that fits snuggly around the sandwiches. Or press down on the panini with a spatula to seal the sandwiches. Cook until the sandwiches are golden brown on one side, 2 to 3 minutes, and then turn them. The sandwiches are done when they are crispy and golden brown on the outside, and the cheese has melted and oozed a bit. Cut the sandwiches into halves diagonally before serving.

Banana–Peanut Butter French Toast

Imagine peanut butter sandwiches soaked in beaten eggs with vanilla, cinnamon, and nutmeg; gently sautéed; and then topped with caramelized bananas, whipped cream, and chopped peanuts. Now imagine this as the perfect dish for your next family brunch. If you want to include an ode to Elvis, serve some hickory-smoked bacon on the side. This recipe will knock everybody's socks off!

Makes 4 servings

French Toast

8 ½-inch-thick brioche or challah slices

8 or more tablespoons creamy peanut butter

1½ cups heavy cream

3 large eggs

3 large egg yolks

2 teaspoons pure vanilla extract

1 teaspoon ground cinnamon

¼ teaspoon ground nutmeg

Banana-Caramel Sauce

8 tablespoons (1 stick) unsalted butter, cut into 5 or 6 pieces

½ cup (packed) light brown sugar

2 teaspoons pure vanilla extract

1 teaspoon ground cinnamon

Pinch of ground nutmeg

3 bananas, sliced diagonally into ½-inch pieces

4 to 6 tablespoons (½ to ¾ stick) unsalted butter, cut into 4 to 6 pieces

1 cup whipped cream (see page 260)

⅓ to ½ cup chopped salted peanuts

Preheat the oven to 200°F.

To make the French toast, spread each of 4 slices of the bread with 1 to 2 tablespoons of the peanut butter. Top each with another bread slice. Place the sandwiches in a single layer in a baking dish.

To make an egg custard, whisk together the cream, eggs, egg yolks, vanilla, cinnamon, and nutmeg in a bowl. Pour the custard over the sandwiches, turning them to make sure that they are well coated. Let the sandwiches sit in the custard for 10 to 15 minutes, turning them a few times.

To make the sauce, melt the 8 tablespoons butter in a saucepan over medium heat. Add the brown sugar, vanilla, cinnamon, and nutmeg and mix until the sugar is dissolved. Reduce the heat if the sauce starts to bubble too much. Once the sugar is dissolved, add the bananas and stir to coat, taking care not to smash them. Keep warm on low heat while making the French toast.

To complete the French toast, melt 2 tablespoons butter in a skillet over medium heat. Let any excess custard drip off the sandwiches before adding them to the skillet. Cook the sandwiches in batches until golden brown, 2 to 3 minutes on each side. Lower the heat if they are getting too dark too quickly. Wipe out the skillet with a paper towel between batches. Melt additional butter as needed. Transfer the French toast to a baking dish and keep warm in the oven. Top the French toast with the banana-caramel sauce, whipped cream, and chopped peanuts before serving.

Strawberry–Cream Cheese Stuffed French Toast FAN FAVORITE

When I was in college, breakfast was often "a bagel à la Bama"—a toasted bagel with cream cheese and Bama strawberry jelly. Those same creamy textures and sweet flavors are brought together in this updated French toast. I spread cream cheese and strawberry jelly, and add some fresh strawberries, between slices of bread before cooking them in a skillet or on a griddle. If that isn't enough strawberry goodness, I drizzle strawberry-orange sauce on top of each serving. Oh my, this is so good!

Makes 5 servings

Strawberry-Orange Sauce

2 cups sliced fresh strawberries

⅓ cup sugar

½ teaspoon orange zest

1 tablespoon fresh orange juice

French Toast

12 ounces cream cheese, softened

3 tablespoons seedless strawberry jam

½ teaspoon pure vanilla extract

10 ¾-inch-thick challah or brioche slices

1¼ cups sliced fresh strawberries

4 large eggs

¾ cup whole milk

2 tablespoons fresh orange juice

1 tablespoon sugar

Unsalted butter

To make the sauce, combine the strawberries, sugar, orange zest, and orange juice in a saucepan and bring to a boil. Reduce the heat and simmer until the strawberries are soft and the syrup is slightly thickened, 10 to 12 minutes. Allow the mixture to cool.

To make the French toast, whisk together the cream cheese, strawberry jam, and vanilla until smooth. Spread the cream cheese mixture on the 10 bread slices. Top 5 of the bread slices with ¼ cup each of the sliced strawberries, then put the remaining bread slices on top like sandwiches.

Whisk together the eggs, milk, orange juice, and sugar in a shallow bowl. Melt the butter in a skillet over medium heat. Dip the sandwiches into the egg mixture and allow to soak for a few seconds on each side. Cook the sandwiches until light golden brown, 3 to 4 minutes per side. Transfer to serving plates and drizzle the sauce on top. Serve warm.

Breakfast Quesadillas with Creamy Salsa Verde Topping FAN FAVORITE

When I want to wake up my guests' taste buds at brunch, I serve these Southwestern-inspired quesadillas filled with scrambled eggs, potatoes, sausage, and cheese. Then, to really make the quesadillas pop, I top them with a salsa verde and sour cream sauce. A pitcher of Rosé Sangria (page 71), a bowl of guacamole, and a big platter of tropical fruit round out this mid-morning meal.

Makes 12 servings

Dipping Sauce

½ cup sour cream

3 tablespoons salsa verde

2 tablespoons seeded and chopped jalapeño, preferably red for color

1 tablespoon chopped fresh chives

Pinch of cayenne

Quesadillas

1 tablespoon unsalted butter

2 uncooked bacon slices, finely chopped

¼ cup shredded potatoes

¼ cup smoked sausage, finely chopped

2 scallions, sliced

4 large eggs, beaten

Pinch of paprika

Vegetable oil spray

2 12-inch flour tortillas

½ cup (2 ounces) shredded pepper Jack or jalapeño Cheddar

To make the dipping sauce, whisk together the sour cream, salsa verde, jalapeño, chives, and cayenne in a bowl.

To make the quesadillas, melt the butter in a large skillet over medium heat. Add the bacon pieces and cook for 3 to 4 minutes, until slightly crisp. Add the potatoes, sausage, and scallions, and cook for an additional 2 minutes, stirring frequently until the potatoes develop some color. Add the eggs and paprika. Cook until the eggs are set. Remove the egg mixture to a bowl. Wipe the skillet clean.

Spray the skillet with vegetable oil spray. Place a tortilla in the skillet and fill half of the tortilla with half of the eggs. Top with half of the cheese. Fold the tortilla in half and cook for 2 to 3 minutes on each side. Remove from the pan and keep warm. Repeat with the remaining ingredients. Cut the quesadillas into 4 wedges and serve with the dipping sauce.

Piña Colada Muffins

When I travel to the Caribbean, my vacation doesn't really start until I'm resting on a lounge chair under a palm tree and there's a piña colada in my hand. My love for this tropical cocktail was the inspiration for these creative muffins. They're filled with coconut and plump pieces of fresh pineapple, sprinkled with a coconut topping, and drizzled with a coconut glaze that brings all these tropical flavors together in every bite. Since I make these at home when I'm *not* on vacation, I usually wash them down with a glass of cold milk.

Makes 12

Topping

1 cup sweetened flaked coconut

⅓ cup all-purpose flour

¼ cup (packed) light brown sugar

4 tablespoons (½ stick) unsalted butter, melted

Muffins

2 cups all-purpose flour, sifted

¼ cup (packed) light brown sugar

2 teaspoons baking powder, sifted

½ teaspoon baking soda, sifted

½ teaspoon table salt

1 large egg, beaten

¾ cup coconut milk

¾ cup Coco Lopez coconut cream

4 tablespoons (½ stick) unsalted butter, melted

1½ teaspoons rum extract

½ teaspoon pure vanilla extract

1¾ cups ¼-inch cubes fresh pineapple

¾ cup sweetened flaked coconut

Glaze

½ cup confectioners' sugar

1½ tablespoons coconut milk

¼ teaspoon rum extract

Preheat the oven to 375°F. Line a 12-cup muffin tin with paper liners.

To make the topping, combine the coconut, flour, and brown sugar in a bowl. Using a fork, stir in the melted butter. The mixture will be slightly lumpy.

To make the muffins, stir together the flour, brown sugar, baking powder, baking soda, and salt in a bowl. In another bowl, whisk together the egg, coconut milk, coconut cream, butter, rum extract, and vanilla. Make a well in the center of the flour mixture and pour in the egg mixture. Using a fork, mix the batter together until just combined. Do not overmix. Fold in the pineapple cubes and flaked coconut.

Evenly divide the muffin batter among the muffin cups. Divide the topping among the muffins. Bake for 20 to 25 minutes, until a toothpick inserted into the center of a muffin comes out clean. Transfer the muffin tin to a wire rack and let cool for 5 minutes before turning out the muffins. Let the muffins cool completely on the wire rack.

To make the glaze, whisk together the confectioners' sugar, coconut milk, and rum extract until no lumps remain. If the glaze is too thick to drizzle, whisk in ¼ teaspoon water to thin it out. Drizzle the glaze over the cooled muffins.

Apple-Cinnamon Muffins with Caramel Sauce

When the September air suddenly turns crisp and fallen leaves are crunching under my feet, it's time to gather the gang and go apple picking. Fortunately, there are a number of you-pick-'em fruit orchards within a short drive from my home. There are rows and rows of apple varieties with familiar names (Gala, Empire, and Red Delicious) as well as unusual ones (Summer Rambo, Jazz, and Keepsake), each with its own distinct bite, aroma, and flavor. I get so carried away by all the choices that I always come home with way too much fruit. I get busy making Apple, Pear, and Fig Chutney (page 130) to spread on sandwiches and give as gifts. Apple, Gorgonzola, Red Onion, and Candied Walnut Salad with Pomegranate Vinaigrette (page 241) frequently appears on my autumn table. I also use some of my apple bounty to bake these irresistible muffins, made with two kinds of apples, plenty of cinnamon and nutmeg, and a caramel drizzle for the perfect reminder of autumn.

Makes 12

Vegetable oil spray

Muffins

2 cups all-purpose flour

2 teaspoons baking powder

½ teaspoon table salt

½ teaspoon ground nutmeg

1½ teaspoons ground cinnamon

⅓ cup canola oil

1½ cups granulated sugar

½ cup (packed) light brown sugar

1 large egg

1 large egg white

1 cup whole milk

1 cup peeled and diced Granny Smith apples

2 cups peeled and diced Gala or Honeycrisp apples

Topping

⅓ cup all-purpose flour

⅓ cup (packed) light brown sugar

⅓ cup chopped walnuts (optional)

½ teaspoon ground cinnamon

3 tablespoons unsalted butter, at room temperature

Caramel Sauce

8 ounces soft caramel candies, papers removed

1½ tablespoons heavy cream

Preheat the oven to 350°F. Generously spray a 12-cup muffin tin with vegetable oil spray.

To make the muffins, sift together the flour, baking powder, salt, nutmeg, and 1 teaspoon of the cinnamon in a bowl. Sift again for light, airy muffins. Whisk together the canola oil, 1 cup of the granulated sugar, the brown sugar, egg, egg white, and milk in a bowl. Gradually add the flour mixture to the egg mixture, stirring just until mixed. Toss the chopped apples with the remaining ½ cup granulated sugar and ½ teaspoon cinnamon in a bowl. Gently fold the diced apple mixture into the batter. Do not overmix.

To make the topping, mix together the flour, brown sugar, walnuts (if using), and cinnamon in a bowl. Add the butter and, using your fingers, blend the ingredients together until crumbly.

Divide the batter evenly among the muffin cups. Top the muffins with the cinnamon sugar mixture. Bake for 20 to 25 minutes, until a tester inserted into the center of a muffin comes out clean. Let the muffins cool in the tin for 10 minutes. Remove the muffins from the cups and let cool on a wire rack while making the caramel drizzle.

To make the caramel sauce, place the caramels and cream in a microwave-safe bowl. Microwave on high for 1 to 2 minutes, stirring every 30 seconds until the caramels are melted. Drizzle the caramel sauce over the cooled muffins.

Breakfast Poppers with Grits and Bacon FAN FAVORITE

When I was growing up in the South, not a week went by when I didn't eat bacon and grits for breakfast. Since I'm always looking for ways to shake things up in the kitchen, I came up with these bite-size poppers. They're heaven in a small bite—crunchy on the outside, creamy on the inside, and include plenty of bacon smokiness. These fry up pretty quickly, so preheat the oil and have a big batch of poppers ready as soon as your hungry guests arrive.

Makes 40

8 slices thick-cut bacon

3 cups whole milk

¾ teaspoon kosher salt

¾ teaspoon freshly ground black pepper

1 cup instant grits

2 cups (8 ounces) shredded Cheddar

⅔ cup chopped scallions

⅓ cup cream cheese, at room temperature

4 to 6 cups canola oil, for frying

2 cups panko bread crumbs

1 cup all-purpose flour

4 large eggs

Cook the bacon in a skillet over medium heat until crisp, 4 to 5 minutes on each side. Drain the bacon on paper towels. Reserve 3 tablespoons bacon fat in the skillet. When the bacon is cool enough to handle, chop it into small pieces.

Combine the milk, the reserved bacon fat, salt, and pepper in a saucepan and bring to a boil. Reduce the heat to a simmer, add the grits, and cook for 5 minutes, stirring occasionally. Remove the grits from the heat and stir in the chopped bacon, the Cheddar, scallions, and cream cheese. Spread the mixture into a 9 x 13-inch baking dish. Cover and refrigerate for at least 2 hours.

Preheat a deep fryer to 350°F. Or, clip a deep-frying thermometer to the side of a heavy deep pot. Add the canola oil to the pot and slowly heat the oil to 350°F.

Place the bread crumbs in a food processor and process until finely ground. Pour the bread crumbs into a shallow bowl. Put the flour in another shallow bowl. Put the eggs in a third shallow bowl and beat lightly. Remove the grits from the refrigerator. Using your hands, take 2 tablespoons of the mixture and shape it into a ball. Repeat with the remaining grits. There should be 40 balls.

Roll the balls in the flour, then dip them into the eggs, followed by the bread crumbs. Using a slotted spoon, add 6 to 8 poppers to the hot oil and fry for 4 minutes, or until golden brown on all sides. Drain on paper towels and repeat with the remaining poppers. Serve immediately.

Cheese, Please!

Since cheeses such as Cheddar, Gouda, Parmesan, and others are sold by weight, not by volume, it's important to know that 8 ounces of shredded or grated cheese equals 2 cups in volume. As a reminder, here's a chart to simplify your shopping:

Weight	Volume
1 pound cheese	4 cups shredded
8 ounces	2 cups shredded
4 ounces	1 cup shredded
3 ounces	¾ cup shredded
2 ounces	½ cup shredded
1 ounce	¼ cup shredded

Shake & Stir

When hosting a cocktail party, a dinner, brunch, or barbecue, I often create a signature cocktail for the event. Greeting guests with a tray of these drinks says, "I'm so glad you're here. Let's get this party started!"

I start by thinking how I can give a traditional cocktail my own spin, twist, shake, or stir. For instance, a cosmopolitan is my favorite drink. It's traditionally made with cranberry juice, vodka, triple sec, and a bit of lime juice, but I decided to sweeten it with a touch of agave syrup and blend everything with ice for a frozen margarita-like texture.

When I added some mango nectar to mojitos, they became a sunny orange color and even more tropical. Inspired by best-loved American desserts, I created soda fountain treats such as Red Velvet and Chocolate Chip Cookie Milk Shakes. Rosé Sangria and Summer Peach Tea Punch turn into unique crowd-pleasers for large gatherings. You can also make kid-friendly versions without the alcohol. So make up a batch or two or three. *Cent'anni! Nastrovia! Cheers! L'chaim! Salud! Skol!* No matter how you say it—bottoms up!

Prosecco-Pomegranate Cocktails

Prosecco, a crisp, dry sparkling wine from northeastern Italy, is an inexpensive alternative to Champagne from France. Prosecco can be enjoyed on its own or paired with fruit juice in cocktails. I wanted to create a festive drink to serve friends and family, especially at the holiday season. What better way than to combine prosecco, pomegranate juice, and a hint of orange in this colorful cocktail. Blood orange bitters can be found in wine and gourmet stores. Fresh, ruby red pomegranate seeds are now available in many markets year-round and save you the trouble of seeding the fruit.

Makes 6

6 sugar cubes

6 tablespoons blood orange bitters

6 ounces pomegranate juice

1 750 ml bottle prosecco, chilled

6 orange twists

Pomegranate seeds

Place 1 sugar cube in each of six champagne flutes. Cover each sugar cube with 1 tablespoon blood orange bitters. Pour 1 ounce pomegranate juice into each flute and stir with a long-handled spoon. Slowly fill each flute with prosecco. Garnish each drink with an orange twist and a few pomegranate seeds.

Do the Twist

To make professional-looking citrus—orange, lemon, lime, grapefruit—twists for cocktails, purchase a channel knife at any kitchen specialty shop. Drag the channel knife from the top of the fruit to its opposite end for a perfect ⅛-inch slice of peel. Gently wrap the peel around a pencil or pen for the perfect citrus twist.

Mango Mojitos

I had my first mojito, a minty Cuban cocktail, while people-watching at a Miami Beach sidewalk café on Ocean Drive. Since I love to create cocktails, I decided to punch up the drink by adding mango nectar. It's an unbeatable tropical treat that combines the bright pop of mango juice with the tingle of fresh mint, lime, and rum. You can almost feel the cool ocean breeze as you sip one.

Makes 4

¼ cup simple syrup (recipe follows)

2 limes, quartered and seeded

1 large bunch of fresh mint, 12 sprigs for muddling and 4 sprigs for garnish

1 cup white rum

1 cup mango nectar or mango pulp

1 mango, thinly sliced

Club soda

Place the simple syrup, lime quarters, and 12 mint sprigs in a glass pitcher. Using a muddler or the back of a wooden spoon, muddle, or crush, the ingredients together. Fill the pitcher halfway with ice cubes. Stir in the rum and mango nectar. Fill four old-fashioned glasses with ice, add 2 or 3 mango slices to each, and divide the mojitos among the glasses. Add a splash of club soda. Garnish each with a sprig of mint before serving.

Simple Syrup

Many cocktails and other beverages call for a tablespoon or so of simple syrup. I keep a jar of it in my refrigerator, making it easy to mix drinks at a moment's notice.

All you have to do is boil equal amounts of water and sugar, stirring until the sugar dissolves. That's it. When I make simple syrup, I usually use 2 cups water and 2 cups sugar, but you can make more or less. The syrup can also be used to sweeten iced tea and other drinks.

To make an infused simple syrup, put some mint leaves, raspberries, cinnamon sticks, vanilla beans, or other flavoring into the syrup once the sugar has dissolved, and let it steep. Strain the mixture into a glass jar. Simple syrup will keep in the refrigerator for up to two months.

Summer Peach Tea Punch

Summertime is iced tea time where I come from. Sometimes I give my iced tea an extra taste of the season by using peach nectar and chunks of frozen peaches. *(Freeze the peaches at least eight hours in advance.)* This tea becomes more flavorful the longer it sits because it allows the tea to become infused with the peaches. For a grown-up beverage, add a splash of your favorite vodka to each glass.

Makes approximately 2 quarts

2 peaches, pitted and sliced into ¾-inch pieces

Juice of ½ lemon

⅔ cup simple syrup (see page 67)

4 peach herbal tea bags

2 cups boiling water

2 cups cold water

2 cups peach nectar

⅓ cup frozen lemonade concentrate, thawed

2 cups lemon-lime soda, chilled

Fresh mint sprigs

Line a baking sheet with parchment paper. Toss the sliced peaches and lemon juice together in a bowl. This will stop the peaches from turning brown. Pour ⅓ cup of the simple syrup over the peaches and let rest for 20 minutes, tossing a couple of times. Remove the peach slices from the syrup and arrange in a single layer on the prepared baking sheet. Freeze for at least 8 hours or overnight.

Place the tea bags in a 1-gallon plastic pitcher or container. Pour the boiling water over the tea bags and let steep for 20 minutes. Remove the tea bags and add the cold water. Stir in the peach nectar, the remaining ⅓ cup simple syrup, and the lemonade concentrate. Refrigerate for at least 8 hours or overnight.

Just before serving, add some frozen peach slices to the pitcher. Pour the tea into tall glasses filled with ice and add a splash of lemon-lime soda. Garnish each one with some frozen peach slices and a mint sprig before serving.

Frozen Cosmopolitans

My go-to cocktail is always a cosmopolitan. My frozen version gives this mixed drink a fun twist. Like any cocktail, this one is all about the right balance of ingredients; one flavor shouldn't overpower another. I worked a long time on getting the proportions just right for my favorite drink. The cranberry juice gives this drink a pop of bright red, making it ideal for either a hot summer's day or a winter holiday get-together. Cheers!

Makes 2

2 tablespoons sugar

1 lime wedge

¾ cup cranberry juice

½ cup vodka

¼ cup frozen cranberries

⅛ cup (1 ounce) Cointreau

1½ tablespoons agave syrup

1 tablespoon fresh lime juice

2 lime twists (see page 66)

Pour the sugar onto a small plate. Run the lime wedge around the rims of 2 martini glasses. Dip the rims of the glasses into the sugar to coat.

Put the cranberry juice, vodka, cranberries, Cointreau, agave, lime juice, and 2 cups ice into a blender. Blend until all the ice is crushed, 35 to 40 seconds. Divide the mixture between the two glasses and garnish each with a lime twist before serving.

Rosé Sangria

When I'm hosting a summer dinner party or cocktail gathering in my backyard, I often serve pitchers of homemade sangria. While sangria is traditionally made with red or white wine, I prefer the color and flavor of rosé mixed with fruit, brandy, and an orange simple syrup. All the preparation can be done early in the day, but add the lemon-lime sparkling water at the last moment to keep the bubbles effervescent. This refreshing party drink can carry the evening from hors d'oeuvres right through dinner.

Makes 8 to 10 servings

Orange Simple Syrup

¼ cup sugar

½ teaspoon orange extract

¼ cup water

Sangria

1 Granny Smith or Honeycrisp apple, cored and cut into ½-inch cubes

2 oranges, sliced into ¼-inch half-moons

1 lemon, sliced into ¼-inch half-moons

1 pint strawberries, hulled and cut in half

1 cup blueberries

1 750 ml bottle dry rosé wine

1 750 ml bottle rosé Moscato wine

¼ cup brandy

¼ cup triple sec or other orange liqueur

1 cup lemon-lime seltzer, chilled

To make the simple syrup, combine the sugar, orange extract, and water in a saucepan. Bring to a boil, then reduce the heat and stir until the sugar has dissolved, 2 to 3 minutes. Chill before using. *(The syrup can be made several days ahead and refrigerated.)*

To make the sangria, combine the apple, slices of 1 orange, the lemon slices, strawberries, blueberries, rosé, Moscato, brandy, triple sec, and orange simple syrup in a bowl or pitcher. Mix well. Cover with plastic wrap and chill for 2 to 3 hours. Right before serving, stir in the lemon-lime seltzer. Make sure that each serving has some pieces of fruit, and garnish with an orange half-moon.

Frozen Mint Juleps FAN FAVORITE

The Kentucky Derby is always held on the first Saturday in May. The day is filled with tradition, from what to wear to what to drink. Mint juleps, the go-to cocktails, have been associated with the Derby since 1938. Juleps are usually made with sprigs of mint that are "muddled," or crushed, in a glass to release the herb's essential oils. Instead, I make and refrigerate a mint-flavored simple syrup, so I can whip up frozen versions of this classic cocktail all throughout the summer. And, they're off!

Makes 4 servings

1 cup sugar

1 cup water

20 fresh mint leaves, plus more for garnish

½ cup bourbon

2 tablespoons fresh lemon juice

Place the sugar, water, and mint leaves in a small saucepan and bring the mixture to a boil. Let it boil for 2 to 3 minutes, until the sugar dissolves. Strain the simple syrup into a jar and let cool.

Put 4 cups ice, the bourbon, mint simple syrup, and lemon juice into a blender and pulse until smooth and slushy. Pour into goblets or highball glasses and garnish with mint leaves.

Tropical Fruit–Infused Iced Tea FAN FAVORITE

To me, iced tea is the house wine of the South. Ask for a glass of iced tea below the Mason-Dixon Line and your hostess or server will say, "Do you want that sweet or unsweet?" Having grown up in North Carolina, for me it was sweet tea. Always looking for some way to put an interesting twist on whatever I'm making, I created a perfect sweet tea with tropical fruit flavors. Making ice cubes with fruit and some of the iced tea keeps this beverage from becoming watered down. This is a sweet way to spend a summer afternoon.

Makes 6 to 8 servings

4 cups water

12 mango- or other tropical fruit–
    flavored tea bags

⅓ cup sugar

1 cup chopped fresh mango

1 cup chopped fresh strawberries

2 cups pineapple juice

1 cup fresh orange juice

1 cup sweetened lemonade

Pour the water into a large saucepan and bring it to a boil. Turn off the heat and add the tea bags. Let the tea steep for 10 minutes, then discard the bags. Add the sugar and stir until dissolved.

Pour the sweetened tea into a large pitcher and refrigerate for at least 2 hours.

Put 1 piece each of mango and strawberry in each compartment of two ice cube trays. Fill each compartment with some iced tea and freeze until solid. While the ice cubes are freezing, pour the remaining tea (about 2¼ cups), the pineapple juice, orange juice, and lemonade into a large pitcher and refrigerate. When ready to serve, add the ice cubes to the tea mixture. Or, pour the tea into a punch bowl and add the ice cubes. Serve immediately.

S'mores Martinis

Oh! My! Word! While these decadent drinks may remind you of toasting marshmallows and making s'mores over summer campfires, you can enjoy these grown-up cocktails any time of the year. Yes, Adult Chocolate Milk is just that—chocolate milk with vodka. Ask for it and the marshmallow vodka in wine and spirits stores. Finish a Valentine's Day or an anniversary dinner by serving these for dessert.

Makes 2

¼ cup chocolate syrup

2 graham crackers, finely crushed

2 marshmallows

¼ cup marshmallow vodka

¼ cup Adult Chocolate Milk

¼ cup heavy cream

Put 3 tablespoons of the chocolate syrup on a small plate. Place the crushed graham crackers on another small plate. Dip the rims of two martini glasses in the chocolate syrup, then dip the rims into the graham cracker crumbs. Quickly turn the martini glasses right side up and drizzle the remaining 1 tablespoon chocolate syrup in a spiral design on the insides of the glasses. Put the glasses in the freezer for 1 hour to let the chocolate harden.

Remove the glasses from the freezer. Heat a small nonstick skillet over medium-high heat. Put each marshmallow on the end of a skewer. Place the skewers in the skillet with a flat side of the marshmallows facing down, until the marshmallows turn golden, about 45 seconds. Remove the skewered marshmallows from the pan and, using the tines of a fork, push 1 marshmallow into each martini glass.

Fill a cocktail shaker halfway with ice, half of the marshmallow vodka, half of the Adult Chocolate Milk, and half of the cream. Shake well and strain the mixture into one of the glasses. Repeat for the second drink.

Red Velvet Milk Shakes

There is probably no more popular cake in America than red velvet. What you may not know is that the cake is actually a rich chocolate cake that turns red, thanks to a little red food coloring. (I use red cake decorating gel.) So, how can you top red velvet cake? By blending the ingredients into a frosty, creamy red velvet milk shake. For a vintage ice cream parlor touch, I serve them in tall glasses with long parfait spoons and striped paper straws.

Makes 2

6 scoops French vanilla ice cream (about 3 cups)

¼ cup red velvet cake mix

2 tablespoons cream cheese, at room temperature

2 or 3 drops red cake-decorating gel

3 tablespoons chocolate syrup

1¼ cups whole milk

1 teaspoon pure vanilla extract

Whipped cream (see page 260), red and white sprinkles, and maraschino cherries

Put the ice cream, cake mix, cream cheese, decorating gel, chocolate syrup, milk, and vanilla into a blender. Blend well, adding more milk for thinner milk shakes. Divide the mixture between two tall glasses. Garnish with the whipped cream, sprinkles, and cherries.

Chocolate Chip Cookie Milk Shakes

My mother used to make these for my brother, my sister, and me when we were sick and didn't have much of an appetite. What kid—sick or not—would turn down a milk shake? What Mom didn't tell us at the time was that she blended an egg into the milk shakes so we'd get some protein and some extra nutrition while we were on the mend. This version combines America's favorite cookie with the beloved soda fountain drink. Sorry, Mom, I now get my eggs by using rich French vanilla ice cream, which is made with eggs and specks from vanilla beans.

Makes 2

6 scoops French vanilla ice cream (about 3 cups)

6 soft-baked chocolate chip cookies, broken into pieces

2 tablespoons chocolate syrup

1¼ cups whole milk

Whipped cream (see page 260)

Combine the ice cream, pieces of 5 of the cookies, the chocolate syrup, and milk in a blender. Blend well. Divide the mixture between two tall glasses. Garnish with the whipped cream and the remaining chocolate chip cookie bits.

Strawberry-Vanilla Smoothies

We all have those days when we're on the go from the minute we wake up in the morning to falling into bed at the end of the day. On those days, I still need a quick, satisfying breakfast or mid-afternoon pick-me-up that's creamy, tasty, and soothing. Smoothies to the rescue! My favorite combines strawberries and strawberry yogurt with a heaping scoop of protein powder to keep me going. A smoothie really fills me up so I'm not so tempted by unhealthy snacks.

Makes 2

10 frozen strawberries

1 6-ounce container nonfat or low-fat strawberry yogurt

1 cup 2% milk

6 tablespoons vanilla protein powder

1 tablespoon agave nectar

Put the strawberries, yogurt, milk, protein powder, and agave in a blender. Blend on high until the drink is smooth and creamy, about 1 minute. Divide the smoothie between two tall glasses.

Frozen Peanut Butter Hot Chocolate `FAN FAVORITE`

Hot chocolate in hot weather may sound a little crazy, but *frozen* hot chocolate is something altogether different and fabulous. It's got everything I love—the richness of hot chocolate and the nuttiness of peanut butter in one glass. When it's hot out there, you deserve this cool, tasty treat.

Makes 4 servings

1 3-ounce dark chocolate bar (70% cacao), chopped

2 1.5-ounce packages peanut butter cups, chopped

2 tablespoons creamy peanut butter

1 tablespoon sugar

1½ cups whole milk

1 tablespoon hot chocolate mix

Whipped cream (see page 260), chopped peanut butter cups, and chocolate sauce (optional)

Mix the dark chocolate, peanut butter cups, peanut butter, sugar, and ½ cup of the milk in a microwave-safe bowl. Microwave on high in 20-second intervals, stirring occasionally, until the chocolate is melted and evenly incorporated. Add the hot chocolate mix and stir until thoroughly blended. Place the mixture in the refrigerator to cool.

Place the remaining 1 cup milk, the cooled chocolate mixture, and 2½ cups ice in a blender and mix until completely smooth. Pour into tall glasses and top each with a spoonful of whipped cream, chopped peanut butter cups, and a drizzle of chocolate sauce, if desired.

Quick & Easy

Like many folks, my mom owned an old-fashioned, stovetop pressure cooker that whistled and hissed. Afraid that her pressure cooker would literally pop its top, Mom never allowed us in the kitchen when she was using it. For a long time, pressure cookers were inexpensively made, especially after World War II and well into the 1950s, when quality metals were scarce.

Boy, oh boy, how times and pressure cookers have changed! Today's models are electric, safe, reliable, and time saving. Once the machine is plugged in and the lid is tightly sealed, pressure builds up and the temperature rises. Heat, in the form of steam, is quickly created and evenly infuses the food with the recipe's spices and seasonings. As a result, soups, stews, vegetables, puddings, and beans that once took hours are ready in a fraction of the time, and the flavors are not to be believed. I even use my pressure cooker during the summer, when I don't want to turn on the oven and heat up my kitchen. Cleanup is a snap. You won't believe the amazing meals you'll be able to serve your family even on weeknights. Do I need to say anything else to convince you that using a pressure cooker is a cook's dream?

Pressure Cooker Tips

· The recipes in this chapter were tested in a 6-quart electric pressure cooker. Any pressure cooker, however, can be used, as long as you follow the manufacturer's manual.

· Some recipes instruct you to sear meat or cook bacon before combining the ingredients in the pressure cooker. I find that searing large pieces of beef, pork, and chicken in a separate skillet over medium-high heat imparts a rich, brown crust that is the first step to a successfully braised dish. Some pressure cookers, however, have a setting that allows you to do this in the machine, so it's up to you.

· Layer the ingredients in the pressure cooker in the order directed.

· Never fill the pressure cooker more than two-thirds full with food and liquid. The steam needs space to build up and thoroughly cook the food.

· Two techniques—quick release and natural release—are used to release pressure, and I specify which one to use in each recipe. "Quick release" means that all the pressure escapes at one time when the steam valve is opened. "Natural release" means that the pressure cooker sits once it's finished cooking and the pressure slowly and naturally cools down. This can take up to fifteen minutes.

Chicken Soup with Gnocchi

Chicken soup is the ultimate comfort food whether you're chilled to the bone on a frigid winter's day, suffering from a cold, or need a little TLC after a bad day. This chicken soup has everything—rich, golden broth; pieces of tender chicken; fragrant herbs and vegetables; and plump, Italian potato dumplings—you could possibly want in a bowl of hot goodness. The best part is you don't have to wait hours for the soup to simmer. Since this soothing soup is made in the pressure cooker, it's ready in just thirty minutes.

Makes 4 to 6 servings

2 pounds boneless, skinless chicken breasts

1 teaspoon kosher salt

1 teaspoon freshly ground black pepper

2 tablespoons canola oil

1 cup finely chopped onions

½ cup finely chopped carrots

½ cup finely chopped celery

6 cups chicken broth

1 teaspoon onion powder

½ teaspoon garlic salt

3 tablespoons fresh thyme leaves

2 tablespoons chopped fresh rosemary

2 tablespoons minced fresh parsley

1 1-pound package potato gnocchi

1 cup (4 ounces) grated Parmigiano-Reggiano

Season the chicken with the salt and pepper. Heat the canola oil in the pressure cooker or in a skillet over medium heat. Brown the chicken on both sides, then transfer to a plate. Add the onions, carrots, and celery and sauté until soft, 4 to 5 minutes.

Place the chicken, vegetables, chicken broth, onion powder, garlic salt, thyme, rosemary, and parsley in the pressure cooker. Cover and lock the lid. Set the pressure to high for 8 minutes. Do a quick release. Open the lid. Transfer the chicken to a serving bowl and, using two forks, shred the chicken. Return the shredded chicken to the pressure cooker. Add the gnocchi and Parmesan. Close the lid. Set the pressure to low for 4 minutes. Do a quick release. Open the lid and ladle the soup and gnocchi into bowls.

Smoked Gouda, Bacon, and Pea Risotto

Risotto is a rib-sticking rice dish that can be served as an entrée or as a side. As much as I love risotto, I don't always have time to make it the traditional way. This Italian rice classic requires a good thirty minutes of constant stirring while adding hot broth until each grain is creamy and tender. The pressure cooker cuts the cooking time in half and leaves your hands free to make a crisp green salad and set the table. A couple of tips: Use a short-grain rice like Arborio. Make sure that each grain of rice is coated with the bacon fat before adding the wine and broth. I stir in some bright green peas for a nice pop of color.

Makes 6 to 8 servings

½ pound center-cut bacon slices, diced

2 garlic cloves, minced

¼ cup minced shallots

2 cups Arborio rice

¼ cup dry white wine

4 cups chicken broth

1 teaspoon fresh thyme leaves

1 teaspoon kosher salt

½ teaspoon freshly ground black pepper

1½ cups (6 ounces) shredded smoked Gouda

½ cup (2 ounces) grated Parmigiano-Reggiano

1 cup hot whole milk

2 cups frozen peas, thawed

Cook the bacon in the pressure cooker on high until crisp. Remove the bacon, but leave the fat. Add the garlic and shallots and sauté until soft, 3 to 4 minutes. Add the rice and stir well to make sure that all the rice is coated with the fat. Add the white wine and cook until the rice absorbs all but 2 tablespoons.

Add the chicken broth, bacon, thyme, salt, and pepper and stir well until all the ingredients are combined. Close the lid and set the pressure to high for 8 minutes. Do a quick release. Open the lid. Add the Gouda, Parmesan, milk, and peas at the same time, but stir only once. Overmixing will cause the risotto to clump; it should be smooth and creamy. Ladle into bowls and serve immediately.

Pressure Cooker "Clambake"

A traditional clambake takes a lot of time and planning. You have to dig a pit in the sand, fill it with large rocks, build a fire, wait for the rocks to become hot, add the food, and cover the whole thing with seaweed and a canvas. Then, you still have to wait hours for the food to be ready. By filling a pressure cooker with clams, shrimp, mussels, corn, and potatoes, you can have a clambake on the table in a fraction of the time. I'd finish this meal with Peach Melba Icebox Pie (page 261) or Key Lime Pie (page 259).

Makes 4 servings

1 cup water

6 to 8 small red potatoes

4 small ears frozen corn (do not thaw)

1½ teaspoons kosher salt

4 tablespoons (½ stick) unsalted butter, cut into cubes

1 pound frozen jumbo (21/25 count) shrimp, peeled and deveined

1 pound littleneck or other hard clams, scrubbed

1 pound cultivated mussels, scrubbed

Lemon wedges

Place the water, potatoes, and corn, in that order, in the pressure cooker. Sprinkle the salt and butter cubes over the potatoes and corn. Add the shrimp, clams, and mussels, in that order, to the pressure cooker. Close the lid and set the pressure to high for 3 minutes. Do a quick release. Open the lid. Ladle the seafood and broth into large bowls and serve with lemon wedges.

Chili con Carne

As far as I'm concerned, you can't have too many chili recipes in your repertoire. Tex-Mex chili con carne—chili with meat—is all about the layers of flavors from the earthy cumin, smoked paprika, pungent oregano, and a couple tablespoons of sofrito, a Mexican blend of tomatoes, peppers, cilantro, and other ingredients. (Look for jarred sofrito in the Mexican food aisle.) Offer shredded sharp Cheddar, sour cream, diced and seeded jalapeños, and finely chopped white onions on the side. Whether you serve it by the bowlful or use it as a topping on hot dogs, this pressure cooker version is a standout in my book.

Makes 8 to 10 servings

2 pounds 80% lean ground beef

2 cups chopped white onions

1 large red bell pepper, seeded and cut into ¼-inch cubes

4 garlic cloves, minced

1 tablespoon ground cumin

1 tablespoon smoked paprika

1 tablespoon chipotle chili powder

1 teaspoon Mexican dried oregano

½ cup beef broth

1 28-ounce can diced tomatoes

2 tablespoons jarred sofrito

3 tablespoons tomato paste

1½ tablespoons kosher salt

1 tablespoon canned mild or hot jalapeños, drained

1 bay leaf

1 14.5-ounce can dark red kidney beans, drained and rinsed

1 14.5-ounce can light (or pink) kidney beans, drained and rinsed

Brown the beef in the pressure cooker. Using a slotted spoon, remove the beef and leave 2 tablespoons of fat in the pressure cooker. Add the onions and bell pepper to the pressure cooker and sauté until soft, 4 to 5 minutes. Add the garlic, cumin, paprika, chili powder, oregano, and beef broth and cook until fragrant, 2 to 3 minutes. Return the beef to the pressure cooker and add the tomatoes, sofrito, tomato paste, salt, jalapeños, bay leaf, dark red kidney beans, and light kidney beans to the pressure cooker. Close the lid and set the pressure to high for 8 minutes. Do a quick release. Open the lid. Discard the bay leaf. Ladle the chili into bowls and serve while hot with your choice of toppings.

Chicken in a Pot

One way my mom got weeknight dinner on the table was by cooking a whole chicken in her pressure cooker. Even my brother, my sister, and I couldn't finish the whole bird at one meal, so there was always enough for her to make Mom's Chicken and Rice Casserole (page 182), chicken noodle soup, or chicken and dumplings later in the week. This recipe will become your go-to, quick-chicken solution.

Makes 4 to 6 servings

3 tablespoons garlic salt

¾ teaspoon freshly ground black pepper

1 4- to 5-pound chicken

2 to 3 tablespoons canola oil

2½ cups chicken broth

1 tablespoon Better Than Bouillon Chicken Base

2 carrots, cut diagonally into ½-inch slices

2 or 3 celery stalks, cut diagonally into ¼-inch slices

1 large white onion, cut into 6 to 8 thick wedges

Bouquet garni of 1 bay leaf, 4 large rosemary sprigs, 4 large thyme sprigs, 4 parsley sprigs, and 4 sage leaves tied in a piece of cheesecloth

Place the roasting rack in the pressure cooker. Combine the garlic salt and pepper in a bowl. Season the chicken inside and out with the garlic salt mixture. Heat the canola oil in a skillet over medium-high heat. Sear the chicken on all sides. Transfer the chicken to a plate and pour any skillet drippings into the pressure cooker.

Add the chicken broth and bouillon base to the pressure cooker. Place the chicken in the pressure cooker. Add the carrots, celery, and onion to both sides of the chicken. Add the bouquet garni. Close the lid and set the pressure to high for 30 minutes. Do a natural release. Open the lid and transfer the chicken to a large bowl. The chicken will be falling-apart tender, so there's no need for carving. Strain the vegetables from the broth, discard the bouquet garni, and reserve the liquid. Serve the chicken with the vegetables and some cooking liquid over the chicken.

Honey Dijon Chicken

Honey Dijon mustard adds just the right balance of spiciness and sweetness to chicken parts cooked in a pressure cooker. Kid-friendly, quick, and perfect for a last-minute weeknight meal, this will become a popular dish that everyone will ask you to prepare. Round out the meal with steamed broccoli or asparagus and some wild rice or buttered noodles.

Makes 6 to 8 servings

4 pounds bone-in, skinless chicken thighs and breasts

2 teaspoons kosher salt

½ teaspoon freshly ground black pepper

2 tablespoons canola oil

½ cup Dijon mustard

¼ cup honey

1 tablespoon cider vinegar

2 tablespoons minced fresh parsley, plus more for garnish

1 tablespoon (packed) light brown sugar

1 cup chicken broth

1 tablespoon cornstarch

Season the chicken with the salt and pepper. Heat the canola oil in a skillet over medium-high heat. Brown the chicken on both sides, then transfer the pieces to the pressure cooker. Whisk together ¼ cup of the mustard, 2 tablespoons of the honey, the vinegar, parsley, and brown sugar in a bowl. Pour the mustard sauce over the chicken and stir to coat well. Let the chicken marinate in the sauce for 15 minutes, stirring occasionally.

Add the chicken broth to the pressure cooker. Close the lid and set the pressure to high for 8 minutes. Do a natural release. Open the lid and transfer the chicken to a serving platter. Whisk 3 tablespoons of the mustard and the remaining 2 tablespoons honey into the pressure cooker. To make a slurry, whisk together ⅓ cup hot broth from the pressure cooker, the cornstarch, and the remaining 1 tablespoon mustard. Whisk the slurry into the pressure cooker, bring to a boil, and stir until the sauce has thickened slightly. Serve the chicken with the sauce and garnish with additional parsley, if desired.

Sunday Pot Roast

When Mom made pot roast for dinner every other Sunday, she seared the meat on the stove and then slowly braised it in the oven for four to five hours, until it was tender and falling apart. The pressure cooker makes short work of this classic, taking just a little more than an hour, and infuses flavor into every comforting bite. Mom used a boneless bottom round roast, but I find that a boneless top round offers the best results. While the pressure cooker is doing its thing, make a batch of biscuits to mop up the sauce.

Makes 4 to 5 servings, with leftovers

1 3-pound trimmed, boneless top round Angus sirloin roast

3 garlic cloves, thinly sliced

1 tablespoon kosher salt

1 teaspoon freshly ground black pepper

2 tablespoons all-purpose flour

2 tablespoons canola oil

2 cups thickly sliced onions

2 cups beef broth

1 1-ounce package onion soup mix

2 tablespoons Worcestershire sauce

1 tablespoon Better Than Bouillon Beef Base

5 red potatoes, quartered

4 carrots, cut diagonally into ½-inch pieces

Make ten to twelve 1-inch-deep slits all over the roast and place the sliced garlic in the slits. Season the roast well with the salt and pepper. Next, dust the roast with the flour. Heat the canola oil in a skillet over high heat. Sear all sides of the roast until brown. Transfer the roast to the pressure cooker. Add the onions to the skillet and cook until translucent, 5 to 6 minutes. Deglaze the skillet with ½ cup of the beef broth, scraping any bits from the bottom of the pan. Transfer the onions and any juices from the skillet to the pressure cooker. Add the remaining 1½ cups beef broth, the onion soup mix, Worcestershire sauce, and beef base to the pressure cooker. Close the lid and set the pressure to high for 40 minutes. Do a quick release. Open the lid. Add the potatoes and carrots, close the lid, and set the timer for 15 additional minutes. Do a natural release. Open the lid and transfer the roast to a platter. Cover with aluminum foil and let rest for 10 minutes before slicing. Once the meat is sliced, arrange it along with the onions, potatoes, and carrots on the platter and serve with the gravy.

Beef Bourguignon

In the movie *Julie & Julia,* Amy Adams plays Julie Powell, who spent a year cooking her way through Julia Child's (Julia played by Meryl Streep) *Mastering the Art of French Cooking.* One of the more notable recipes that Julie spent a lot of time on was Child's *boeuf bourguignonne,* a dish she prepared for a very important dinner party. As someone who cooks on TV, I owe a great deal to Julia Child, who inspired me as well as millions of others with her skills, honesty, and charm. Here's my effortless pressure cooker spin on this French stew classic. Serve it on a bed of buttered noodles or mashed potatoes. *Bon appétit!*

Makes 4 to 5 servings

2 to 2½ pounds beef chuck roast, trimmed and cut into 1-inch cubes

1½ tablespoons kosher salt

1 teaspoon freshly ground black pepper

6 slices thick-cut bacon, diced

20 pearl onions, peeled

3 garlic cloves, minced

1 pound cremini mushrooms, quartered

2 tablespoons extra-virgin olive oil, plus more if needed

½ cup all-purpose flour

2 cups beef broth

3 cups red wine

2 to 3 carrots, cut diagonally into ½-inch pieces

1 bay leaf

1 teaspoon dried thyme, crushed

1 teaspoon dried rosemary, crushed

4 tablespoons (½ stick) unsalted butter, at room temperature

Season the beef with 1 tablespoon of the salt and ¾ teaspoon of the pepper. Cook the bacon in a skillet until crispy. Using a slotted spoon, remove the bacon, leaving the fat in the pan. Add the onions and sauté for 3 to 4 minutes. Add the garlic and sauté until fragrant, about 1 minute. Remove the onions and garlic from the skillet to a bowl, leaving the fat. Add the mushrooms to the skillet and sauté for 2 to 3 minutes. Remove the mushrooms and add to the onions and garlic. Turn the heat off for a moment.

Heat 1 tablespoon of the olive oil in the same skillet over medium-high heat. Dredge the beef in ¼ cup of the flour. Brown the beef in batches in the skillet, adding the remaining 1 tablespoon olive oil, if needed. Be sure not to overcrowd the pan. As you brown the meat, add a bit more oil as needed. Remove the beef from the skillet. Add ⅓ cup of the beef broth and deglaze the skillet, scraping up all the brown bits from the bottom of the pan. Add this to the pressure cooker. Add the beef, bacon, onions, garlic, mushrooms, red wine, the remaining 1⅔ cups beef broth, the carrots, bay leaf, thyme, and rosemary to the pressure cooker. Close the lid and set the pressure to high for 20 minutes.

While the beef is cooking, blend together the butter and the remaining ¼ cup flour in a bowl. Once the stew is finished cooking, do a quick release. Open the lid. Discard the bay leaf. Stir in the flour-butter mixture and the remaining ½ tablespoon salt and ¼ teaspoon pepper before serving.

Osso Buco

I once took a cooking class to learn how to make this Italian classic. The teacher admonished us to be on time, because the osso buco—bone with a hole—had to braise in the oven for hours before it would be ready to eat at the end of class. In this recipe, the pressure cooker comes to the rescue! Osso buco can be on the table in less than an hour. Purchase veal shanks of the same size so they cook evenly. Gremolata, a traditional condiment of garlic, herbs, and lemon, is sprinkled on top of the veal shanks just before serving. Spoon the veal shanks and plenty of gravy onto a bed of orzo. It just doesn't get any better.

Makes 4 servings

4 veal shanks (3 to 4 pounds total)

1 tablespoon kosher salt

2 teaspoons freshly ground black pepper

3 tablespoons all-purpose flour

1 teaspoon garlic powder

1 teaspoon dried thyme

1 teaspoon minced fresh sage

½ pound pancetta, cut into ¼-inch cubes

3 to 4 tablespoons extra-virgin olive oil, as needed

1 cup finely chopped carrots

1 cup finely chopped celery

2 cups finely chopped onions

3 garlic cloves, minced

1 tablespoon tomato paste

1 cup dry white wine

1 cup chicken broth

½ cup chopped fresh basil

1 bay leaf

1 14.5-ounce can crushed tomatoes with basil, garlic, and oregano

Gremolata

Leaves of 2 or 3 fresh thyme sprigs

¼ cup minced fresh parsley

Zest of 1 lemon

2 garlic cloves, minced

1 teaspoon kosher salt

½ teaspoon freshly ground black pepper

To make the osso buco, season the veal shanks with the salt and pepper. Combine the flour, garlic powder, thyme, and sage in a shallow bowl.

Put the pancetta in a skillet and sauté over medium-high heat until cooked and just crispy, 3 to 4 minutes. Using a slotted spoon, remove the pancetta, leaving the drippings in the pan, to a bowl. Add enough olive oil to coat the bottom of the skillet. Dredge the shanks in the flour mixture, shaking off any excess, and put them in the skillet to sear on all sides. Once the veal shanks are brown, transfer them to a platter. Stir the carrots, celery, onions, garlic, and tomato paste into the skillet and sauté just until soft, 4 to 5 minutes. Add the white wine and chicken broth and cook, scraping up the brown bits from the bottom of the pan, until the liquid has reduced by about one third, 4 to 5 minutes. Pour the vegetable mixture into the pressure cooker. Add the veal shanks, pancetta, basil, bay leaf, and tomatoes to the pressure cooker. Close the lid and set the pressure to high for 30 minutes. Do a natural release. Open the lid and transfer the veal shanks to a platter. Discard the bay leaf. Use a handheld immersion blender to blend the sauce in the pressure cooker.

To make the gremolata, put the thyme, parsley, lemon zest, garlic, salt, and pepper into a mini food processor. Pulse until coarsely ground. Transfer to a small bowl.

To serve, place the veal shanks in shallow bowls and spoon some sauce over each serving. Pass the gremolata so everyone can sprinkle on the desired amount.

Asian Pulled Pork

At Chinese restaurants, I often start with some sweet-and-sour barbecued spareribs. I wondered if I could combine this Chinese American classics with the flavors of Southern-style pork. I wanted instant gratification—no waiting for the pork to cook low and slow in the oven—so I successfully experimented with my pressure cooker.

Makes 8 to 10 servings

Asian Barbecue Sauce

1 cup hoisin sauce

⅓ cup soy sauce

½ cup fresh orange juice

2 tablespoons (packed) dark brown sugar

3 garlic cloves, minced

¼ cup sweet Thai chili sauce

4 or 5 drops Sriracha sauce

1 tablespoon rice vinegar

1 tablespoon grated fresh ginger

Pulled Pork

1 4- to 5-pound Boston butt, trimmed and cut into 4 or 5 pieces

1 tablespoon kosher salt

1 teaspoon freshly ground black pepper

1 tablespoon sesame oil

1 tablespoon canola oil

1 medium onion, thinly sliced

1 cup chicken broth

Kaiser, brioche, or slider rolls

2 scallions, thinly sliced diagonally

To make the sauce, whisk together the hoisin sauce, soy sauce, orange juice, brown sugar, garlic, chili sauce, Sriracha, rice vinegar, and ginger in a bowl.

To make the pork, season the pork pieces with salt and pepper. Put the sesame oil and canola oil in a large skillet over medium-high heat. In batches, sear the pork pieces on all sides. Put the pork into the pressure cooker. Add the onion to the skillet and cook until translucent, 5 to 6 minutes. Add the chicken broth and deglaze, scraping up any brown bits from the bottom of the skillet. Add the onion and skillet drippings to the pressure cooker. Pour 1 cup of the Asian barbecue sauce into the pressure cooker and stir well to coat the pork. Reserve the remaining sauce to pour over the pork after it is cooked. Close the lid and set the pressure to high for 50 minutes. Do a natural release. Open the lid and transfer the pork to a large bowl. Using two forks, shred the pork. Heat the remaining barbecue sauce in a saucepan. Serve the pork on toasted rolls with additional sauce and garnish with the scallions.

Pork Chops with Marinara Sauce

Because pork chops were affordable and quick to prepare, we ate them at least once a week when I was growing up, usually on Wednesday nights. Mom fried them in a big cast-iron skillet, then cooked some hominy in the pork fat and served them with some green beans from a Mason jar that my Grandmother Burnzie had put up during the summer.

I'm always looking for new ways to prepare pork chops. Cooking them in the pressure cooker means dinner can be on the table in no time. Serve with a side of spaghetti and a crisp salad of romaine or mixed greens. *Buon appetito!*

Makes 4 servings

4 6- to 8-ounce bone-in center-cut pork chops

2 teaspoons kosher salt

½ teaspoon freshly ground black pepper

1 tablespoon extra-virgin olive oil

1 medium onion, thinly sliced

3 garlic cloves, minced

½ cup chicken broth

1 teaspoon tomato paste

1 28-ounce can crushed tomatoes with basil and oregano

1 14.5-ounce can quartered artichoke hearts, drained

Season the pork chops with the salt and pepper. Heat the olive oil in a large skillet over medium-high heat. Brown the pork chops on both sides and transfer to a plate. Add the onion and garlic to the skillet and sauté until soft, 4 to 5 minutes. Transfer the onion and garlic to another plate.

Put the chicken broth and tomato paste in the pressure cooker and stir well. Add the pork chops, then top them with the onion, garlic, and tomatoes. Close the lid and set the pressure to high for 9 minutes. Do a quick release. Transfer the pork chops to a platter. Stir the artichokes into the sauce and heat until warm. Spoon the artichokes and sauce over the pork chops and serve immediately.

Golden Beets with Molasses and Brown Sugar

My guess is that people turn up their noses when offered beets because they've eaten them only right from the can or when cooked too long. Cooking beets under pressure retains their natural sweetness and their antioxidant richness. I cook them with cider vinegar, molasses, and brown sugar to give them a tangy taste. If you've had only red beets, give bright, golden yellow beets a try. They're delicious and won't stain your hands or cutting board. Serve them with Grilled Kielbasa, Pepper, and Onion Sandwiches with Barbecue Sauce (page 138), Parmesan Pork Cutlets (see page 214), or Turkey Meat Loaf (page 210).

Makes 6 to 8 servings

6 golden beets, leave ½-inch stem

3½ tablespoons cider vinegar

1 tablespoon extra-virgin olive oil

⅓ cup molasses

2 tablespoons (packed) dark brown sugar

4 tablespoons (½ stick) cold unsalted butter, cut into 4 or 5 pieces

Place the beets in the pressure cooker. Add 1 to 1½ cups water, enough to cover the beets halfway. Close the lid and set the pressure to high for 20 minutes. Do a quick release. Open the lid. The beets should be tender when pierced with a fork. If not, close the lid and set the timer for an additional 5 minutes. When the beets are cool enough to handle, rinse under cool running water and remove the skins. The skins should slide right off. Cut the beets into large chunks and put them in a bowl. Gently toss with 1 tablespoon of the vinegar and the olive oil.

Combine the molasses, brown sugar, and the remaining 2½ tablespoons vinegar in a saucepan over medium heat, stirring continuously. Once the sugar has melted, stir in the butter, one piece at a time. Spoon the sauce over the warm dressed beets and serve immediately.

Ratatouille

In Disney's *Ratatouille*, the culinary genius Remy the rat saves the day—and Gusteau's restaurant—by making a ratatouille so extraordinary that the snotty food critic Anton Ego is immediately transported back to his mother's kitchen. Voilà! That's what the best comfort food does: One perfect bite of macaroni 'n' cheese, red beans and rice, or ratatouille brings back memories and warm feelings. Ratatouille, a vegetable stew of eggplant, summer squash, bell peppers, and tomatoes, is the best way I know to use up your end-of-summer garden vegetables. It freezes well and makes a great omelet filling or pasta topping,.

Makes 6 to 8 servings

2 to 3 tablespoons extra-virgin olive oil

1 large onion, finely chopped

4 to 5 small eggplants, cut into ½-inch cubes

3 garlic cloves, minced

1 large yellow squash, cut into ½-inch cubes

1 large zucchini, seeded and cut into ½-inch dice

1 large red bell pepper, seeded and cut into ¼-inch dice

1 large yellow bell pepper, seeded and cut into ¼-inch dice

3 cups (1½ to 2 pounds) diced plum tomatoes

¼ cup chopped sun-dried tomatoes

1 cup canned crushed tomatoes

½ cup vegetable broth

2 tablespoons balsamic vinegar

1 tablespoon kosher salt

1 teaspoon red pepper flakes

2 tablespoons minced fresh oregano

Leaves of 4 or 5 fresh thyme sprigs, coarsely chopped

½ cup julienned fresh basil leaves

Grated Parmigiano-Reggiano

Heat the olive oil in the pressure cooker. Add the onion and sauté until translucent, 5 to 6 minutes. Add the eggplant and sauté until softened slightly, 2 to 3 minutes. Add the garlic and sauté until fragrant, about 1 minute. Add the yellow squash, zucchini, red bell pepper, yellow bell pepper, tomatoes, vegetable broth, vinegar, salt, red pepper flakes, oregano, and thyme. Close the lid and set the pressure to high for 5 minutes. Do a quick release. Stir in the basil and let simmer for 1 minute before serving with the cheese.

White Chocolate–Cherry Rice Pudding FAN FAVORITE

The first time I ate rice pudding was when I went to sleepaway summer camp as a little boy. Until then, I had eaten rice only as a side dish with savory foods. The pudding at camp was a silky custard dotted with soft rice and lots of raisins. I add white chocolate to keep the pudding pearly white and dried cherries instead of raisins. As soon as you release the steam valve on the pressure, your family will come running to see what smells so good.

Makes 6 to 8 servings

1½ cups Arborio rice

2 cups whole milk

½ cup heavy cream

½ teaspoon table salt

¾ cup sugar

1½ teaspoons pure vanilla extract

¼ teaspoon ground cinnamon

8 ounces white chocolate, finely chopped

¾ cup dried cherries

Put the rice, milk, cream, salt, sugar, vanilla, cinnamon, and white chocolate in the pressure cooker. Stir well. Close the lid and set the pressure to low for 20 minutes. Do a natural release and don't open the lid for 5 minutes. Open the lid, stir in the dried cherries, and let stand for 5 minutes before spooning into bowls.

Low & Slow

After a long day, especially in the cooler months, I look forward to something comfy and hearty for dinner. For me, there's nothing better than French Onion Soup that's been simmering all day or a big platter of tender beef ribs. The question is how can you baste, braise, stir, add extra broth, and otherwise tend to dishes like these if you're at work or tending to the kids?

The slow cooker comes to the rescue. This appliance does the work for you so you have time to do the other important things in your life. Electric slow cookers are simple to use—just add the ingredients as directed, set the timer, and off you go. You don't have to remember to baste a braising roast or add liquid to soups and stews so they don't scorch. With a slow cooker, all the moisture stays in the food; nothing dries out and all the flavors are locked in. My mom used her slow cooker to make pork roast or stew. She just put everything in the slow cooker in the morning before heading off to work. When I let myself in the house after school, it was all I could do to wait until dinnertime because of the mouthwatering aromas.

The slow cooker is a money saver—tougher, less expensive cuts of meat become oh-so-tender when cooked for hours on end. An added plus is that the slow cooker frees up the oven and stovetop for other dishes, especially at the holidays. This really is set-it-and-forget-it cooking.

Slow Cooker Tips

- These recipes were tested in a 6-quart electric slow cooker with settings for high and low. Any slow cooker, however, can be used; just be sure to read the manual that comes with your appliance to make sure you understand how it works.

- To maximize flavor and get the best results, brown meat and sauté some ingredients as directed in a separate skillet before putting them into the slow cooker.

- One hour on the high setting is equivalent to two hours on the slow setting.

- One of the great things about using a slow cooker is that you never have to stir or baste whatever is cooking. Removing the lid while the slow cooker is on will cause the temperature to drop and additional cooking time may be necessary. Remove the lid only when instructed to do so.

- Adding more ingredients than listed will cause the timing and the temperature to be off. Fill the slow cooker no more than two-thirds full.

- For safe consumption, the temperature of cooked beef should reach 140°F and poultry and pork should reach 160°F. If you have any doubts, insert an instant-read thermometer into the meat or poultry. If the temperature is lower than mentioned, set the timer for additional cooking time.

French Onion Soup FAN FAVORITE

The secret to this classic soup is to cook onions low and slow in butter for at least thirty minutes so they release their water content and become soft, golden, and sweet, or caramelized. Once the onions are caramelized, they're cooked in broth. The soup is ladled into bowls and slices of French bread are placed on top. Each bowl is topped with shredded cheeses and browned in the oven until the cheeses are melted and gooey.

Makes 6 servings

4 tablespoons (½ stick) unsalted butter

1 tablespoon canola oil

2½ to 3 pounds yellow onions, thinly sliced

1 teaspoon kosher salt

¼ teaspoon freshly ground black pepper

2 garlic cloves, minced

1 cup dry white wine

2 bay leaves

2 quarts beef broth

1 tablespoon Better Than Bouillon Beef Base

Asiago Croutons (recipe follows)

4 cups (1 pound) shredded Gruyère

¼ cup (1 ounce) shredded Asiago

Melt the butter with the canola oil in a Dutch oven over low heat. Add the onions and season with salt and pepper. Increase the heat to medium and cook the onions, stirring occasionally, until the onions are caramelized, 25 to 30 minutes. Add the garlic and sauté until fragrant, 1 to 2 minutes. Raise the heat to high and stir in the white wine. Once the liquid has reduced by half, pour the onion mixture into the slow cooker. Add the bay leaves, beef broth, and beef base. Cover and cook on high for 7 hours.

When the timer goes off, preheat the oven to broil. Arrange six ovenproof bowls on a baking sheet. With a slotted spoon, transfer the cooked onions to the bowls, being sure to discard the bay leaves. Ladle the hot soup into the bowls, leaving about ¼ inch of space at the tops. Place 2 or 3 croutons on top of each bowl. Pile the Gruyère and sprinkle the Asiago on top of the croutons. Put the bowls under the broiler and broil until the cheeses melt and become bubbly and brown, 2 to 3 minutes. Serve the soup hot with additional croutons.

Asiago Croutons

Makes 18 to 24

1 day-old baguette, cut diagonally into
    ½-inch slices

½ cup extra-virgin olive oil

1 tablespoon chopped fresh parsley

½ teaspoon garlic salt

½ teaspoon freshly ground black pepper

½ teaspoon onion powder

1 cup (4 ounces) grated Asiago

Preheat the oven to 400°F.

Arrange the bread slices on a baking sheet. Whisk together the olive oil, parsley, garlic salt, pepper, and onion powder. Brush the oil-herb mixture onto the bread slices. Sprinkle the Asiago evenly over the croutons. Bake until lightly brown and the cheese is melted, 9 to 12 minutes. Watch the croutons carefully to make sure the cheese doesn't burn.

Chicken Tortilla Soup FAN FAVORITE

While the list of spices may look long, know that each one plays a supporting role that results in a full-flavored soup. Enjoy the hearty soup on its own or serve it with cheese quesadillas or grilled cheese sandwiches. There's no better way to make your house a home than having something warm and comforting simmering all day long in the slow cooker. When your family walks in the door, they'll say, "Boy, that smells great! How long before dinner?"

Makes 6 to 8 servings

Chicken

1 teaspoon paprika

1 teaspoon dried oregano

1 teaspoon ground cumin

1 teaspoon chili powder

⅛ teaspoon cayenne

½ teaspoon kosher salt

1 tablespoon extra-virgin olive oil

4 boneless, skinless chicken breasts

Soup

4 garlic cloves, minced

1 large onion, cut into small dice

1 red bell pepper, cut into small dice

1 green bell pepper, cut into small dice

1 jalapeño, seeded and minced

2 canned chipotle peppers in adobo sauce, minced

1 28-ounce can petite diced tomatoes

4 cups chicken broth

1 cup frozen corn kernels

1 teaspoon dried oregano

½ teaspoon ground cumin

1 teaspoon chili powder

1 19-ounce can red kidney beans, drained and rinsed

2 tablespoons coarsely ground cornmeal

2 tablespoons fresh lime juice

1½ cups coarsely chopped fresh cilantro leaves

Shredded Monterey Jack, crushed corn tortilla chips, chopped avocado, sour cream, and lime wedges

Preheat the oven to 375°F.

To make the chicken, combine the paprika, oregano, cumin, chili powder, cayenne, salt, and olive oil in a bowl to make a paste. Rub the chicken breasts generously with the paste and place in a baking dish. Roast the chicken until completely cooked through, about 20 minutes. When it is cool enough to handle, shred or dice the chicken.

To make the soup, put the shredded chicken, garlic, onion, red bell pepper, green bell pepper, jalapeño, chipotles, diced tomatoes, chicken broth, corn, oregano, cumin, chili powder, kidney beans, cornmeal, and lime juice in the slow cooker. Cover and cook on high for 3½ hours. When finished, stir in the cilantro. Ladle the soup into bowls and serve accompanied by the cheese, tortilla chips, avocado, sour cream, and lime wedges.

Chicken Soup with Matzo Balls

The first time I ate chicken soup with matzo balls was when I was presenting a cookbook years ago on QVC. What amazed me was how similar it was to my mother's chicken and dumplings. Matzo is an unleavened cracker-like bread eaten during the Jewish holiday of Passover. According to the Bible, when Pharaoh expelled the Jews from Egypt, they had to leave in such a hurry that they didn't have time for their bread to rise, so they baked the unleavened dough on hot desert stones. Fortunately for us, we can simply go to the grocery store and purchase matzo meal in the kosher foods aisle.

Makes 8 to 10 servings

Soup

1 4- to 5-pound roasting chicken, cut into quarters

6 to 8 fresh thyme sprigs

6 to 8 fresh parsley sprigs

3 bay leaves

4 to 5 black peppercorns

3 garlic cloves, cut in half

1 cup diced carrots

1 cup diced celery

1½ cups finely chopped onions

1 quart chicken broth

2 tablespoons Better Than Bouillon Chicken Base

Kosher salt, as needed

Matzo Balls

1 cup matzo meal

¼ cup chicken fat, skimmed from the soup, *or* ¼ cup rendered chicken fat (7-ounce containers are found near frozen kosher meat)

4 large eggs, separated

1 tablespoon minced fresh thyme leaves

¼ cup minced fresh parsley

1½ teaspoons kosher salt, plus more if needed

¼ teaspoon freshly ground black pepper

To make the soup, put the chicken, thyme, parsley, bay leaves, peppercorns, garlic, carrots, celery, onions, chicken broth, and chicken base in the slow cooker in the order listed. Add enough water to fill the slow cooker almost to the top. Cover and cook on low for 6 hours. Open the lid and skim off the fat, reserving ¼ cup for the matzo balls. Drain the chicken, vegetables, and herbs in a colander set over a large bowl. Add the broth back into the slow cooker. Remove and shred the meat from the chicken bones and add to the soup. Discard the skin and bones. Add the vegetables back into the slow cooker as well. Taste the soup and add salt, if necessary.

To make the matzo balls, mix together the matzo meal, chicken fat, egg yolks, thyme, parsley, salt, and pepper in a bowl. Put the egg whites in the bowl of a standing mixer with the whisk attachment and beat to stiff peaks. Using a spatula, fold the egg whites into the matzo mixture until no streaks remain. Cover the bowl with plastic wrap and refrigerate to firm up for 30 minutes.

Using a small ice cream scoop or wet hands, form the matzo mixture into 1-inch balls and gently lower them into the hot soup. Set the slow cooker to high and cook for 1½ to 2 hours. To serve, ladle 1 or 2 matzo balls and some chicken, vegetables, and broth into bowls. If there are any leftover matzo balls, store them separately from the soup.

Vegetarian Black Bean Soup FAN FAVORITE

When I'm hosting *In the Kitchen with David,* many viewers call in or join our live chats and ask me for more hearty meals without meat. This comforting black bean soup can be served to vegetarians and vegans alike. Puréeing just some of the soup makes it creamy but leaves the rest of the beans and vegetables with plenty of texture. I serve this with some crusty artisan bread.

Makes 4 to 6 servings

1 16-ounce bag black beans

½ teaspoon sugar

6 cups vegetable broth or water

¾ teaspoon kosher salt

¾ teaspoon freshly ground black pepper

2 teaspoons adobo seasoning (choose any except the bitter orange and lemon flavors)

5 garlic cloves, minced

¾ cup chopped onion

½ cup chopped celery

½ cup chopped red bell pepper

½ cup chopped green bell pepper

1 tablespoon hot sauce

⅓ cup fresh cilantro, chopped, plus more for garnish

Sour cream

Place the beans, sugar, 5 cups of the vegetable broth, the salt, pepper, adobo, garlic, onion, celery, red bell pepper, green bell pepper, and hot sauce in the slow cooker. Cover and cook on high for 2½ hours. Ladle 3 cups of the soup and the remaining 1 cup vegetable broth into a blender and blend until smooth. Add the puréed soup back into the slow cooker. Stir in the cilantro. Ladle the soup into bowls and serve with sour cream and additional chopped cilantro.

White Bean Chicken Chili   `FAN FAVORITE`

A lighter alternative to beef-and-bean chili is tender chicken with creamy cannellini beans. These white beans are perfect for slow cooking as they hold their shape when heated. They're also high in protein and vitamin B. A good dose of spices adds layers of flavor while still keeping it light. Serve it with corn bread or crusty bread to make sure you don't miss a single drop of goodness.

Makes 4 to 6 servings

2 tablespoons extra-virgin olive oil

1 pound boneless, skinless chicken breasts, cut into 1-inch pieces

1½ teaspoons kosher salt

¼ teaspoon freshly ground black pepper

1 large onion, chopped

4 large garlic cloves, chopped

1 tablespoon ground cumin

1 teaspoon dried oregano

½ teaspoon red pepper flakes

3 15-ounce cans cannellini (white kidney) beans, drained and rinsed

1 cup chicken broth

1 7-ounce can diced green chiles, drained

⅓ cup diced red bell pepper

½ cup heavy cream

Shredded Cheddar, sour cream or plain yogurt, chopped fresh cilantro, and crushed tortilla chips

Heat the olive oil in a skillet over medium-high heat. Season the chicken with ½ teaspoon of the salt and the pepper. Add the chicken to the skillet and sauté, stirring frequently, until brown, 5 to 7 minutes. Put the cooked chicken, the onion, garlic, cumin, oregano, red pepper flakes, beans, chicken broth, chiles, bell pepper, and the remaining 1 teaspoon salt in the slow cooker. Cover and cook on high for 3½ hours. Before removing the chili from the slow cooker, stir in the cream. Ladle the chili into bowls and let each person add Cheddar, sour cream, cilantro, and tortilla chips as desired.

Cincinnati Chili

Whenever I travel for work or pleasure I like to eat regional specialties. When I had the opportunity to visit Cincinnati with QVC, I had my first plate of the local chili. Invented by Cincinnati's Greek immigrants, Cincinnati chili is more of a sauce than a thick stew, features cinnamon, cocoa, cumin, and cloves, and is served on a bed of spaghetti. Cincinnatians even have their own language for ordering this favorite: "Two-way" is chili and spaghetti. "Three-way" is chili, spaghetti, and thinly shredded cheese. "Four-way" is chili, spaghetti, cheese, and diced raw onions. "Five-way" is chili, spaghetti, cheese, raw onions, and kidney beans. Oyster crackers accompany every order.

Makes 6 servings

2 tablespoons canola oil

3 cups finely chopped white onions

3 garlic cloves, minced

2 pounds ground beef

1 28-ounce can crushed tomatoes

1 cup beef broth

1 tablespoon unsweetened cocoa powder

2 teaspoons chili powder

½ teaspoon ground cumin

½ teaspoon ground cinnamon

Pinch of ground cloves

1 teaspoon chopped canned jalapeño

1 bay leaf

2 tablespoons Worcestershire sauce

1 tablespoon cider vinegar

1 tablespoon kosher salt

1 pound spaghetti, cooked

2 cups (8 ounces) finely shredded sharp Cheddar

Oyster crackers

Heat the canola oil in a skillet over low heat. Add 2 cups of the onions and cook until translucent, 5 to 6 minutes. Add the garlic and sauté until fragrant, about 1 minute. Transfer the onions and garlic to a plate. Add the ground beef to the skillet and sauté just until the meat loses its color. Drain the meat well through a colander and add to the slow cooker. Add the onions, garlic, tomatoes, beef broth, cocoa, chili powder, cumin, cinnamon, cloves, jalapeño, bay leaf, Worcestershire sauce, vinegar, and salt to the slow cooker. Cover and cook on high for 5 hours. Remove and discard the bay leaf. Serve the chili over hot spaghetti and let everyone add the cheese, the remaining 1 cup onions, and the oyster crackers.

Pulled Chicken

Just like its pork counterpart, pulled chicken is tender and melt-in-your-mouth wonderful. I always use chicken thighs because they remain moist and provide great flavor. The sauce is tangy, spicy, and has just the right touch of heat. Serve this as an entrée or pile it high on sandwiches. Just be sure to remember the coleslaw.

Makes 6 to 8 servings

2 teaspoons chili powder

1 teaspoon kosher salt

1 teaspoon smoked paprika

½ teaspoon cayenne

2½ pounds boneless, skinless chicken thighs, fat trimmed

Barbecue Sauce (page 121)

Seeded hamburger buns, toasted

Mix the chili powder, salt, paprika, and cayenne together in a bowl. Sprinkle the spice mixture over the chicken thighs to coat thoroughly. Put the chicken thighs in the slow cooker. Add 1 cup of the barbecue sauce and toss well. Cover and cook on low until the chicken is tender, about 5 hours.

Transfer the chicken pieces to a platter, leaving the sauce in the slow cooker. Using two forks, shred the chicken into bite-size pieces. Skim off any fat from the sauce in the slow cooker. Return the shredded chicken to the slow cooker. Heat the remaining barbecue sauce in a saucepan and pour 1 cup over the shredded chicken and mix well. Serve the chicken and additional sauce on toasted buns.

Barbecue Sauce

I find that most store-bought barbecue sauces are too sweet or too spicy or too smoky, so I prefer to make my own. I use my barbecue sauce on Pulled Chicken (page 119), Kansas City–Style Smoked Chicken (page 136), and Grilled Kielbasa, Pepper, and Onion Sandwiches with Barbecue Sauce (page 138). Feel free to add more or less of the ingredients listed below until the balance of flavors is just right for you. This makes more than you need for my recipes, but barbecue sauce keeps well in the refrigerator for a month.

Makes 3 to 3½ cups

2½ cups ketchup

½ cup (packed) dark brown sugar

¼ cup molasses

3 tablespoons cider vinegar

1 tablespoon Worcestershire sauce

1 teaspoon liquid smoke

1 teaspoon kosher salt

⅛ teaspoon cayenne

Put the ketchup, brown sugar, molasses, vinegar, Worcestershire sauce, liquid smoke, salt, and cayenne in a saucepan over high heat. Stir continuously until the sugar has dissolved and the ingredients are well combined. Lower the heat to medium and cook for 5 to 10 minutes, stirring occasionally.

Barbecued Short Ribs

Like lots of fathers, my dad loved his grill. Nothing made Dad happier than slow cooking big beef ribs in his homemade barbecue sauce on a Sunday afternoon. (This sauce is a bit different from the one on page 121.) After getting the charcoal to the right temperature, he spent hours feeding the fire and turning and basting the ribs. Dad's love of ribs inspired this recipe. I prefer short ribs, which have more meat and smaller bones than beef ribs, and let the slow cooker do all the work. While the cooking time is long, the ribs self-baste and stay moist.

Makes 4 to 6 servings

Barbecue Sauce

3 cups ketchup

1 cup molasses

¼ cup (packed) dark brown sugar

¼ cup cider vinegar

¼ cup Worcestershire sauce

2 tablespoons Dijon mustard

2 tablespoons liquid smoke

1 teaspoon cayenne

Ribs

3 pounds beef short ribs

2 tablespoons kosher salt

1 teaspoon freshly ground black pepper

2 tablespoons canola oil

1 large white onion, cut into small chunks

3 garlic cloves, thinly sliced

To make the barbecue sauce, put the ketchup, molasses, brown sugar, vinegar, Worcestershire sauce, mustard, liquid smoke, and cayenne in a saucepan over medium heat. Stir continuously until the sugar has dissolved and the ingredients are well combined.

To make the ribs, season the ribs with the salt and black pepper. Heat the canola oil in a large skillet over high heat. Sear the ribs on all sides. This may have to be done in several batches. Transfer the ribs to the slow cooker. Add the onion and garlic to the slow cooker. Pour half of the barbecue sauce over the ribs in the slow cooker and toss well. Cover and cook on high until tender when pierced with a fork, 4 to 5 hours. When the ribs are done, transfer them and the sauce to a platter. Heat the remaining barbecue sauce in a saucepan and serve with the ribs.

Guinness Beef Stew `FAN FAVORITE`

I once went on a QVC buying trip to Ireland in search of handcrafted collectibles. After filming on a rainy, cold day, one family invited us to join them for a dinner of hearty Irish beef stew. When I entered their cottage, my mouth began to water from the aroma of the stew that had been simmering on the back of their stove. Whenever I make this dish, I'm reminded of that family's hospitality.

Makes 6 to 8 servings

¼ cup all-purpose flour

1½ teaspoons kosher salt

¾ teaspoon freshly ground black pepper

1½ pounds beef stew meat, cut into 1½-inch cubes

1½ tablespoons canola oil

1¼ teaspoons dried thyme

1 bay leaf

1¼ cups beef broth

1 14.9-ounce can stout, such as Guinness

2½ tablespoons tomato paste

¼ cup chopped celery

½ large onion, chopped

1 garlic clove, minced

4 carrots, cut into ½-inch slices

1 pound russet potatoes, peeled and cut into ½-inch pieces

2 tablespoons (¼ stick) unsalted butter

2 tablespoons chopped fresh parsley

Put 2 tablespoons of the flour, ¾ teaspoon of the salt, and ½ teaspoon of the pepper in a bowl. Add the beef cubes and toss to coat.

Heat the canola oil in a skillet over medium-high heat. Working in batches, brown the beef cubes on all sides, 5 to 7 minutes. Transfer the beef to the slow cooker. Add the thyme, bay leaf, beef broth, stout, tomato paste, celery, onion, garlic, carrots, the remaining ¾ teaspoon salt, and the remaining ¼ teaspoon pepper. Stir to coat the meat. Cover and cook on high for 2½ hours. When the timer goes off, add the potatoes and cook for an additional 1½ hours. When the timer goes off again, remove 2 cups of the sauce.

Melt the butter in a saucepan over medium heat. Whisk in the remaining 2 tablespoons flour and cook, whisking constantly, for about 1 minute. Add the 2 cups sauce and simmer until thick. Pour the sauce into the slow cooker and stir well. Ladle the stew into bowls and garnish with the parsley.

Peppers Stuffed with Beef and Orzo

Stuffed peppers are popular comfort food the world over, from Spain to Sweden, from the Middle East to the Mediterranean. Mine feature colorful bell peppers filled with a mixture of ground beef, Italian rice-shaped orzo, Danish Havarti with dill, and zesty tomatoes with chiles. Once the peppers are filled, the slow cooker takes care of the rest. Spoon some of the sauce over the peppers before serving.

Makes 6 servings

2 14.5-ounce cans diced tomatoes with basil and garlic

1 cup beef broth

3½ teaspoons kosher salt

1 pound 80% lean ground beef

¾ cup orzo, cooked

1½ cups crumbled feta

1 cup (4 ounces) plus 6 tablespoons shredded Havarti with dill

1 cup finely chopped onions

3 garlic cloves, minced

1 large egg, beaten

1 medium zucchini, seeded and chopped into ¼-inch cubes (about 1 cup)

1 medium yellow squash, seeded and chopped into ¼-inch cubes (about 1 cup)

1 14.5-ounce can Ro*Tel tomatoes, drained

1 tablespoon chopped canned jalapeños

1 teaspoon freshly ground black pepper

1 teaspoon dried oregano

6 large bell peppers, such as yellow, green, or red

Add the diced tomatoes, beef broth, and 1 teaspoon of the salt to the slow cooker and stir.

Combine the ground beef, cooked orzo, feta, 1 cup of the Havarti, the onions, garlic, egg, zucchini, yellow squash, Ro*Tel tomatoes, jalapeños, the remaining 2½ teaspoons salt, the pepper, and oregano in a bowl. Mix well.

Cut the tops off the peppers and hollow them out, removing all the seeds. Divide the filling among the peppers, pushing the mixture into the cavities. Stand the filled peppers, meat side up, in the slow cooker. Divide the remaining 6 tablespoons Havarti and sprinkle it on top of the peppers. Cover the slow cooker and cook on high for 5 hours.

Remove the peppers to individual bowls. Using a handheld immersion blender, purée the sauce in the slow cooker. Pour the sauce over the peppers before serving.

Red Beans and Rice with Andouille

In New Orleans, Monday was traditionally wash day. Across the city a pot of beans and a leftover ham bone from Sunday's dinner simmered on the stove while the week's clothes were laundered. Red beans and rice remains a New Orleans tradition. New Orleans music legend Louis Armstrong even signed his autograph "Red Beans and Ricely Yours." There's no reason to wait for Monday to serve it up. A slow cooker allows the beans and andouille to cook all day.

Makes 8 to 10 servings

½ pound red beans, soaked overnight in water

½ pound red kidney beans, soaked overnight in water

1 quart chicken broth

1 pound andouille sausage, cut diagonally into ¾-inch pieces

2 cups finely chopped white onions

1 cup diced green bell peppers

1 cup diced celery

6 garlic cloves, minced

1 ham hock

1 tablespoon jarred sofrito

2 teaspoons Creole seasoning

2 bay leaves

Cooked white rice

2 scallions, sliced diagonally into ¼-inch pieces

Hot sauce

Rinse the red beans and kidney beans. Place the beans, chicken broth, and 2 cups water in the slow cooker.

Brown the sausage in a skillet over high heat. Remove the sausage from the skillet and add to the slow cooker, leaving the fat in the skillet. Add the onions, bell peppers, celery, and garlic to the skillet and sauté over medium-high heat until lightly brown. Add the vegetables with the cooking fat, the ham hock, sofrito, Creole seasoning, and bay leaves to the slow cooker. Cover and cook on high for 6 hours. Remove the slow cooker lid, discard the bay leaves, and, using a potato masher, mash up some beans to give the sauce a more creamy consistency. Replace the lid and cook for 1 additional hour.

Ladle some red beans and sausage on top of cooked rice in a shallow bowl. Let each person add the scallions and hot sauce, as desired.

Pork Chops with Sauerkraut, Apples, and Potatoes

Every culture has its favorite foods to ring in the New Year. I live and work near Lancaster County, Pennsylvania, home to many Amish and Mennonites. Eating pork and sauerkraut on New Year's is believed to ensure health and blessings. There's no reason to wait until New Year's to eat this hearty dish. I add apples and apple juice to my slow cooker version to mellow the sauerkraut's strong flavor.

Makes 4 to 6 servings

6 to 8 red potatoes, cut into 2-inch chunks

2 cups apple juice or apple cider

1 32-ounce package sauerkraut, drained

3 tablespoons (packed) dark brown sugar

3 tablespoons whole grain Dijon mustard

2 Granny Smith apples, peeled, cored, and cut into 1-inch slices

2 Gala apples, peeled, cored, and cut into 1-inch slices

4 to 6 ¾-inch-thick pork chops on the bone

4 teaspoons kosher salt

2 teaspoons freshly ground black pepper

2 tablespoons canola oil

2 bay leaves

1 large onion, sliced

Put the potatoes and apple juice in the slow cooker. Mix together the sauerkraut, brown sugar, mustard, Granny Smith apples, and Gala apples in a bowl and toss well. Place half of this mixture on top of the potatoes and apple juice.

To prevent the edges of the pork chops from curling, cut two 1-inch slits at each end. Season the chops with 2 teaspoons of the salt and 1 teaspoon of the pepper. Heat the canola oil in a skillet over high heat. Once the oil is smoking, sear the chops, 30 to 40 seconds on each side. Put the chops on top of the apple-sauerkraut mixture in the slow cooker. Tuck the bay leaves around the chops.

Add the onions to the skillet. Season with the remaining 2 teaspoons salt and 1 teaspoon pepper. Sauté the onions until they start to brown, 6 to 8 minutes. Put the onions on top of the pork chops. Top with the remaining apple-sauerkraut mixture. Cover and cook on high for 5 to 6 hours. Remove and discard the bay leaves before serving.

Candied Sweet Potatoes   FAN FAVORITE

Candied sweet potatoes are the perfect side dish with holiday ham or turkey. The tough part is finding space in the oven for this dish. Sitting on the countertop, the slow cooker does a beautiful job of mingling all the flavors with these tender spuds. I add pineapple chunks for a fresh pop of color and great flavor.

Makes 10 to 12 servings

3 pounds sweet potatoes, peeled and cut into 2-inch chunks

2 8-ounce cans pineapple chunks, drained and liquid reserved

½ cup (packed) dark brown sugar

½ teaspoon ground cinnamon

⅛ teaspoon ground nutmeg

8 tablespoons (1 stick) unsalted butter, melted

½ cup molasses

3 tablespoons cornstarch

1½ cups walnut pieces, toasted

Place the sweet potatoes and pineapple in a large bowl.

Combine ¼ cup of the reserved pineapple juice, the brown sugar, cinnamon, nutmeg, butter, and molasses in a bowl, then add the mixture to the sweet potatoes. Toss to coat.

Spoon the sweet potatoes into the slow cooker. Cover and cook on high for 2½ to 3 hours, stirring gently every 30 minutes. Whisk the cornstarch and the remaining pineapple juice together in a bowl to make a slurry. Add the slurry to the sweet potatoes, mixing gently, but thoroughly, to combine. Simmer the sweet potatoes for 3 to 5 minutes. Before serving, carefully fold in the walnuts and avoid breaking apart the sweet potatoes.

Apple, Pear, and Fig Chutney

When I think of autumn, chutney comes to mind. This sweet-and-tangy recipe fills my house with seasonal aromas as it gently simmers in the slow cooker. It's just the ticket as a condiment with pork chops or as a stuffing for pork roast. For a last-minute appetizer or snack, I spread some on crackers or crostini and top each one with a little piece of Brie or Cheddar. Or put some in jars to give as holiday or hostess gifts from your kitchen.

Makes approximately 2 quarts

1 tablespoon canola oil

¾ cup chopped shallots

4 Granny Smith apples, peeled, cored, and cut into ¼-inch cubes

3 Bartlett pears, peeled, cored, and cut into ¼-inch cubes

½ cup golden raisins

12 ounces dried figs, finely chopped

2 tablespoons honey

½ teaspoon dried thyme

1 tablespoon chopped fresh parsley

½ to ¾ cup apple juice

2 tablespoons balsamic vinegar

½ cup (packed) dark brown sugar

¼ teaspoon ground allspice

¼ cup brandy

Heat the canola oil over medium-high heat in a skillet. Add the shallots and sauté until soft and tender, 4 to 5 minutes. Put the cooked shallots in the slow cooker. Add the apples, pears, raisins, figs, honey, thyme, parsley, apple juice, vinegar, brown sugar, allspice, and brandy in the order listed. Cover and cook on high until thick and jam-like, 4 to 5 hours.

Smoke & Fire

As soon as it feels like spring is giving way to summer, it's time for one of my favorite warm weather activities: firing up my grill and my smoker at my home in Pennsylvania. It seems that once I start cooking outdoors, I rarely use my oven until autumn rolls around. From Memorial Day to the Fourth of July to Labor Day, it's smoked ribs, chicken, and brisket, or grilled burgers, chicken, fish, steaks, potatoes, corn, and even fruit. I can't get enough of that woodsy, smoky, charred flavor no matter what I'm cooking. Grilling and smoking are two of the things that make summer, well, summer.

After a long, cold winter and chilly, damp spring, it's so wonderful to be out in the yard with my grill and smoker, hearing the buzz of lawn mowers, the laughter of kids in their wading pools, the bells of passing bikes, and the sounds of my friends and neighbors enjoying their yards, patios, decks, or whatever outdoor space they have.

If you live in one of the warmer areas of the country, chances are good that you're lucky enough to be grilling and smoking food all year round. Just know that I'm so envious. And hungry. I'll be right over.

Smoked Brisket

Since brisket isn't the most tender cut of meat, it requires long, low, and slow cooking, making it ideal for smoking. First, I rub, score, and poke the fat on top of the brisket so my homemade herb rub seeps down into the meat, and then I let everything marinate overnight. Next, I wrap the brisket, some beef broth, and any remaining rub in aluminum foil so the meat can steam and become tender and smoky as it cooks. I remove the foil, save the drippings to make a gravy, and smoke the meat, fat side up, until it is infused with smoky flavor and becomes meltingly tender. Yes, smoked brisket takes a long time to cook. Is it worth it? You bet.

Makes 8 to 10 servings

Rub

⅓ cup (packed) dark brown sugar

3 tablespoons smoked paprika

3 tablespoons chili powder

3 tablespoons garlic powder

3 tablespoons onion powder

2 tablespoons kosher salt

1 tablespoon coarsely ground black pepper

1 teaspoon cayenne

Beef Brisket

1 6- to 7-pound beef brisket

2 cups mesquite wood chips

1½ quarts beef broth

2 medium onions, thickly sliced, plus 3 cut into 1-inch pieces

To make the rub, combine the brown sugar, paprika, chili powder, garlic powder, onion powder, salt, black pepper, and cayenne in a bowl.

To make the brisket, score the fat on top of the brisket. Use a large meat fork and pierce the brisket all over, making sure to push the tines of the fork all the way through. Pat three quarters of the rub on both sides of the brisket. Coat the brisket well. Wrap the brisket with plastic wrap, place in a dish, and refrigerate for 6 to 24 hours. Reserve the remaining rub.

Add the wood chips to the smoker according to the manufacturer's directions. Preheat the smoker to between 250°F and 275°F.

About 1 hour before putting the brisket in the smoker, stir together 2 cups of the beef broth and the remaining rub in a saucepan over medium heat until the rub is dissolved. Let the broth cool. About 1 hour before putting the brisket in the smoker, remove it from the refrigerator and let it come to room temperature. Wrap the brisket, sliced onions, and seasoned beef broth in 2 sheets of heavy-duty aluminum foil. Place the brisket in the smoker, fat side up, and set the timer for 4 to 5 hours. Put the remaining 1 quart beef broth and the onion pieces in a pan on the bottom rack of the smoker.

Remove the brisket from the smoker. Put the brisket on a platter and pour the juices and onions into a blender. Purée until smooth and pour into a saucepan. Place the uncovered brisket, fat side up, directly on a rack in the smoker. Smoke until the brisket is crusty, 2 to 3 hours. Add a handful of additional wood chips to the smoker every 30 minutes. Remove the brisket from the smoker, cover with foil, and let it rest for at least 30 minutes. Heat the pureed sauce. Slice the brisket against the grain and serve with the gravy.

Woodn't It Be Nice: Wood Chips

It's hard to beat that extra layer of flavor that wood chips bring to grilling and smoking. Any hardwood that is free of sap can be used for smoking, especially chips from fruit and nut trees. Apple wood gives your food a nice mellow, slightly fruity flavor. Mesquite imparts a much more intense smokiness. Pecan and walnut wood chips, not surprisingly, add a little nutty touch to the smoke. Hickory is most synonymous with smoking and barbecuing, but since it has such a strong flavor, I like to combine it with apple or cherry chips. Feel free to try your own wood combinations and develop a backyard family flavor all your own. Purchase prepackaged wood chips and follow the directions or saw small pieces of dried wood to use when cooking over fire.

Kansas City–Style Smoked Chicken FAN FAVORITE

With more than one hundred barbecue restaurants and joints, Kansas City takes its barbecue very seriously. K.C. folks smoke anything and everything—brisket, pulled pork, beef ribs, and turkey—but I have to say that their smoked chicken is my favorite. When smoked properly, the whole chicken is moist and fall-apart tender. Serve smoked chicken with traditional barbecue fare—baked beans, potato salad, and, of course, coleslaw.

Makes 4 to 6 servings

Dry Rub

¼ cup (packed) light brown sugar

¼ cup paprika

2 teaspoons kosher salt

1½ teaspoons freshly ground black pepper

1 teaspoon garlic powder

1 teaspoon onion powder

1 teaspoon dry mustard

1 teaspoon chili powder

¼ teaspoon cayenne

1 4½- to 5-pound chicken, trussed (ask your butcher to do this)

Barbecue Sauce (page 121), at room temperature

To make the dry rub, combine the brown sugar, paprika, salt, pepper, garlic powder, onion powder, dry mustard, chili powder, and cayenne in a bowl. Pour ¼ cup rub into a smaller bowl and store the remaining rub in a container for future use.

Preheat the smoker to 250°F. Coat the entire surface of the trussed chicken with the reserved rub. Place the chicken in the smoker and smoke for 3½ hours.

Brush the chicken with half of the barbecue sauce and continue to smoke for another 30 minutes, or until an instant-read thermometer inserted into the thickest part of the chicken registers 165°F. Remove the chicken from the smoker to a cutting board. Tent the chicken with aluminum foil and let rest for 5 to 10 minutes. Heat the remaining barbecue sauce in a saucepan. Remove the twine, carve the chicken, and serve with the remaining sauce.

Grilled Kielbasa, Pepper, and Onion Sandwiches with Barbecue Sauce

When friends are coming over, but I haven't had time to put a meal together, I turn to these quick-and-easy grilled sausage sandwiches. They're just like the smoky treats sold at street fairs and church bazaars, where you can smell them blocks away. Brush the sausages with some barbecue sauce and cook them on one half of the grill. Put the vegetables in a grill basket so they don't fall through the grate, and grill them on the other half. Once everything is done, put some sausages and vegetables on toasted hero rolls and add a good squeeze of tangy mustard.

Makes 4 servings

2 cups hickory wood chips, soaked in water for at least 30 minutes

1 cup Barbecue Sauce (page 121)

¼ cup whole grain Dijon mustard, plus more for serving

1 green bell pepper, seeded and cut into ¼-inch strips

1 red bell pepper, seeded and cut into ¼-inch strips

1 large onion, halved and cut into ¼-inch slices

2 tablespoons extra-virgin olive oil

1 teaspoon kosher salt

½ teaspoon freshly ground black pepper

2 14-ounce packages kielbasa, each sausage cut into 4-inch pieces

6 hero rolls, toasted on the grill

Place the soaked wood chips in the grill and preheat the grill to medium heat.

Whisk together the barbecue sauce and mustard in a bowl. Toss the green bell pepper, red bell pepper, onion, olive oil, salt, and black pepper in a bowl.

Put the kielbasa pieces on one half of the grill. Brush with the barbecue sauce mixture. Grill until grill marks appear on each side of the kielbasas, 4 to 5 minutes, while turning and basting regularly with the barbecue sauce.

Place a grill basket on the other half of the grill. Add the bell pepper mixture. Shaking the basket constantly, grill the vegetables until the bell peppers and onion become charred on the edges, 3 to 5 minutes.

While the grill is hot, toast the buns for 1 minute. Put the grilled kielbasas on the toasted buns. Top each with some grilled peppers and onion and serve with mustard.

Grilled Chicken and Pesto Flatbread Pizzas

I took a cooking class and learned how to make pizza dough from scratch. Once the dough was rolled out and fresh toppings were added, the pizzas were grilled to thin, crispy perfection. While making pizza dough is fun, waiting for the dough to rise does take time, and when I want my pizza, I want it now! I realized that I could quickly have my pizza and eat it, too, if I used fresh or frozen naan, an airy Indian flatbread. While you can use any favorite toppings, I find that pesto, instead of a traditional red sauce, pairs well with grilled chicken. Naan means pizza in no time!

Makes 4 servings

2 garlic cloves

1 tablespoon fresh lemon juice

1 tablespoon Dijon mustard

1 shallot, minced

1 tablespoon fresh rosemary leaves

1 teaspoon kosher salt

¼ teaspoon freshly ground black pepper

1 cup extra-virgin olive oil

¾ to 1 pound skinless, boneless chicken thighs, about ¾ inch thick

½ cup jarred roasted red bell peppers, drained and chopped

⅛ cup balsamic vinaigrette dressing

Pesto

2 garlic cloves

1½ cups (packed) fresh basil leaves

⅛ cup toasted walnuts

¾ cup (3 ounces) grated Parmigiano-Reggiano

½ teaspoon fresh lemon juice

½ teaspoon kosher salt

¼ cup extra-virgin olive oil

4 garlic-flavored naan flatbreads

1 pound fresh mozzarella, thinly sliced

To make the chicken, put the garlic cloves in a food processor and pulse 2 or 3 times to mince. Add the lemon juice, mustard, shallot, rosemary, salt, and pepper and pulse to combine. Add the olive oil and blend to combine.

Put the chicken thighs in a resealable plastic bag and add the garlic-mustard marinade. Close and shake well to coat the chicken. Refrigerate for 3 to 4 hours or even overnight, flipping the bag from time to time.

Combine the roasted bell peppers and balsamic vinaigrette in a bowl.

To make the pesto, put the garlic in a food processor or blender and pulse to mince. Add the basil, toasted walnuts, ¼ cup of the Parmesan, the lemon juice, and salt and process until the basil is finely chopped. With the machine running, slowly pour in the olive oil and blend until a paste forms.

Preheat the grill to medium-high heat.

Remove the chicken from the marinade and discard the marinade. Grill the chicken until cooked through, 6 to 8 minutes on each side.

In an empty spot on the grill, grill the naan on each side for 1 to 2 minutes. Remove the naan from the grill and spread about 2 tablespoons pesto on each piece, leaving a ¼-inch border. Top each piece of naan with 3 or 4 slices mozzarella, some grilled chicken, red peppers, and a sprinkle of the remaining ½ cup Parmesan. Transfer the naan to the grill and close the lid to melt the cheese. Cook for 2 to 3 minutes before serving.

The Ultimate Gourmet Cheese Hamburgers

There are cheeseburgers and then there are ultimate cheeseburgers. Like perfect meatballs, these beauties begin with a combination of ground beef, veal, and pork. Veal and pork balance the beef's flavors and keep the burgers from being too dense. Then I take them over the top with a filling of onion, garlic, and three kinds of cheese. Yes, I am a wild man when it comes to cheese. Be warned: Your family will never stand for humdrum cheeseburgers again.

Makes 6 servings

2 tablespoons canola oil

1 medium Spanish onion, finely chopped

3 garlic cloves, minced

1 pound 80% lean ground beef

½ pound ground veal

½ pound ground pork

1 cup (4 ounces) shredded yellow extra-sharp Cheddar

2 tablespoons grated Parmigiano-Reggiano

2 tablespoons Worcestershire sauce

1 teaspoon kosher salt

½ teaspoon freshly ground black pepper

½ cup (2 ounces) shredded whole milk mozzarella

4 kaiser rolls, toasted

Boston Bibb lettuce, sliced tomatoes, and sliced red onions

Heat the canola oil in a skillet over low heat. Add the onion and cook until translucent, 5 to 6 minutes. Add the garlic and sauté until fragrant, about 1 minute. Remove from the heat and let cool.

Put the beef, veal, pork, Cheddar, Parmesan, Worcestershire sauce, salt, and pepper in a bowl. Using a slotted spoon, transfer half of the onion-garlic mixture to the bowl, leaving as much of the oil as possible in the skillet. Using your hands, blend the ingredients, but do not overmix.

Combine the mozzarella and the remaining onion-garlic mixture in a separate bowl, again leaving as much oil as possible in the skillet.

Divide the meat mixture into 6 parts. Roll each into a ball. Using your thumb, make an indentation in the center of each ball and fill it with the mozzarella-onion mixture. Roll each ball to enclose the filling, then flatten the balls into patties about ¾ inch thick. Cover and refrigerate the burgers for 2 to 3 hours before grilling.

About 30 minutes before grilling, preheat the grill to high heat.

Grill each burger for 5 to 6 minutes on each side to desired doneness, turning just once. Serve on the toasted kaiser rolls with the traditional burger condiments—lettuce, tomatoes, and red onions.

Grilled New York Strip Steak with Herb Butter

There are two secrets to cooking a great steak: really high heat (not flames) and the right seasoning. You need plenty of heat to get that great sear on the outside and tender, juicy goodness on the inside, so I always cook steaks on my outdoor grill. I find that an indoor broiler just doesn't get hot enough. I rub the steaks with a homemade herb blend before grilling them. Then each cooked steak gets a pat of savory herb butter that starts to melt as soon as it lands on the meat.

Makes 4 servings

Herb Butter

4 tablespoons (½ stick) unsalted butter, at room temperature

1 teaspoon chopped fresh parsley

1 teaspoon fresh thyme leaves

¼ teaspoon kosher salt

Rub

1 tablespoon garlic powder

¼ cup kosher salt

3 tablespoons freshly ground black pepper

2 teaspoons chili powder

2 teaspoons dried thyme

2 teaspoons dried rosemary, crushed

4 10- to 12-ounce bone-in, ¾- to 1-inch-thick New York strip steaks

To make the herb butter, put the butter, parsley, fresh thyme, and salt in a food processor and pulse to combine. Using a rubber spatula, scrape the butter mixture onto a piece of plastic wrap and shape it into a log. Freeze the log until firm.

To make the rub, combine the garlic powder, salt, pepper, chili powder, dried thyme, and rosemary in a small bowl. Coat both sides of the steaks with the rub. Let the steaks sit at room temperature for 30 minutes before grilling.

Preheat the grill to high heat.

Grill the steaks. For medium-rare, grill the steaks until an instant-read thermometer registers 125°F to 130°F, 4 to 6 minutes per side. For medium, grill the steaks until the thermometer registers 140°F to 145°F, 6 to 8 minutes per side.

Remove the steaks from the grill and let rest for 5 to 6 minutes to reabsorb their juices. Slice the herb butter into rounds and serve atop the steaks.

Hot Dogs: Three Ways

Hot dogs! Hot dogs! Hot dogs! We've got 'em three ways: chili cheese dogs! Southern slaw dogs! Chicago-style dogs! Toppings know no limits when it comes to wieners, franks, red hots, or whatever they're called in your part of the country. Here are three of my favorite ways to dress them up. You can make any or all of the toppings in advance, so everyone can assemble their own combinations. I have always preferred all-beef dogs because I love their rich flavor. Hot diggity dogs!

Makes 24 servings

24 all-beef hot dogs

16 plain and 8 poppy seed hot dog buns

Preheat the grill to high heat.

Evenly score 16 hot dogs along their length. For the Chicago hot dogs, use a knife to make an X at both ends of 8 hot dogs. Grill all of the hot dogs for 4 minutes per side. Toast the buns.

Chili Cheese Hot Dogs

Chili

2 tablespoons canola oil

1 cup finely chopped onions

2 garlic cloves, minced

½ pound 80% lean ground beef

1 1-ounce packet chili seasoning

¼ teaspoon cayenne

1 14.5-ounce can crushed tomatoes

1 cup canned kidney beans, drained and rinsed

½ teaspoon kosher salt

½ cup (2 ounces) shredded yellow extra-sharp Cheddar

½ cup (2 ounces) shredded pepper Jack

Spicy mustard

To make the chili, heat the canola oil in a large skillet over medium-high heat. Add ½ cup of the onions and sauté until soft, 4 to 5 minutes. Add the garlic and cook until fragrant, about 1 minute. Add the beef and cook until the meat loses its pink color, using a wooden spoon to break up the beef as it cooks. Add the chili seasoning and cayenne and stir well. Add the tomatoes, kidney beans, and salt and bring to a boil. Lower the heat and simmer for 5 to 6 minutes.

To assemble the Chili Cheese Hot Dogs, put the hot dogs on 8 toasted plain buns and top each with some chili, a sprinkle of Cheddar and pepper Jack, chopped onion, and a squeeze of spicy mustard.

Southern Slaw Hot Dogs

Coleslaw

2 tablespoons cider vinegar

½ cup mayonnaise

¼ cup buttermilk

2 tablespoons sugar

¼ teaspoon celery salt

½ teaspoon kosher salt

½ teaspoon freshly ground black pepper

1 14-ounce bag coleslaw mix, finely chopped

1 16-ounce can baked beans with bacon, onions, and brown sugar

Spicy mustard

To make the coleslaw, whisk together the vinegar, mayonnaise, buttermilk, sugar, celery salt, kosher salt, and pepper in a bowl. Add the coleslaw mix and toss well. Cover and refrigerate for 1 hour before serving.

Put the baked beans in a saucepan over low heat and let simmer for 20 minutes.

To assemble the Southern Slaw Hot Dogs, put the hot dogs on 8 toasted plain buns and spoon some beans and coleslaw onto each one, followed by a squirt of spicy mustard.

Chicago-Style Hot Dogs

¼ cup yellow mustard

8 dill pickle spears, cut in half lengthwise

1 large tomato, cut into ¼-inch slices

¼ cup sweet pickle relish

16 peperoncini sweet peppers, cut in half

½ cup finely chopped red onion

Celery salt

To assemble the Chicago-Style Hot Dogs, put the hot dogs on the toasted poppy seed buns and squirt some yellow mustard on each one. Top each with 2 pickle halves, 2 tomato slices, some pickle relish, 2 sweet peppers, some red onion, and a sprinkle of celery salt.

Grilled Teriyaki Pork Chops `FAN FAVORITE`

In Japan, "teriyaki" refers to a popular method of grilling or broiling food with a soy sauce, rice wine, and sugar glaze. *Teri* means "to shine"; *yaki* means "to grill." I love the way the sauce caramelizes on the pork chops, giving them a sweet, salty flavor as well as a beautiful shine. These chops look gorgeous and taste even better than they look. But don't stop at pork chops; you can also use this sauce on chicken cutlets, salmon steaks, or vegetables.

Makes 4 servings

1 cup soy sauce

1¼ cups pineapple juice

¾ cup (packed) light brown sugar

¼ cup Worcestershire sauce

3 tablespoons white or rice vinegar

3 tablespoons canola oil

¼ cup onion powder

Pinch of red pepper flakes

2 garlic cloves, minced

1 tablespoon grated fresh ginger

4 6- to 8-ounce pork chops (bone-in or boneless)

1 tablespoon cornstarch

1 tablespoon cold water

Whisk together the soy sauce, pineapple juice, brown sugar, Worcestershire sauce, vinegar, canola oil, onion powder, red pepper flakes, garlic, and ginger in a dish large enough to hold the pork chops in a single layer. Stir the marinade until the sugar dissolves. Transfer 1 cup of the marinade to a saucepan, cover, and refrigerate. Add the pork chops to the marinade in the dish, cover, and refrigerate for 30 minutes to 3 hours, turning the chops from time to time. (Don't marinate the chops any longer or they will become mushy.)

Preheat the grill to medium heat.

Remove the chops and the saucepan with the marinade for the glaze from the refrigerator. Heat the glaze in the saucepan over medium heat. To make a slurry, dissolve the cornstarch in the cold water in a small bowl. Whisk the slurry into the hot glaze. Place the pork chops on the grill and discard the marinade from the baking dish. Grill the chops on both sides, brushing them frequently with the glaze until cooked through, 6 to 8 minutes.

Tuna Burgers with Lemon-Dill Mayonnaise

There are a couple of tips to keep in mind when making tuna burgers. Buy top-quality, sushi-grade tuna. Don't overcook them; these burgers should be served just shy of medium-rare. They're delicate, so turn them carefully. Finally, do you know what's really good on a tuna burger? A couple of slices of cooked smoked bacon.

Makes 4 servings

Mayonnaise

1 cup mayonnaise

Zest of 1 lemon

1 teaspoon fresh lemon juice

1½ tablespoons chopped fresh dill

1 teaspoon kosher salt

⅛ teaspoon freshly ground black pepper

Burgers

3 tablespoons extra-virgin olive oil

½ cup chopped shallots

½ cup dry white wine

2 tablespoons fresh lemon juice

3 tablespoons capers, drained and chopped

1 pound ahi tuna steaks, chilled and chopped into ½-inch pieces

¼ cup panko bread crumbs

1 large egg, beaten

2 tablespoons chopped fresh dill

½ teaspoons kosher salt

¼ teaspoon freshly ground black pepper

Vegetable oil spray

4 to 6 kaiser rolls or seeded hamburger buns, toasted on the grill

Lettuce, sliced avocado, and sliced tomatoes

To make the mayonnaise, whisk together the prepared mayonnaise, lemon zest, lemon juice, and dill in a bowl and mix thoroughly. Season with the salt and pepper.

To make the burgers, heat the grill to medium-high. Heat the olive oil in a skillet over medium-high heat. Add the shallots and cook until soft and lightly brown, 2 to 3 minutes. Add the white wine and lemon juice and, using a wooden spoon, scrape all the brown bits off the bottom of the pan. Continue cooking until 3 tablespoons of wine remain. Remove the skillet from the heat and stir in the capers. Let the mixture cool.

Combine the tuna, bread crumbs, egg, dill, salt, and pepper in a bowl. Stir in the shallot-caper mixture. Shape the mixture into 4 burgers. Refrigerate the burgers for

15 to 20 minutes before grilling. This will help to keep them from falling apart when grilling.

Preheat the grill to medium-high.

Lightly spray the burgers with vegetable oil spray. Place the burgers on the grill for 3 to 4 minutes per side for medium-rare.

Serve the burgers on the rolls, accompanied by the mayonnaise, lettuce, avocado, and tomatoes.

Grilled Scallops with Citrus Marinade

Pearly white sea scallops are usually sautéed, poached, or fried. My go-to preparation is to marinate them in orange juice and honey and then grill them for just a few minutes so they're caramelized on the outside, yet still tender inside. For a first course, start with the Stuffed Artichokes (page 225), and some Coconut Cream Pie (page 257) to finish.

Makes 4 servings

1½ pounds sea scallops, dried well

Zest of 1 orange

1 cup fresh orange juice

3 tablespoons honey

1 tablespoon minced fresh parsley

1 teaspoon jarred green peppercorns, drained and crushed

½ teaspoon kosher salt

½ cup canola oil

3 cups mixed salad greens

Put the scallops in a dish large enough to hold them in a single layer. Whisk together the orange zest, orange juice, honey, parsley, peppercorns, and salt in a bowl. Slowly drizzle in the canola oil, whisking until well incorporated. Remove ¼ cup of the marinade to the dish with the scallops.

Refrigerate and marinate the scallops for 1 hour, turning them several times. (Don't marinate for any longer or the scallops will "cook" and become tough.)

Heat the remaining marinade in a saucepan over low heat. Simmer for 20 to 25 minutes, until the liquid has reduced by one quarter and has thickened slightly.

Preheat the grill to medium-high heat.

Place the scallops in a grill basket and grill them for 3 to 4 minutes per side, until grill marks appear. Discard the marinade that the scallops were in. Don't overcook the scallops or they will become tough and dry. Divide the mixed salad greens and scallops among four plates. Spoon the reduced marinade over the scallops and serve immediately.

Surf and Turf Kebabs

Surf (lobster) and turf (steak) was a classic served at steak houses across the country. I changed the surf from lobster to shrimp for these kebabs. Cutting everything into similar sizes results in even cooking. Be aware that the beef will take a few more hours to marinate than the shrimp. While making kebabs means a little more work on the front end, the presentation when your guests sit down is worth it. Choose from cooked rice, Grilled Sweet Potato Fries with Ranch Yogurt Sauce (page 157), or Roasted Potatoes with Lemon and Herbs (page 227) as a side dish.

Makes 12

Marinade

1 cup soy sauce

1 cup rice vinegar

⅔ cup (packed) light brown sugar

2 tablespoons toasted sesame oil

¼ cup grated fresh ginger

2 garlic cloves, minced

2 tablespoons white sesame seeds

Kebabs

1 pound jumbo (21/25 count) shrimp, peeled and deveined, with tails on

1 pound top sirloin steak, cut into 1½-inch cubes

½ pineapple, cut into ¾-inch pieces

2 large red onions, cut into 6 wedges and separated into slices

2 red bell peppers, seeded and cut into 2-inch squares

12 12-inch metal or thick wooden skewers (soak wooden skewers in water for 1 hour)

2 yellow bell peppers, seeded and cut into 2-inch squares

Toasted white sesame seeds

2 scallions, sliced diagonally

To make the marinade, whisk together the soy sauce, rice vinegar, brown sugar, sesame oil, ginger, garlic, and sesame seeds in a saucepan over medium-high heat. Bring to a boil, then reduce the heat and simmer for 10 to 15 minutes, until the mixture is reduced slightly. Transfer the marinade to a bowl and refrigerate for 30 minutes.

Place the shrimp and the steak in separate bowls. Pour half of the marinade over the shrimp and the other half over the steak. Marinate the beef for at least 2 hours, and up to 8 hours, in the refrigerator. Marinate the shrimp for 30 minutes, turning occasionally.

Preheat the grill to medium heat.

To make the kebabs. remove the shrimp from the marinade, but reserve the marinade. Alternately thread the shrimp, pineapple, half of the red onions, and red bell peppers onto the skewers 3 or 4 times, starting and ending with a shrimp.

Remove the beef from the marinade, but reserve the marinade. Alternately thread the beef, red onions, and yellow bell peppers onto the skewers 3 or 4 times, starting and ending with the beef. Brush the skewers with some reserved marinade and use the rest to brush the kebabs while they're grilling.

Grill the shrimp skewers, basting occasionally with the remaining marinade, for 2 to 3 minutes per side, until the shrimp are pink. Grill the beef skewers, basting occasionally with the remaining marinade, for 4 to 5 minutes per side for medium doneness and 6 to 7 minutes per side for medium-well. Discard any leftover marinade.

Remove the skewers from the grill and sprinkle the kebabs with the toasted sesame seeds and sliced scallions before serving.

Grilled Corn on the Cob, Mexican Style

Elote—pronounced *hel-low-tay*—refers to the Mexican street food version of grilled corn on the cob. Once the corn silks are removed, the corn and husks are grilled or boiled. Then the corn is slathered with a rich combination of mayonnaise, cayenne, lime juice, and butter. You've never had corn on the cob like this. Cotija is a Mexican hard cheese sold in blocks or rounds, then grated. Queso fresco or Parmesan can be substituted.

Makes 4 servings

4 ears corn, husks intact

¼ cup mayonnaise

¼ teaspoon cayenne, plus more for garnish

Juice of 1 lime

1½ teaspoons minced fresh cilantro

2 tablespoons (¼ stick) unsalted butter, melted

½ cup grated Cotija cheese

Carefully pull down the corn husks and remove only the silks. Pull the husks back on the corn. Submerge the corn in a bucket of cold water for 30 minutes. Make sure the corn is fully covered with water.

Whisk together the mayonnaise, cayenne, lime juice, and cilantro in a bowl.

Preheat the grill to medium-high heat.

Remove the corn from the water and shake off any excess. Grill the corn for 18 to 20 minutes, rotating the ears every 3 to 4 minutes to make sure the corn is cooking on all sides. Remove the corn from the grill. Using mitts, remove the husks, leaving the core attached at the end to make a holder. To char the corn, return the ears to the heat and grill, watching carefully and turning occasionally so the corn doesn't burn, for 1 to 2 minutes.

Spread each ear with 1½ teaspoons melted butter, followed by 1 tablespoon mayonnaise mixture. Sprinkle each ear with 2 tablespoons grated cheese and extra cayenne just before serving.

Bacon-Wrapped Asparagus Bundles

Asparagus are most flavorful when grilled. They're even better when wrapped in bacon before grilling, then given a good squeeze of fresh lemon for brightness. These bundles go well with other fired-up dishes—Grilled New York Strip Steak with Herb Butter (page 145), Tuna Burgers with Lemon-Dill Mayonnaise (page 150), and Grilled Scallops with Citrus Marinade (page 152).

Makes 6 servings

2 pounds thick asparagus, trimmed

¼ cup extra-virgin olive oil

2 teaspoons Montreal Steak Seasoning

12 slices center-cut bacon

2 to 3 lemon wedges

Preheat the grill to medium-high heat.

Place the asparagus, olive oil, and steak seasoning in a large bowl and toss to coat thoroughly.

Divide the asparagus into 12 bundles of 5 or 6 spears each. Wrap 1 piece of bacon around the center of each bundle, leaving 1½ to 2 inches of asparagus showing on each end. Tuck in the bacon ends, using a toothpick, if needed, to secure the bacon. (If using toothpicks, soak them in water for 30 minutes before using so they won't burn.)

Grill the bacon bundles, tucked-in sides down, away from direct heat, for 3 to 4 minutes per side, for a total of 9 to 12 minutes, until the bacon is cooked and the asparagus is tender. For crisper bacon, move the bundles to a hotter spot, but watch them carefully to avoid flare-ups. Before serving, squeeze the lemon wedges over the asparagus bundles.

Grilled Sweet Potato Fries with Ranch Yogurt Sauce

Mom served sweet potatoes, usually in a casserole, on Thanksgiving, and then we didn't see them for another year. I've since discovered their versatility and how healthy they are. I grill sweet potato wedges until they're crisp and serve them with a creamy ranch-style yogurt dressing. Sometimes I serve them as an appetizer, while the rest of the meal is cooking, or as an accompaniment to grilled steak, Tuna Burgers with Lemon-Dill Mayonnaise (page 150), or Grilled Teriyaki Pork Chops (page 149). No matter how many of these crispy treats I make, they disappear in minutes. For even cooking, it's important that the sweet potatoes be cut into wedges of the same size. The creamy dipping sauce can be used on other vegetables—asparagus, broccoli, or carrots.

Makes 6 to 8 servings

Vegetable oil spray

Dipping Sauce

2 cups whole milk plain Greek yogurt

3 tablespoons heavy cream

1 1-ounce packet ranch dip and seasoning mix

2 teaspoons sugar

½ teaspoon kosher salt

¼ teaspoon freshly ground black pepper

Sweet Potato Fries

6 medium orange sweet potatoes, peeled and cut into ½-inch wedges

2 to 3 tablespoons extra-virgin olive oil

1 teaspoon kosher salt

½ teaspoon freshly ground black pepper

Preheat the oven to 400°F. Line a baking sheet with parchment paper and spray with vegetable oil spray. Preheat the grill to high heat.

To make the sauce, whisk together the yogurt, cream, seasoning mix, sugar, salt, and pepper in a bowl.

To make the sweet potatoes, toss the sweet potato wedges, olive oil, salt, and pepper in a bowl and coat well. Arrange the sweet potatoes in a single layer on the prepared baking sheet. Bake for 15 to 20 minutes. Transfer to the hot grill and grill the sweet potatoes until they are fork tender, 2 to 3 minutes. Serve with the dipping sauce.

Grilled Eggplant and Tomato Bundles

What do I do when my garden hands me a bounty of eggplants and tomatoes by summer's end? Thinly slice the vegetables, layer them with smoked mozzarella, and give them a turn on the grill. Serve these as a first course while the Grilled New York Strip Steak (see page 145) and Grilled Sweet Potato Fries (see page 157) are cooking on the grill.

Makes 6 servings

6 tablespoons extra-virgin olive oil

3 tablespoons balsamic vinegar

2 garlic cloves, finely minced

⅛ teaspoon dried thyme

⅛ teaspoon dried basil

⅛ teaspoon dried dill

⅛ teaspoon dried oregano

1 teaspoon plus 1 tablespoon kosher salt

1 teaspoon plus 1 tablespoon freshly ground black pepper

1 large eggplant, sliced ½ inch thick

1 16-ounce round smoked mozzarella, thinly sliced

2 large tomatoes, sliced

½ cup (2 ounces) grated Parmigiano-Reggiano (optional)

Preheat the grill to medium heat.

Combine the olive oil, vinegar, garlic, thyme, basil, dill, oregano, 1 teaspoon of the salt, and 1 teaspoon of the pepper in a bowl. Brush both sides of the eggplant with the olive oil–vinegar mixture.

Arrange half of the eggplant slices on a baking sheet and top each with a slice of mozzarella, followed by a slice of tomato. Sprinkle the tomatoes with the remaining 1 tablespoon salt and 1 tablespoon pepper. Top the tomatoes with mozzarella, followed by the remaining eggplant slices.

Place the bundles on the grill and grill for 5 to 7 minutes. Carefully turn the bundles and grill until the bundles can be pierced with a fork, 5 to 7 minutes. Remove the bundles to salad plates and garnish with a generous sprinkle of Parmesan, if desired, before serving.

Gather & Share

As you've read and cooked your way through this book, I'm sure you've noticed that many of my recipes are based on dishes that my mom and other relatives prepared when I was growing up. These comfort classics are much more than a trip down memory lane. Study after study shows that people have better relationships and families are more closely knit when they gather at the table and share what's going on in their lives. But I don't need a study to convince me that sitting down at the table and sharing a meal feeds our souls as well as our bodies.

One of my goals on *In the Kitchen with David* and in my cookbooks is to encourage families to return to the dinner table. Yes, it's a commitment and can take effort to get a meal on the table, especially during the week when time is at a premium. For those nights, I created a speedy Five-Cheese, Fifteen-Minute Stovetop Mac 'n' Cheese and Stir-Fry Hoisin Chicken and Broccoli. If you and your gang have more time, say, on a weekend, go for the Beef Potpies or Meat Lasagna Roll Ups. However you do it, remember that eating dinner with your loved ones helps build shared experiences, teaches manners, and creates memories that will last forever.

Baked Perciatelli with Mini Meatballs

While I adore meatballs and spaghetti, I find that spaghetti is a little too thin to stand up to hefty meatballs, especially when everything is baked together in a casserole. I prefer perciatelli, which are long, hollow pasta strands that are thicker than spaghetti. To save time, I brown fully cooked frozen mini meatballs before combining them with the perciatelli, tomato sauce, and, of course, plenty of cheese. The only thing to do while this is baking is to make a quick green salad and heat a loaf of garlic bread.

Makes 8 to 10 servings

1 tablespoon unsalted butter

2 tablespoons extra-virgin olive oil

30 fully cooked, cocktail-size frozen Italian beef meatballs

1 cup finely chopped white onions

2 garlic cloves, minced

1 28-ounce can puréed tomatoes

1 28-ounce can diced tomatoes

½ teaspoon dried oregano

1 heaping tablespoon chopped fresh basil

1½ teaspoons plus 2 tablespoons kosher salt

½ teaspoon red pepper flakes

1 pound perciatelli

½ cup (4 ounces) whole milk ricotta cheese

2 cups (8 ounces) shredded mozzarella

½ cup (2 ounces) grated Asiago

½ cup (2 ounces) shredded Italian Fontina

Preheat the oven to 350°F. Butter the bottom and sides of a 4-quart baking dish. Line a platter with paper towels.

Heat the olive oil in a skillet over high heat. Add the meatballs and brown them, 3 to 4 minutes. When the meatballs are brown, transfer them to the paper towel–lined dish. Do not clean out the skillet.

To make the sauce, add the onions to the same skillet the meatballs were cooked in. Sauté until the onions are soft, 4 to 5 minutes. Add the garlic and sauté until fragrant, about 1 minute. Stir in the puréed and diced tomatoes, the oregano, basil,

1½ teaspoons salt, and red pepper flakes and bring to a boil. Reduce the heat and simmer for 10 to 15 minutes.

While the sauce is cooking, bring a large pot of water to a boil. Add the remaining 2 tablespoons salt and the pasta, and cook until the pasta is al dente, 8 to 10 minutes. Drain the pasta well.

To make the casserole, combine the browned meatballs, perciatelli, ricotta, 1½ cups of the mozzarella, and ¼ cup of the Asiago. Stir in all but 2 cups tomato sauce and mix everything together until well combined. Reserve the 2 cups sauce to serve with the casserole. Pour the mixture into the prepared baking dish. Sprinkle on the remaining ½ cup mozzarella, ¼ cup Asiago, and the Fontina. Cover the prepared casserole with aluminum foil.

Bake for 20 minutes. Remove the foil and bake for an additional 10 to 15 minutes, until the cheese is brown and the sauce is bubbly. Let the baking dish sit at room temperature for 5 to 10 minutes before serving with the remaining sauce.

Five-Cheese, Fifteen-Minute Stovetop Mac 'n' Cheese

Anyone who knows me knows that I love macaroni and cheese. It is, hands down, my favorite dish in the world. But, I have to admit, mac 'n' cheese takes time to make and bake, so I decided to create a streamlined, stovetop version that doesn't skimp on flavor or creaminess. The best part—besides its scrumptious goodness—is that it takes just fifteen minutes. I use five cheeses—smoky Gouda, nutty Gruyère, fruity Asiago, and two sharp Cheddars. *Gemelli,* which means "twins" in Italian, are a short double-twisted pasta shape that holds on to the sauce. If you love melted cheese, sprinkle some additional Cheddar on top and place the pot under a preheated broiler for 3 to 4 minutes. Of course, I would always recommend adding some divine swine—like cooked, crumbled bacon on top!

Makes 6 to 8 servings

3 tablespoons unsalted butter

2 tablespoons all-purpose flour

1 teaspoon dry mustard

2 cups heavy cream, warmed

1 cup (4 ounces) shredded smoked Gouda

½ cup (2 ounces) shredded Gruyère

¼ cup (1 ounce) shredded Asiago

1 cup (4 ounces) shredded yellow extra-sharp Cheddar

2 cups (8 ounces) shredded white sharp Cheddar

1 pound gemelli or other pasta twists, cooked

½ cup sour cream

1 teaspoon kosher salt

½ teaspoon white pepper

Melt the butter in a Dutch oven over medium heat. Add the flour and mustard and stir with a wooden spoon or whisk until a thick paste forms, 2 to 3 minutes. Stir in the cream and bring the mixture to a simmer, stirring until the sauce becomes thick. Add the Gouda, Gruyère, Asiago, yellow Cheddar, and white Cheddar, stirring the cheeses until melted and the sauce is smooth. Add the cooked pasta and stir well to combine. Stir in the sour cream, salt, and white pepper and cook until the ingredients are combined and hot, 2 to 3 minutes. Serve immediately.

Italian Wedding Casserole

I love to spend time in my kitchen experimenting with ingredients and coming up with a twist on a favorite dish. One day, I challenged myself to take the mini meatballs and spinach from Italian wedding soup and make a casserole. I replaced the chicken broth with Alfredo sauce and combined everything with farfalle, butterfly-shaped pasta, before turning the mixture into a baking dish. Simmering the meatballs in chicken broth keeps them moist. The results? A creamy, cheesy casserole with meatballs and spinach in every bite. Do take the time to make the chicken meatballs from scratch; it will make all the difference.

Makes 8 to 10 servings

Chicken Meatballs

2 tablespoons extra-virgin olive oil

1 cup finely chopped white onions

2 garlic cloves, minced

1 pound ground chicken

1 large egg

½ cup Italian seasoned fine bread crumbs

1 tablespoon chopped fresh parsley

1 teaspoon kosher salt

¼ teaspoon freshly ground black pepper

1 quart chicken broth

Spinach

2 tablespoons extra-virgin olive oil

2 shallots, finely chopped

2 garlic cloves, minced

6 cups baby spinach

¾ teaspoon plus 2 tablespoons kosher salt

¼ teaspoon freshly ground black pepper

1 pound farfalle

Vegetable oil spray

2 15-ounce jars Alfredo sauce

2½ cups (10 ounces) grated mozzarella

1 tablespoon chopped fresh parsley

To make the meatballs, line a baking sheet with parchment paper. Heat the olive oil in a skillet over low heat. Add the onions and sauté until translucent, 5 to 6 minutes. Add the garlic and sauté until fragrant, about 1 minute. Remove from the heat.

Combine the cooked onions and garlic, the chicken, egg, bread crumbs, parsley, salt, and pepper in a bowl. Using your hands, mix well until the ingredients are combined. Shape the mixture into ½-inch balls and place on the prepared baking sheet. Refrigerate the chicken meatballs for 1 hour to firm up.

Bring the chicken broth to a boil in a Dutch oven. Add the meatballs and lower the heat to a simmer. Simmer until the meatballs are cooked through, 8 to 10 minutes. Drain, reserving ½ cup broth. Let the meatballs cool in a single layer on a sheet tray.

To make the spinach, heat the olive oil in a large skillet or sauté pan over medium-high heat. Add the shallots and sauté until soft, 2 to 3 minutes. Add the garlic and sauté until fragrant, about 1 minute. Add the spinach, the ¾ teaspoon salt, and the pepper, and, using tongs, cook, tossing the spinach just until it begins to wilt. Let the spinach drain in a colander.

Put the Alfredo sauce in a saucepan and heat over medium-low heat. Meanwhile, preheat the oven to 350°F.

Bring a large pot of water to a boil. Add the 2 tablespoons salt and the farfalle, and cook until the pasta is al dente, 8 to 10 minutes. Drain the pasta well.

To make the casserole, spray a 4-quart baking dish with vegetable oil spray.

Combine the cooked spinach, Alfredo sauce, the ½ cup reserved chicken broth, farfalle, and the meatballs in a bowl. Add 1½ cups of the mozzarella. Mix well and pour into the prepared baking dish. Sprinkle the top with the remaining 1 cup mozzarella. *(The casserole can be prepared to here, wrapped well, and frozen for 1 month.)*

Bake until the cheese is melted and the sauce is bubbly, 20 to 25 minutes. Cover the dish with aluminum foil the last 10 minutes if the cheese is starting to get too brown. Let the dish sit for 5 to 10 minutes and sprinkle the parsley on top before serving.

Meat Lasagna Roll Ups

Just about the only Italian food my mom cooked was spaghetti with meat sauce. Whenever I was invited over to my buddy Frank's house, I hoped that his mom would make her lasagne. It was love at first bite.

Lasagne is traditionally made by layering sauce, noodles, and cheese with more sauce, noodles, and cheese. But in my version, you spoon sauce and cheese onto cooked lasagna noodles, roll them up, and place them in a baking dish. Each rolled bundle then becomes an easy-to-serve generous portion.

Makes 8 to 12 servings

Meat Sauce

2 tablespoons extra-virgin olive oil

1 cup finely chopped white onions

⅓ cup minced carrot

⅓ cup minced celery

3 garlic cloves, minced

3 tablespoons tomato paste

⅛ cup red wine

1 pound 80% lean ground beef

½ pound ground pork

½ pound ground veal

1 28-ounce can puréed tomatoes with basil

1 28-ounce can diced tomatoes with basil

2½ teaspoons kosher salt

½ teaspoon freshly ground black pepper

Lasagna Roll Ups

12 lasagna noodles

Vegetable oil spray

1 15-ounce container whole milk ricotta cheese

1 large egg, beaten

1½ cups (5 ounces) grated Parmigiano-Reggiano

2½ cups (10 ounces) shredded mozzarella

½ teaspoon freshly ground black pepper

Heat the olive oil in a Dutch oven over medium-high heat. Add the onions, carrot, and celery and sauté, stirring occasionally, until the onions are translucent, 5 to 6 minutes. Add the garlic and sauté until fragrant, about 1 minute. Stir in the tomato paste and sauté until the tomato paste turns a deep red, about 5 minutes. Add the red wine, stirring to scrape up any brown bits from the bottom of the pot, and cook until the wine evaporates, 4 to 5 minutes. Using a slotted spoon, transfer the vegetables from the pot to a bowl.

Add the beef, pork, and veal to the Dutch oven and, using a wooden spoon to break up the meat, cook until the meat loses its pink color. Once all the meat is cooked, remove any excess fat with a ladle or spoon. Return the vegetables to the pot and add the tomatoes and their juices, the salt, and the pepper to the meat mixture. Simmer over low heat for 20 to 30 minutes, stirring occasionally. Remove the sauce from the heat.

While the meat sauce is simmering, cook 12 lasagna noodles according to the package directions. Drain and lay out the noodles in a single layer on a clean towel so they don't stick to one another.

Preheat the oven to 350°F. Lightly spray the bottom of a 9 x 13-inch baking dish with vegetable oil spray. Spoon about 3 cups meat sauce into the baking dish.

Mix together the ricotta, egg, ¾ cup of the Parmesan, 1 cup of the mozzarella, and the pepper in a bowl. Evenly spread about ¼ cup of the cheese mixture over each noodle. Next, evenly spread about 2 tablespoons meat sauce over the ricotta. Roll up each noodle like a jelly roll. Place each one, seam side down, in the prepared dish. They should fit snuggly in the dish. Top each roll with 2 tablespoons meat sauce. Sprinkle the remaining 1½ cups mozzarella and ¾ cup Parmesan on top. Cover the dish with aluminum foil and bake until the cheese is melted and the sauce is bubbly, 35 to 40 minutes. Remove the foil for the last 10 minutes. Let rest for 5 to 10 minutes before serving.

Stir-Fry Hoisin Chicken and Broccoli

I believe that making food at home is always better than takeout. Sure, it's easy to order in, but with your own fresh ingredients, you get to decide how your food tastes and adjust the seasonings for kids and grown-ups. Hoisin sauce is a Chinese condiment made with soybean paste, garlic, chiles, spices, and often a little sugar and vinegar that's used for dipping or adding to recipes. When stir-frying, make sure to cut all the ingredients to the same size. The actual cooking time can be measured in minutes, while it will take just seconds for the smiles to spread around your dinner table.

Makes 4 servings

⅓ cup hoisin sauce

¼ cup sesame oil

2 tablespoons (packed) dark brown sugar

2 tablespoons soy sauce

1 tablespoon rice vinegar

1 tablespoon grated fresh ginger

1 teaspoon red pepper flakes

1 garlic clove, minced

1 pound boneless, skinless chicken breasts, cut into ½-inch strips

2 cups cut-up broccoli

½ medium red onion, sliced ⅛ inch thick

1 red bell pepper, seeded and thinly sliced

1 yellow bell pepper, seeded and thinly sliced

1 carrot, cut into julienne strips

½ cup chicken broth

Kosher salt and freshly ground black pepper

4 cups rinsed and cooked jasmine rice

1 cup cashews

1 scallion, sliced diagonally into ⅛-inch pieces

Whisk together the hoisin sauce, 2 tablespoons of the sesame oil, the brown sugar, 1 tablespoon of the soy sauce, the rice vinegar, ginger, red pepper flakes, and garlic in a shallow dish. Add the chicken and let marinate at room temperature while cooking the vegetables.

Fit a steamer basket into a saucepan and bring 1 inch water to a boil. Add the broccoli, cover tightly, and steam until crisp-tender, about 2 minutes. Using a slotted spoon, transfer the broccoli to a bowl. Heat the remaining 2 tablespoons sesame oil in a large skillet over medium-high heat until almost smoking. Add the onion, red bell pepper, yellow bell pepper, and carrot and sauté, stirring constantly, until crisp, 4 to 5 minutes. Transfer the vegetables to the bowl with the broccoli.

Add the chicken and marinade to the skillet and cook until the chicken is no longer pink and is cooked through, 4 to 6 minutes. Stir in the chicken broth and let simmer, 2 to 3 minutes. Add all of the vegetables and toss gently. Add the remaining 1 tablespoon soy sauce and toss gently. Cook until the vegetables are cooked through, an additional 2 to 3 minutes. Season with salt and pepper. Serve over hot rice and garnish with the cashews and scallion.

Chicken Thighs with Red Bell Pepper Sauce

Mom cooked a fair number of one-pot meals because they were a time saver for her and for us kids, who had to wash the dishes after every meal. A one-pot meal means less work for everyone. Moist, juicy, and tender chicken thighs cook quickly, making them ideal for weeknight dinners. Just put the skillet right on the table and serve the chicken and sauce over some rice, noodles, or quinoa with a side of green beans. Don't be concerned about the amount of garlic in this dish. As the garlic cooks, it softens, mellows, and adds just the right amount of flavor.

Makes 4 to 6 servings

8 bone-in, skin-on chicken thighs

2½ teaspoons kosher salt

¾ teaspoon freshly ground black pepper

¼ cup all-purpose flour

2 to 3 tablespoons extra-virgin olive oil

2 to 4 tablespoons (¼ to ½ stick) unsalted butter

8 garlic cloves, gently smashed

3 shallots, thinly sliced

Leaves from 4 to 5 fresh thyme sprigs

½ cup dry white wine

3 tablespoons room-temperature plus 1½ cups hot chicken broth

2 tablespoons cornstarch

1 7-ounce jar roasted red bell peppers, cut into 1-inch strips

4 cups cooked white rice

Minced fresh parsley

Preheat the oven to 375°F.

Season both sides of the chicken thighs with the salt and pepper. Lightly dredge the chicken thighs in the flour, shaking off any excess. Heat 2 tablespoons of the olive oil and 1 tablespoon of the butter in an ovenproof skillet over medium heat. Working in batches, sear both sides of the chicken until brown, 3 to 4 minutes on each side. Transfer the seared chicken to a plate. Add more butter and oil between batches and lower the heat, if necessary. Add the garlic, shallots, and thyme to the hot skillet and sauté for 2 to 3 minutes. Add the white wine, stirring to scrape up any brown bits from the bottom of the pot, and cook until the wine is reduced to 3 tablespoons. To make a slurry, whisk the 3 tablespoons chicken broth and the cornstarch together in a bowl. Add the slurry, the remaining 1½ cups chicken broth, and the roasted bell peppers to the skillet and bring to a boil. Reduce the heat and simmer for 5 to 6 minutes. Return the chicken, skin side up, to the skillet and simmer, spooning some cooking liquid over the chicken thighs, for 3 to 5 minutes. Place the skillet in the oven and bake until the chicken is cooked through, 20 to 30 minutes. About halfway through the cooking time, baste the chicken with the sauce. Spoon the chicken and sauce into shallow bowls over the rice and sprinkle with the parsley before serving.

Turkey Breast with Roasted Vegetables

Sometimes I have a hankering for turkey, but I just don't have the time or the need to roast an entire bird. A turkey breast with roasted vegetables always fits the bill. For tender meat and the crispiest skin, I rub herb butter between the skin and the meat. This is some good turkey; it makes enough for a meal plus plenty for sandwiches the next day. And the gravy? Just taste it, and your smile will spread from ear to ear.

Makes 8 to 10 servings

Vegetable oil spray

Turkey

6 tablespoons (¾ stick) unsalted butter, at room temperature

4 teaspoons kosher salt

2 teaspoons freshly ground black pepper

Leaves from 2 fresh sage sprigs, plus 2 or 3 fresh sage sprigs

Leaves from 2 fresh thyme sprigs, plus 2 or 3 fresh thyme sprigs

Leaves from 2 fresh rosemary sprigs, plus 2 or 3 fresh rosemary sprigs

1 4- to 5-pound boneless, skin-on turkey breast

4 medium baking potatoes, skin on, cut into 1½-inch pieces

2 to 3 carrots, cut diagonally into 1½-inch pieces

2 medium white onions, cut into 6 to 8 wedges

About ¼ cup extra-virgin olive oil

1 cup chicken broth

Gravy

Reserved drippings from the cooked turkey

3 tablespoons all-purpose flour

2 cups hot chicken broth

1 tablespoon unsalted butter

Kosher salt and freshly ground black pepper

Preheat the oven to 375°F. Using the vegetable oil spray, lightly coat a roasting pan large enough to hold the turkey breast and vegetables.

To make the turkey, combine the butter, 2 teaspoons of the salt, 1 teaspoon of the pepper, the sage leaves, rosemary leaves, and thyme leaves in a mini food processor. Pulse until combined, about 30 seconds.

Place the turkey in the center of the prepared roasting pan, breast side up. Using

your fingers, gently loosen the skin from the meat of the turkey breast. Evenly spread half of the herb butter under the turkey skin.

To make the roasted vegetables, place the potatoes, carrots, and onions in a large bowl and toss with the olive oil, the remaining 2 teaspoons salt, and the remaining 1 teaspoon pepper. Surround the turkey breast with the vegetables and the sage sprigs, thyme sprigs, and rosemary sprigs. Pour the chicken broth into the pan.

Roast the turkey breast until an instant-read thermometer inserted into the thickest part registers 165°F, 1 to 1½ hours. After the first 20 minutes, spread the remaining herb butter on the turkey skin. Baste the turkey and the vegetables with the pan juices every 20 minutes. Transfer the turkey and vegetables to a serving platter and cover with aluminum foil while making the gravy. Let rest for 10 minutes before slicing.

To make the gravy, place the roasting pan with the drippings over medium-high heat. Using a wooden spoon, stir in the flour and scrape up any brown bits from the bottom of the roasting pan, 3 to 4 minutes. Whisk in 1½ to 2 cups chicken broth and the butter and bring to a boil. Continue stirring and taste for seasoning, adding salt and pepper as necessary. For a velvety, smooth gravy, strain the gravy through a fine-mesh strainer; pour into a gravy boat, and serve alongside the turkey and vegetables.

Open-Face Turkey Reuben Melts

A Reuben is a super popular deli sandwich, but when I make it at home, I want a lighter version, but with the same flavors. I substitute sliced smoked turkey for the corned beef and keep the Swiss cheese, Russian dressing, and coleslaw. Reubens are one of the best ways I know to use up leftover turkey, like Turkey Breast with Roasted Vegetables (page 175).

Makes 6 servings

Coleslaw

2 tablespoons cider vinegar

½ cup mayonnaise

¼ cup buttermilk

2 tablespoons sugar

½ teaspoon kosher salt

½ teaspoon freshly ground black pepper

¼ teaspoon celery salt

1 small head of cabbage, finely shredded (about 5 cups)

½ cup finely shredded carrots

¼ cup finely diced red onion

Russian Dressing

¼ cup ketchup

3 tablespoons chili sauce

1 cup mayonnaise

¼ cup sweet pickle relish

½ teaspoon kosher salt

¼ teaspoon freshly ground black pepper

Sandwiches

4 tablespoons (½ stick) unsalted butter, at room temperature

6 slices marble rye bread

1½ pounds smoked turkey, thinly sliced

½ pound Swiss cheese, thinly sliced

To make the coleslaw, whisk together the vinegar, mayonnaise, buttermilk, sugar, salt, pepper, and celery salt in a large bowl. Add the cabbage, carrots, and red onion and toss well. Cover and refrigerate for at least 1 hour, or up to 2 days.

To make the dressing, whisk together the ketchup, chili sauce, mayonnaise, pickle relish, salt, and pepper in a small bowl. Cover and refrigerate for up to 1 week.

To make the sandwiches, preheat the oven to 350°F. Line a baking sheet with parchment paper.

Butter both sides of the bread. Heat a large skillet over medium-high heat. Add the bread to the skillet and lightly toast both sides. Or, toast the bread in the preheated oven. Place the toasted bread on the prepared baking sheet. Spread about 2 tablespoons Russian dressing on each slice of bread. Layer 4 to 5 turkey slices on each bread slice. Using a slotted spoon, place about ¼ cup coleslaw on the turkey. Top each sandwich with 3 slices of Swiss cheese.

Place the baking sheet in the oven and bake for 8 to 10 minutes, until the cheese starts to melt. Turn the oven to broil and cook until the cheese is melted and bubbly, 1 to 2 minutes. Serve immediately.

Shrimp and Chorizo Paella

Spanish paella is traditionally cooked in a wide, flat pan over an open fire. It was originally made with chicken, rabbit, and game, because it comes from the inland city of Valencia. Today, paella includes duck, lobster, clams, and mussels. There are even vegetarian versions. Here's my preferred combination—large shrimp and zesty chorizo.

Makes 6 to 8 servings

2 tablespoons extra-virgin olive oil

1 pound chorizo, sliced diagonally into ½-inch pieces

1 pound large (31/35 count) shrimp, peeled, deveined, and tails removed

Kosher salt and freshly ground black pepper

1½ cups chopped Spanish onions

1 cup diced red bell peppers

2 garlic cloves, minced

½ cup dry white wine

2 cups long-grain white rice

3½ cups chicken broth, warmed

1 15-ounce can petite diced tomatoes

2 pinches of saffron

2 bay leaves

1 cup frozen peas, thawed

1 tablespoon minced fresh parsley

Lemon wedges

Heat the olive oil in a large skillet over medium-high heat for 30 seconds. Add the chorizo and cook until the fat begins to render, 3 to 4 minutes. While the chorizo is cooking, lightly season the shrimp with salt and pepper. Add the shrimp to the skillet and continue cooking, stirring occasionally, until they turn pink. Remove the shrimp and chorizo to a plate and cover with aluminum foil to keep warm.

Add the onions and bell peppers to the same skillet and cook until the onions are translucent, 5 to 6 minutes. Add the garlic and cook until fragrant, about 1 minute. Pour in the white wine and use a wooden spoon to scrape up all the brown bits from the bottom of the pan. Cook for an additional 2 minutes. Stir in the rice and cook for 1 minute, making sure the rice is thoroughly coated. Add the chicken broth, diced tomatoes, saffron, ½ teaspoon salt, and the bay leaves and bring to a boil. Cover with a lid, reduce the heat to low, and simmer until the rice is cooked, 20 to 25 minutes. (Don't peek at the rice while it's cooking.)

Remove the pan from the heat. Discard the bay leaves. Add the chorizo and shrimp, and the peas. Cover the pan, return it to the stove, and let rest for 5 minutes. Using a fork, stir together the ingredients and season to taste with salt and pepper. Garnish with the minced parsley and lemon wedges. Serve immediately.

Mom's Chicken and Rice Casserole

As I've said, Mom made a lot of freezer-to-oven-to-table casseroles when I was growing up. One of us kids would pop a frozen casserole into the oven so by the time Mom got home from work, all she had to do was prepare a green vegetable. I can picture us eating this casserole around our kitchen table with Mom, still dressed in her white nurse's uniform. This dish is classic Venable family comfort food.

Makes 6 to 8 servings

Vegetable oil spray

4 cups water

2 cups long-grain white rice

1 tablespoon canola oil

1 cup small-diced onions

1 garlic clove, minced

1 rotisserie chicken, skin and bones removed, meat shredded

2 10¾-ounce cans cream of chicken soup

½ cup mayonnaise

2 tablespoons fresh lemon juice

½ cup chicken broth

1 teaspoon dried thyme

½ teaspoon kosher salt

1 teaspoon freshly ground black pepper

1 cup panko bread crumbs

½ cup slivered almonds

8 tablespoons (1 stick) unsalted butter, melted

Preheat the oven to 350°F. Spray a 4-quart baking dish with vegetable oil spray.

Bring the water to a boil in a saucepan over high heat. Stir in the rice and bring back to a boil. Cover, reduce the heat to low so the water doesn't boil over, and simmer until the water is absorbed, 10 to 15 minutes. While the rice is cooking, heat the canola oil in a skillet. Add the onions and garlic and cook until the onions are translucent, 5 to 6 minutes. Put the shredded chicken, cooked rice, sautéed onions and garlic, cream of chicken soup, mayonnaise, lemon juice, chicken broth, thyme, salt, and pepper in a large bowl. Stir to combine the ingredients. Evenly spread the chicken-rice mixture in the prepared baking dish.

Combine the bread crumbs, almonds, and butter in a bowl. Sprinkle the bread crumb mixture over the chicken and rice. Bake for about 1 hour, or until hot, bubbly, and brown on top. Let rest for 5 to 10 minutes before serving.

Baked Shrimp and Feta

A Greek favorite, baked shrimp and feta can be whipped up in no time for a family-friendly weeknight meal or a dinner party. The shrimp are immersed in a flavorful tomato sauce and then topped with feta before going into the oven for a short time. Serve this dish with rice or orzo and some crusty bread to mop up the sauce. If using smaller shrimp, reduce the cooking time by a few minutes.

Makes 4 to 6 servings

3 tablespoons extra-virgin olive oil

1 medium Vidalia onion, finely chopped

3 garlic cloves, minced

½ cup dry white wine

1 15-ounce can diced tomatoes with basil and oregano

½ teaspoon red pepper flakes

½ teaspoon kosher salt

1½ cups (packed) fresh baby spinach

1½ pounds extra jumbo (16/20 count) shrimp, peeled, deveined, and tails removed

1 cup (4 ounces) crumbled feta

3 tablespoons finely chopped fresh parsley

2 tablespoons finely chopped fresh oregano, or 1 teaspoon dried

Preheat the oven to 400°F.

Heat the olive oil in an ovenproof skillet over low heat. Add the onion and cook until translucent, 5 to 6 minutes. Stir in the garlic and sauté until fragrant, about 1 minute. Pour in the white wine and, using a wooden spoon, scrape any brown bits off the bottom of the pan. Continue cooking until all but 1 or 2 tablespoons wine has cooked off. Add the diced tomatoes and bring to a boil. Stir in the red pepper flakes and salt. Reduce the heat and simmer for 10 minutes, stirring occasionally.

Remove the skillet from the heat and stir in the spinach and shrimp. Sprinkle the feta on top. Bake for 15 to 18 minutes, until the shrimp are pink and cooked through and the feta has melted. Remove from the oven and stir in the parsley and oregano before serving.

Beef and Bean Burrito Casserole

I didn't eat much Mexican food until I went to college and tried the many Mexican restaurants in and around Chapel Hill. Burritos became a late-night favorite of mine. This crowd-pleasing casserole was inspired by the fresh, custom-made burritos served up in Mexican restaurants across the country. These hearty wraps are assembled, packed tightly in a baking dish so they hold their shape, and then covered with extra sauce and cheese. You get the taste treat of a burrito with the ease of a casserole.

Makes 4 to 6 servings

Burritos

1 14.5-ounce can Ro*Tel tomatoes, puréed

2 tablespoons canola oil

2 cups finely chopped white onions

2 garlic cloves, minced

1¼ pounds 80% lean ground beef

2 canned chipotle peppers in adobo sauce, seeded and finely chopped

½ teaspoon chili powder

1 teaspoon ground cumin

1 tablespoon adobo sauce

1 14.5-ounce can Ro*Tel tomatoes, drained

1½ cups refried beans

4 cups (1 pound) shredded yellow extra-sharp Cheddar

8 8-inch flour tortillas

Guacamole, salsa, sour cream, minced red onions, and chopped fresh cilantro

Preheat the oven to 375°F. Pour half of the puréed tomatoes on the bottom of a 9 x 13-inch baking dish.

Heat the canola oil in a skillet over low heat. Add the onions and sauté until soft, 4 to 5 minutes. Add the garlic and sauté until fragrant, about 1 minute. Transfer the onions and garlic to a bowl. Add the ground beef to the skillet and cook until brown. Drain off the oil and return the onions and garlic to the skillet. Add 1 of the chopped chipotle peppers, the chili powder, cumin, adobo sauce, and the can of drained tomatoes. Stir well and cook over low heat for 2 to 3 minutes. Remove from the heat.

Heat the refried beans and the remaining chipotle pepper in a saucepan over medium heat, stirring occasionally. Once the beans are hot, add ½ cup of the Cheddar and continue stirring until the cheese is melted.

Microwave the tortillas on high to soften them, 10 to 20 seconds. Arrange the tortillas on a work surface. Put a layer of refried beans, followed by a layer of meat mixture, in the center of the tortillas. Divide and sprinkle 1½ cups of the Cheddar on top. Fold in the sides of the tortillas, then tightly roll up the tortillas. Place the burritos, seam side down, in the prepared baking dish. They should fit snuggly. Pour the remaining puréed tomatoes over the burritos and sprinkle on the remaining 2 cups Cheddar. Bake the casserole for 25 minutes. Turn the oven to broil and broil until the cheese is melted, bubbly, and slightly brown, 3 to 4 minutes. Let rest for 5 to 10 minutes before serving with the guacamole, salsa, sour cream, red onions, and cilantro.

Beef Potpies

I have loved potpies since I was old enough to hold a spoon. As a kid, I'd pull up a chair and sit in front of the glass oven door and wait for my potpie to bubble up and over the sides of the pan. Once at the table, I'd lift the flaky pastry top and watch as the steam floated up. Then I'd take a big spoonful and blow on it until it was cool enough to taste. This is the perfect dish for a crisp autumn evening or a hearty meal on a snowy day. No matter how old I get, potpies will always bring out the kid in me.

Makes 4 servings

1 to 2 large russet potatoes, peeled and cut into ¼-inch cubes (about 2 cups)

1 tablespoon plus 2 teaspoons plus ½ teaspoon kosher salt

1½ pounds ½-inch sirloin beef cubes or leftover steak

1 teaspoon freshly ground black pepper

2 to 4 tablespoons canola oil

1 cup finely chopped white onions

3 garlic cloves, minced

3 tablespoons unsalted butter

3 tablespoons all-purpose flour, plus 2 to 3 tablespoons, for rolling out pastry

2½ cups beef broth, warmed

½ cup heavy cream, warmed

2 tablespoons Worcestershire sauce

3 cups frozen mixed vegetables, thawed

2 tablespoons minced fresh parsley

¾ teaspoon dried thyme

1 sheet puff pastry, thawed

1 large egg

Preheat the oven to 375°F. Line a baking sheet with aluminum foil.

Put the potato cubes and 1 tablespoon salt in a saucepan and cover with water. Bring to a boil, reduce the heat to a simmer, and cook until the potatoes are fork tender but still firm, 5 to 6 minutes. Drain and set aside.

Season the beef cubes with the 2 teaspoons salt and ½ teaspoon of the pepper. Heat the canola oil in a Dutch oven over medium-high heat. Working in two batches, add the beef cubes and brown on all sides. Using a slotted spoon, transfer the beef to a large bowl. Add the onions to the Dutch oven and sauté until translucent, 4 to 5 minutes. Add the garlic and sauté until fragrant, about 1 minute. Using a slotted spoon, remove the onions and garlic and add to the bowl with the beef.

In the same Dutch oven, melt the butter over medium heat. Whisk in

3 tablespoons of the flour and cook, whisking constantly, until the mixture is medium brown in color, 4 to 5 minutes. Whisk in the warm beef broth, cream, and Worcestershire sauce and bring to a slight boil. Reduce the heat and continue stirring until the sauce has thickened slightly, 3 to 4 minutes. Return the beef mixture to the Dutch oven. Add the cooked potatoes, mixed vegetables, parsley, thyme, and the remaining ½ teaspoon pepper. Stir to combine and simmer for 10 to 15 minutes. Divide the beef mixture among four 12- to 14-ounce individual ovenproof crocks.

Using the remaining flour, on a floured surface, roll out the puff pastry sheet to a ⅛-inch thickness. Using a bowl and a paring knife, trace and cut out 4 circles large enough to cover the tops of each crock, allowing for a little to hang over the edges. Place 1 circle on top of each filled crock and crimp the edges. Cut 2 or 3 slits into the top of the pastry to allow steam to escape. Beat the egg with 1 tablespoon water in a small bowl. Brush the egg wash over the top of each pastry shell. Sprinkle with the remaining ½ teaspoon salt.

Place the potpies on the prepared baking sheet. Bake for 30 to 40 minutes, until the pastry is puffed and lightly brown. Remove the potpies from the oven and let cool for 5 to 10 minutes before serving.

Cool It

Cookbook instructions always say to let a pie cool completely before serving. That's because if you've ever tried to lift a hot wedge out of the pie plate, the filling will be soupy and not hold together. The same thing is true of casseroles and gratins if you try to serve them right out of the oven. Let the hot dish sit for 5 to 10 minutes to allow the runny juices or cheeses to be reabsorbed by the rice, pasta, meat, or vegetables. Italian Wedding Casserole (page 166), Better-Than-Ever Tuna Casserole (page 207), and mac 'n' cheese (see page 165) will remain hot and be a whole lot easier to serve if allowed to sit for a bit.

Steak Tacos with Chipotle Slaw and Avocado Salsa FAN FAVORITE

Tacos are a great standby meal, but if you want to make the dish more substantial, add some steak. The lime juice, jalapeño, and garlic give the flank steak a south-of-the-border kick. Serve with a pile of warm tortillas, chipotle slaw, avocado salsa, and Mango Mojitos (page 67). Finish the fiesta with Key Lime Pie (page 259).

Makes 10 to 12 servings

Steak

2 garlic cloves

⅔ cup chopped fresh cilantro

Juice of 2 limes

¼ cup extra-virgin olive oil

½ teaspoon kosher salt

⅛ teaspoon freshly ground black pepper

1 jalapeño, seeded and quartered

1 teaspoon chili powder

1 2- to 2½-pound flank steak

Slaw

1 cup sour cream

2 tablespoons whole milk

2 teaspoons canned chipotle pepper in adobo sauce (or more to taste), chopped

1½ teaspoons white vinegar

6 cups shredded cabbage

Salsa

3 avocados, peeled, pitted, and diced

⅓ cup minced red onion

Juice of 4 limes

½ large jalapeño, seeded and minced

1 teaspoon minced garlic

⅓ cup chopped fresh cilantro

2 tablespoons extra-virgin olive oil

1 plum tomato, seeded and diced

½ teaspoon kosher salt

⅛ teaspoon ground black pepper

10 to 12 8-inch flour tortillas

To make the steak, combine the garlic, cilantro, lime juice, olive oil, salt, pepper, jalapeño, and chili powder in a food processor. Process the marinade until finely minced.

   Place the flank steak in a shallow dish and pour on the marinade. Cover and

refrigerate the steak for a minimum of 2 hours, but not more than 8 hours. If left in the marinade for too long, the meat will become mushy.

To make the slaw, whisk together the sour cream, milk, chipotle, and vinegar in a large bowl until combined. Add the cabbage and toss to coat completely with the dressing. *(The slaw can be refrigerated for 2 hours, but not longer.)*

To make the salsa, combine the avocados, red onion, lime juice, jalapeño, garlic, cilantro, olive oil, tomato, salt, and pepper in a bowl. Toss well. *(The salsa can be made and refrigerated for up to 2 hours prior to serving.)*

To make the tacos, preheat the grill to medium-high heat.

Grill the steaks until desired degree of doneness, 6 to 8 minutes per side. Let the steak rest for 10 minutes before thinly slicing diagonally across the grain. Heat the tortillas on the grill. Serve the sliced steak accompanied by the slaw, the salsa, and the warm tortillas.

Sweet-and-Sour Pork Medallions

When I order sweet-and-sour pork at a Chinese restaurant, the sauce can sometimes be too sweet and lack the right balance of flavors. The saltiness of the soy sauce, the tang of the vinegar, and the sweetness of the pineapple combine to add bright, complex flavors to this version. While a pot of rice is cooking, prep the ingredients—a quick sauce, sliced pork tenderloin, and cut-up vegetables. This dish comes together in just minutes. Serve over white rice, accompanied by some steamed broccoli, and garnish with scallions.

Makes 8 servings

Sauce

½ cup sugar

¼ cup soy sauce

¼ cup ketchup

3 tablespoons white wine vinegar

1 tablespoon honey

1 teaspoon red pepper flakes

Juice from canned pineapple (see "Pork" below)

2 tablespoons cornstarch

2 tablespoons minced fresh parsley

Pork

1 2-pound pork tenderloin, silver skin removed, sliced into ½-inch pieces

2 teaspoons kosher salt

½ teaspoon freshly ground black pepper

¼ cup canola oil, plus more if needed

½ Vidalia or Walla Walla onion, sliced ⅛ inch thick

2 large red bell peppers, seeded and cut into ⅛-inch strips

2 large yellow bell peppers, seeded and cut into ⅛-inch strips

½ pound snow peas

2 garlic cloves, minced

1 14.5-ounce can pineapple chunks, juice reserved for the sauce

2 to 3 tablespoons chicken broth, heated (optional)

4 cups cooked white rice

2 scallions, sliced

To make the sauce, combine the sugar, soy sauce, ketchup, vinegar, honey, and red pepper flakes in a saucepan. Add ½ cup water. Bring to a boil over medium-high heat. To make a slurry, whisk together the canned pineapple juice and cornstarch in a small bowl until dissolved. Add the slurry to the saucepan and continue stirring until the sauce thickens. Stir in the parsley and remove from the heat.

To make the pork, season the pork with the salt and pepper. Heat the canola oil in a skillet over medium-high heat. Add the pork and brown on both sides until almost cooked through, 4 to 5 minutes. Remove the pork from the pan. Add the onion and sauté for 2 to 3 minutes, adding a bit more oil if necessary. Add the red bell peppers, yellow bell peppers, and snow peas and sauté for 3 to 4 minutes. Add the garlic and sauté until fragrant, 2 to 3 minutes, reducing the heat if necessary. Return the pork to the skillet and toss everything together over medium heat. Add the sweet-and-sour sauce and pineapple chunks and simmer until the pork is completely cooked, 4 to 5 minutes. If necessary, you can thin out the sauce slightly with 2 to 3 tablespoons chicken broth. Serve over the white rice and garnish with the scallions.

Light & Bright

Comfort food fills my tummy and gives me a warm, nostalgic feeling. When I dream of comfort foods, the words "diet," "low fat," and "low cal" don't come to mind. There are, however, times when we all have to watch our waistlines. Been there, done that. But who wants to give up all those great flavors and tastes and eat rabbit food? Not me. So, I went into my kitchen and created lighter versions of my favorite classic dishes.

Now you can have Better-Than-Ever Tuna Casserole, Skinny Fried Chicken, and Linguine Carbonara and feel good about eating them. Wait until you try the Lighter Baked Macaroni 'n' Cheese. (You know I can't live without my mac 'n' cheese!) Discover how to cook just about any fish and vegetables in parchment paper for the most flavorful and easy preparation. And, yes, you can have dessert—Angel Food Cake with Berries, Grilled Fruit with Grand Marnier Whipped Topping, and Strawberry-Pineapple Frozen Yogurt.

Chicken Quinoa Soup FAN FAVORITE

Quinoa (pronounced *keen*-wa) is an ancient gluten-free, nutrition-packed seed originally from the Andes Mountains. Hugely popular and now available everywhere, quinoa is known as the "chameleon" of grains, because it takes on the flavors of the herbs, vegetables, and other spices it's mixed with. Quinoa cooks quickly, in just fifteen minutes. To get this filling dish on the table in less than thirty minutes, pick up a store-bought rotisserie chicken on your way home. This soup is hearty and wonderful.

Makes 6 to 8 servings

1½ tablespoons extra-virgin olive oil

½ cup thinly sliced scallions

1 cup shredded carrots

1 cup chopped yellow onions

¾ cup thinly sliced celery

1 14.5-ounce can no-salt-added diced tomatoes, drained

1 teaspoon freshly ground black pepper

3 tablespoons chopped fresh cilantro

½ teaspoon ground cumin

10 cups low-sodium chicken broth

¾ cup quinoa

1 rotisserie chicken, skin and bones removed, shredded into pieces

Heat the olive oil in a Dutch oven over medium heat. Add the scallions, carrots, onions, celery, and tomatoes and sauté until soft, 4 to 5 minutes. Stir in the pepper, cilantro, and cumin and cook for 2 more minutes.

Pour in the chicken broth, add the quinoa, and cook, uncovered, for 15 minutes. Add the shredded chicken and cook for 5 more minutes before serving.

Seven-Layer Taco Salad

While we don't usually think of salads as comfort food, family picnics or parties weren't complete without a seven-layer salad when I was a kid. Popular throughout the South, seven-layer salads are traditionally arranged in and served from a clear glass bowl so everyone can see the layers. My seven-layer salad is not only delicious, but also beautiful to look at all in a crunchy, whole wheat tortilla bowl. The best part is that you can eat the bowl!

Makes 2 servings

Tortilla Bowls

Vegetable oil spray

1 teaspoon low-sodium taco seasoning

1 teaspoon kosher salt

Two 10-inch whole wheat flour tortillas

2 tablespoons extra-virgin olive oil

Ground Beef

2 tablespoons canola oil

½ cup finely chopped white onion

1 teaspoon kosher salt

½ pound 90% lean ground beef

3 tablespoons low-sodium taco seasoning

½ cup beef broth

Lime Vinaigrette

2 tablespoons fresh lime juice

1 teaspoon agave nectar

1 teaspoon Dijon mustard

¼ teaspoon red pepper flakes

¼ teaspoon cayenne

¾ cup canola oil

Salad

2 cups thinly sliced iceberg or romaine lettuce leaves

½ cup canned black beans, drained and rinsed

1 avocado, peeled, pitted, and cut into ¼-inch cubes

½ cup (2 ounces) shredded light sharp Cheddar

½ cup diced plum tomatoes

2 tablespoons minced red onion

¼ cup low-fat sour cream or nonfat yogurt

Preheat the oven to 400°F.

To make the tortilla bowls, place two 6-inch ovenproof bowls, rims down, on a baking sheet. Lightly spray the outsides of the bowls with vegetable oil spray.

Mix together the taco seasoning and salt in a bowl. Microwave the tortillas on high to soften them, 10 to 20 seconds. Lightly brush both sides of each tortilla with the olive oil. Lightly sprinkle the tortillas with the seasoning mixture and drape one over each upside-down bowl. Gently press the tortillas around the bowls to make them fit. Cover the tortillas with aluminum foil. Bake for 8 to 10 minutes, until crisp. Transfer to a wire rack to cool and remove the foil.

To prepare the ground beef, heat the canola oil in a large skillet over low heat. Add the white onion and salt and sauté until soft, 4 to 5 minutes. Add the beef and cook, stirring occasionally, until no longer pink, 6 to 7 minutes. Drain any excess oil. Stir in the taco seasoning mix and beef broth and cook, stirring occasionally, until the liquid has evaporated, 4 to 5 minutes.

To make the vinaigrette, place the lime juice, agave, mustard, red pepper flakes, and cayenne in a food processor and pulse to combine. With the food processor running, add the canola oil in a slow, steady stream until the dressing is emulsified.

To complete the salad, fill each taco bowl in the following order: lettuce, black beans, beef, avocado, cheese, tomatoes, and red onion. Top each bowl with some vinaigrette and serve immediately with the sour cream on the side.

TBLT Salads

After a stretch of too many rich meals, I do find myself craving a simple salad with vegetables, a bit of protein, and a tasty homemade dressing. By replacing regular bacon with turkey bacon and adding just a few croutons instead of two slices of bread, I turn a BLT into a comforting and filling TBLT salad. Just perfect for a light lunch.

Makes 4 main-course servings

Dressing

1 cup nonfat plain Greek yogurt

3 tablespoons light mayonnaise

2 tablespoons white wine vinegar

2 teaspoons sugar

1 teaspoon whole grain Dijon mustard

1 teaspoon fresh lemon juice

1 tablespoon chopped fresh parsley

1 tablespoon chopped fresh chives

½ teaspoon garlic salt

¼ teaspoon freshly ground black pepper

Croutons

½ day-old baguette, cut into ½-inch cubes

¼ cup extra-virgin olive oil

1 teaspoon garlic salt

½ teaspoon freshly ground black pepper

Salad

½ pound turkey bacon slices

1 small head of red leaf lettuce, chopped into bite-size pieces

1 small head of romaine, chopped into bite-size pieces

4 plum tomatoes, cut into ½-inch pieces

½ cup finely chopped red onion

Kosher salt and freshly ground black pepper

Preheat the oven to 400°F. Line a baking sheet with parchment paper.

To make the dressing, whisk together the yogurt, mayonnaise, vinegar, sugar, mustard, lemon juice, parsley, chives, garlic salt, and pepper in a bowl. Cover and refrigerate.

To make the croutons, toss the bread, olive oil, garlic salt, and pepper in a bowl. Arrange the bread cubes on the prepared baking sheet in a single layer. Bake for 6 to 8 minutes, until light golden brown. Let cool.

To make the salad, put the turkey bacon in a single layer on paper towels on a microwave-safe plate. Cover with an additional paper towel. Microwave on high for 2 minutes. If the bacon isn't crisp enough, continue to microwave it at 30-second intervals. When cool enough to handle, chop the bacon.

Combine the red leaf lettuce and romaine in a large bowl and then divide the lettuce among four large plates. Divide the chopped tomatoes among the plates. Sprinkle with equal portions bacon and red onion. Lightly sprinkle with salt and pepper. Drizzle 2 to 3 tablespoons dressing on each salad and sprinkle with about ¼ cup croutons before serving.

Linguine Carbonara

Creamy, cheesy linguine carbonara is a rich pasta dish made with eggs, Parmesan, and bacon. While it's hearty and filling, linguine carbonara isn't a low-calorie dish. I decided to create a lighter version of this Italian comfort classic. An egg substitute stands in for the eggs, while leaner Canadian bacon replaces the traditional fatty bacon. It's still light, creamy, and oh so satisfying. *Mangia!*

Makes 6 to 8 servings

2 tablespoons plus ½ teaspoon kosher salt

1 pound linguine

2 tablespoons (¼ stick) unsalted butter

1 6-ounce piece Canadian bacon, cut in half and then cut into ¼-inch strips

2 tablespoons extra-virgin olive oil

1 cup finely chopped white onions

3 garlic cloves, minced

½ cup dry white wine

1 cup Egg Beaters

1 cup (4 ounces) grated Parmigiano-Reggiano

½ teaspoon freshly ground black pepper

2 tablespoons minced fresh parsley

Bring a large pot of water and 2 tablespoons of the salt to a boil. Add the linguine and cook until al dente. Before draining the pasta, remove ¼ cup cooking water in a measuring cup. Drain the pasta and immediately return it to the warm pot.

While the linguine is cooking, melt the butter in a skillet over medium heat. Add the Canadian bacon and sauté until lightly brown, 3 to 4 minutes. Using a slotted spoon, remove the bacon to a plate. Add the olive oil and heat in the same skillet. Add the onions and sauté until translucent, 5 to 6 minutes. Add the garlic and sauté until fragrant, about 1 minute. Add the white wine and, using a wooden spoon, stir to get any little bits of onion and garlic off the bottom of the pan. Reduce the heat to low and simmer until the wine is reduced to 2 tablespoons.

Whisk together the Egg Beaters, Parmesan, pepper, and the remaining ½ teaspoon salt in a bowl.

Add the cooked pasta and the reserved ¼ cup pasta cooking water to the skillet with the onions and garlic and pour the egg mixture over the pasta over low heat. Using tongs, quickly mix everything together. Add the cooked bacon and the parsley and toss until all is well combined. Serve immediately.

Mandarin Spring Salad with Grapefruit Dressing FAN FAVORITE

If you get tired of the same-old, same-old green salad with vinaigrette, here's one that will perk up any meal. Bright, colorful, tangy, and satisfying, it's a change-up that screams springtime. Add some grilled chicken or shrimp to take it from side dish to main course. This salad is simply beautiful.

Makes 4 servings

Dressing

½ cup fresh grapefruit juice

3 tablespoons extra-virgin olive oil

1 tablespoon honey

1 tablespoon mayonnaise

1 teaspoon Dijon mustard

¼ teaspoon kosher salt

¼ teaspoon freshly ground black pepper

¼ teaspoon grapefruit zest

Salad

1 11-ounce container spring mix salad

½ cup thinly sliced celery

1 avocado, peeled, pitted, and thinly sliced

¼ cup sliced almonds, toasted

1 11-ounce can mandarin orange segments, drained

To make the dressing, put the grapefruit juice, olive oil, honey, mayonnaise, mustard, salt, pepper, and grapefruit zest into a food processor. Process until blended.

To assemble the salad, place the salad mix, celery, avocado, almonds, and oranges in a salad bowl. Just before serving, pour the dressing over the salad and lightly toss to coat.

Skinny Fried Chicken

One of the dishes at the top of my comfort-food food chain is Southern fried chicken. As good as crisp-on-the-outside, moist-on-the-inside fried chicken is, it's not exactly something to eat frequently. The good news is that I've found a way to make flavorful fried chicken with less fat and far fewer calories in every piece. A crispy cornflake coating and just the right spices make this dish a satisfying home run. Now, you can have your fried chicken and eat it, too.

Makes 12 servings

12 boneless, skinless chicken breasts, pounded to ½ inch thick

2 cups buttermilk

1 tablespoon hot sauce

Vegetable oil spray

½ cup all-purpose flour

3 cups cornflake crumbs

1 teaspoon paprika

1 teaspoon kosher salt

½ teaspoon freshly ground black pepper

½ teaspoon cayenne

½ teaspoon garlic powder

½ teaspoon onion powder

1 teaspoon poultry seasoning

Rinse the chicken breasts in cold water, then place them in a resealable plastic bag with the buttermilk and hot sauce. Close the bag, shake until the chicken pieces are fully coated, and refrigerate for at least 2 hours or overnight.

Position a rack in the center of the oven. Preheat the oven to 400°F. Spray a wire rack with vegetable oil spray and place it in a roasting pan or on a baking sheet.

Place the flour on a plate. Mix the cornflake crumbs, paprika, salt, black pepper, cayenne, garlic powder, onion powder, and poultry seasoning in a bowl until the ingredients are evenly distributed. Remove the chicken breasts from the bag and place them on a plate. Pour the marinade into a medium bowl. Dredge each breast with the flour until fully coated, shaking off any excess. Then coat the chicken in the marinade, followed by a dredging in the cornflake mixture.

Arrange the chicken pieces on the prepared wire rack. Bake for 15 minutes. Reduce the oven temperature to 350°F and bake until cooked through and crispy, 15 to 20 minutes.

Stuffed and Grilled Flank Steak FAN FAVORITE

My favorite flank steak preparation is to marinate the steak; cut a pocket in the meat; fill it with a colorful mixture of spinach, bell peppers, and feta; and then grill or broil it to medium-rare. When the meat is sliced, the filling is in the middle.

Makes 6 to 8 servings

1½ pounds flank steak

Marinade

½ cup extra-virgin olive oil

½ cup balsamic vinegar

¼ cup honey

⅓ cup minced fresh rosemary

Stuffing

½ cup crumbled feta

4 garlic cloves, minced

⅔ cup finely diced red bell pepper

½ cup sliced scallions

¼ teaspoon kosher salt

¼ teaspoon freshly ground black pepper

Steak Seasoning

½ teaspoon kosher salt

¼ teaspoon freshly ground black pepper

To cut a pocket into the flank steak, slice an opening on the longer and thicker side of the steak. Turn the steak over and slice deeper into the meat, stopping ½ inch from the three other edges. Place the steak in a 9 x 13-inch baking dish.

To make the marinade, combine the olive oil, vinegar, honey, and rosemary in a bowl and pour it over the steak. Let the steak marinate for 30 minutes.

Preheat the grill to high heat.

To make the stuffing, combine the feta, garlic, bell pepper, scallions, salt, and black pepper in a bowl.

Remove the steak from the marinade. Discard the marinade. Combine the salt and pepper and season the steak. Fill the pocket with the stuffing mixture. To keep the filling from falling out, weave a metal or wooden skewer (soaked in water for 30 minutes) in and out of the steak's opening. Grill the steak for 12 to 14 minutes on each side for medium-rare, or longer if you prefer the steak medium or well-done. Remove the steak to a cutting board and let it stand for 5 to 10 minutes before thinly slicing on the bias.

Better-Than-Ever Tuna Casserole FAN FAVORITE

Nothing says comfort like an old-fashioned tuna casserole, but traditional tuna casserole is usually not on the lighter fare menu. I took on the challenge to make this one better and started changing and adjusting ingredients. I think you'll love the comforting results.

Makes 8 to 10 servings

Vegetable oil spray

1 12-ounce package whole grain egg noodles

2 tablespoons extra-virgin olive oil

1 cup chopped onions

8 ounces button mushrooms, thinly sliced

2 10.75-ounce cans 98% fat-free cream of mushroom soup

1½ cups low-fat milk

½ cup fat-free half-and-half

½ teaspoon dried thyme

1 teaspoon kosher salt

½ teaspoon freshly ground black pepper

¼ teaspoon garlic powder

1 cup (4 ounces) shredded reduced-fat Cheddar

3 5-ounce cans tuna fish, well drained

1½ cups frozen peas

¼ cup seasoned bread crumbs

¼ cup (1 ounce) grated Parmigiano-Reggiano

Preheat the oven to 350°F. Spray a 9 x 13-inch baking dish with vegetable oil spray.

Bring a large pot of water to a boil. Add the noodles and cook until tender but still firm to the bite. Drain the noodles.

Heat the olive oil in a skillet over low heat. Add the onions and mushrooms and sauté until the onions are translucent and the mushrooms are cooked through, 5 to 6 minutes. Let cool.

Combine the cream of mushroom soup, milk, half-and-half, thyme, salt, pepper, and garlic powder in a large bowl. Add the noodles, cheese, tuna, peas, and the onions and mushrooms. Fold the ingredients together until combined.

Transfer the mixture to the prepared dish. Sprinkle the bread crumbs and Parmesan evenly on top. Bake for 40 to 45 minutes, until the top is golden brown and the casserole is bubbly. Let rest for 5 to 10 minutes before serving.

Halibut in Parchment Paper

En papillote is a method of steaming meat, fish, vegetables, and herbs inside a sealed parchment paper package. During baking, the parchment paper browns and puffs up. The best part is the presentation. Each person gets his or her own package, and when the paper is cut open with scissors, fragrant puffs of steam are released and everything inside is cooked to perfection.

Makes 4 servings

Vegetable oil spray

4 6- to 8-ounce, ¾-inch-thick halibut, cod, or scrod fillets

Kosher salt and freshly ground black pepper

2 lemons, sliced into ⅛-inch half-moons

½ small carrot, cut into 2-inch thin strips

½ leek (dark green top removed), cut into 2-inch thin strips

½ yellow bell pepper, cut into 2-inch thin strips

8 small tarragon sprigs

2 tablespoons minced fresh parsley

2 tablespoons (¼ stick) unsalted butter

¼ cup dry white wine

Preheat the oven to 400°F. Cut 4 pieces of parchment into rectangles approximately 12 x 18 inches. Fold the parchment sheets in half the long way. Using scissors, cut the largest half of a heart possible out of each sheet. Open each heart and lightly spray with vegetable oil spray on one side of each heart.

Lightly season each piece of fish with salt and pepper. Place 1 piece of fish on the oiled side of each heart. There should be about a 1-inch border on all sides. On top of each fish piece, shingle 5 or 6 lemon slices, 5 or 6 carrot strips, 4 or 5 leek strips, 4 or 5 bell pepper strips, and 2 tarragon sprigs. Divide the parsley among the 4 pieces of fish. Dot ½ tablespoon butter on top of each piece. Drizzle 1 tablespoon white wine over each piece. Fold over the opposite side of the heart and twist or roll the edges together to seal. Make sure all the edges are sealed well. At the bottom point of the heart, fold the edge under to keep the parchment from coming open while cooking.

Place the packages on a baking sheet. Bake for 8 to 10 minutes. Place each parchment package on a dinner plate. Once everyone is at the table, use a scissors to cut a hole in each package to let the steam escape.

Turkey Meat Loaf

While meat loaf is a classic American comfort food dish, it can sometimes be heavy, dense, and, okay, I'll say it, high in calories. The secret to making a good, light meat loaf all depends on the flavorful ingredients used. I start with ground turkey and add whole wheat bread crumbs and egg whites to bind the meat together. Each bite contains a burst of sun-dried tomato and a pop of creamy queso fresco. The glaze has a touch of spiciness from the mustard counterbalanced by the sweet ketchup and honey. This is my new favorite meat loaf recipe.

Makes 6 to 8 servings

Vegetable oil spray

Meat Loaf

3 pounds 90% lean ground turkey

1 cup whole wheat bread crumbs

2 large egg whites

2 cups (8 ounces) grated queso fresco

1 7-ounce jar sun-dried tomatoes in oil, drained and cut into ⅛-inch strips

1 cup finely chopped onions

½ cup finely chopped celery

½ cup finely chopped carrot

1 tablespoon chopped fresh parsley

1½ teaspoons chopped fresh basil

½ teaspoon dried oregano

1½ teaspoons kosher salt

1 teaspoon freshly ground black pepper

Glaze

1 cup ketchup

2 tablespoons honey

2 tablespoons Dijon mustard

Put one oven rack on the lowest shelf and the other on the shelf just above it. Put a roasting pan on the lowest oven rack. Fill it with water. Spray a 9 x 5-inch loaf pan with vegetable oil spray. Preheat the oven to 350°F.

To make the meat loaf, put the turkey, bread crumbs, egg whites, cheese, sun-dried tomatoes, onions, celery, carrot, parsley, basil, oregano, salt, and pepper in a large bowl. Using clean hands, mix until all of the ingredients are combined. For a tender meat loaf, don't overmix. Put the mixture in the loaf pan and evenly press to form a smooth loaf. Place the loaf pan on the shelf above the one with the pan filled with hot water. This technique keeps the meat loaf from forming a crack on top while baking. Bake for 40 minutes.

To make the glaze, combine the ketchup, honey, and mustard in a saucepan over medium heat. Cook for 2 minutes, stirring occasionally so the glaze doesn't burn.

Remove the meat loaf from the oven and brush the glaze onto the top. Return the meat loaf to the oven and bake until an instant-read thermometer inserted into the center registers 170°F to 180°F. Let the meat loaf rest for 5 to 10 minutes before slicing.

Lighter Baked Macaroni 'n' Cheese

There are times when we all have to back off from rich foods. Since macaroni 'n' cheese is the one dish I could eat every day, I decided to make a lighter version of my all-time favorite comfort food without sacrificing flavor and texture. I worked hard to create a mac 'n' cheese that lives up to my standards. I started with hearty multigrain pasta, which has great flavor. For the cheesy, gooey part, I used part-skim mozzarella, reduced-fat sharp Cheddar, and light garlic cheese spread. For extra creaminess, I added some light sour cream. It all comes together in a guilt-free dish that everyone at the dinner table will love.

Makes 6 to 8 servings

Vegetable oil spray

3 tablespoons kosher salt

1 12-ounce box multigrain elbow macaroni

2 teaspoons cornstarch

2 tablespoons 2% milk

5 tablespoons unsalted butter

⅔ cup finely chopped onion

¼ cup all-purpose flour

1 teaspoon dry mustard

5 cups 2% milk, warmed

1 cup (4 ounces) shredded part-skim mozzarella

4 cups (1 pound) shredded reduced-fat sharp Cheddar

1 6.5-ounce Alouette Light Garlic & Herbs cheese spread

½ teaspoon freshly ground black pepper

1½ cups light sour cream

Preheat the oven to 350°F. Spray a 9 x 13-inch baking dish with vegetable oil spray.

Bring a large pot of water and 2 tablespoons of the salt to a boil. Add the macaroni and bring back to a boil. Reduce the heat slightly and cook until al dente, 5 to 6 minutes. Drain the macaroni and put in a large bowl.

While the pasta is cooking, whisk together the cornstarch and milk to make a slurry. Melt the butter in a large saucepan over low heat. Add the onion and sauté until soft, 4 to 5 minutes. Whisk in the flour and mustard and cook, whisking constantly, for 2 to 3 minutes. Whisk in the 2% milk, bring to a boil, and continue stirring until the sauce has thickened. Whisk in ⅓ cup of the mozzarella, 2 cups of the Cheddar, the garlic-herb cheese spread, the remaining 1 tablespoon salt, the pepper, and the slurry. Bring back to a boil and continue to stir until you have a nice thick, smooth sauce. Remove from the heat.

Add the cooked macaroni to the sauce. Stir in another ⅓ cup of the mozzarella, 1 cup of the Cheddar, and the sour cream. Pour into the prepared baking dish. Top with the remaining ⅓ cup mozzarella and 1 cup Cheddar. Cover with aluminum foil. Bake for 20 minutes. Remove the foil and bake for an additional 20 to 25 minutes, until the cheeses are bubbly and brown. Let rest for 5 to 10 minutes before serving.

Parmesan Pork Cutlets with Tomato-Basil Salad and Broccoli Rabe

I've always believed that pork and Parmesan go together well. Like a lighter version of Wiener schnitzel, these pork cutlets are pounded until thin, then gently dredged in flour, dipped in egg whites, and coated with whole wheat bread crumbs and Parmesan cheese before they are baked, rather than fried. Then the flavors are really ramped up with some chopped tomato and basil and a side of broccoli rabe.

Makes 4 servings

Vegetable oil spray

Pork Cutlets

4 6- to 8-ounce boneless pork chops, trimmed and pounded to ½-inch thickness

1 teaspoon kosher salt

½ teaspoon freshly ground black pepper

¼ cup all-purpose flour

2 large egg whites, beaten

½ cup fine whole wheat bread crumbs

1 cup (4 ounces) grated Parmigiano-Reggiano, plus more for garnish

1 teaspoon ground sage

1 tablespoon chopped fresh parsley

Tomato-Basil Salad

3 plum tomatoes, quartered, seeded, and diced

2 tablespoons extra-virgin olive oil

2 garlic cloves, minced

1 teaspoon kosher salt

¼ teaspoon freshly ground black pepper

⅛ cup balsamic vinegar

3 or 4 large basil leaves, cut into thin strips

Broccoli Rabe

1 quart low-sodium chicken broth

2 bunches of broccoli rabe, stems trimmed

2 tablespoons extra-virgin olive oil

3 garlic cloves, minced

3 tablespoons minced shallots

½ teaspoon kosher salt

¼ teaspoon red pepper flakes

Preheat the oven to 350°F. Line a baking sheet with aluminum foil and place a wire rack on top. Generously spray the rack with vegetable oil spray.

To make the pork cutlets, season the cutlets on both sides with the salt and pepper. Spread the flour in a shallow bowl. Put the egg whites in a shallow bowl and beat with a fork. Mix the bread crumbs, Parmesan, sage, and parsley in a third bowl. Dredge the cutlets in the flour, then in the egg whites, and then in the bread crumb mixture. Place the cutlets on the wire rack above the prepared baking sheet. Bake for 30 to 40 minutes, turning the cutlets after 15 or 20 minutes. Remove from the oven and let rest for 5 to 10 minutes before serving.

To make the tomato-basil salad, put the tomatoes, olive oil, garlic, salt, pepper, and vinegar in a bowl and toss gently. Add the basil and toss gently.

To make the broccoli rabe, bring the chicken broth to a boil in a saucepan. Fill a bowl with cold water and ice as described below. Add the broccoli rabe to the pan and cook until tender and bright green in color, 3 to 4 minutes. Drain in a colander and plunge into the ice bath to stop the cooking. Drain again. Heat the olive oil in a skillet over medium heat. Add the garlic and shallots and sauté until fragrant, 2 to 3 minutes. Add the broccoli rabe, salt, and red pepper flakes and sauté to heat through, 3 to 4 more minutes.

To serve, place a pork cutlet on each plate and top with the tomato-basil salad. Divide the broccoli rabe among the plates and serve with additional Parmesan.

Taking a Plunge Can Be a Shock!

Blanching, or shocking, vegetables is the technique of plunging them into ice water to keep them from cooking more once they're done. If you just remove the pot from the heat, the vegetables will keep cooking. Submerging broccoli, asparagus, carrots, and other vegetables locks in their flavor, color, and texture. No more drab green beans or overcooked peas.

While the water is coming to a boil for cooking the vegetables, fill a large bowl three-quarters full with ice and cold water. Add the prepared vegetables to the boiling water. After 30 seconds, remove a piece and immediately plunge it into the ice water. Take a bite. If the vegetable is cooked to your liking, strain the hot water from the vegetables or use a slotted spoon to transfer the vegetables to the bowl with the ice water. If not, continue cooking and taste another piece every 30 seconds. Cook the remaining vegetables to desired doneness. Let the vegetables cool in the ice water for 1 minute, then drain them through a colander. When entertaining, it's nice to know that your vegetables need just a quick reheating with butter or oil, herbs, or any other ingredients. Blanched vegetables also make a nice alternative to raw vegetables when served with dips.

Angel Food Cake with Berries

I have never really been a big fan of angel food cake—it's usually just too plain and a little too bland for my taste. To give it some zing I add blueberries to the batter for pops of color and a bright berry flavor in every bite. Then each slice gets a big spoonful of mixed berry sauce. Angel food cake now becomes absolutely heavenly.

Makes 8 to 10 servings

Mixed Fruit

1 pint blueberries

1 pint strawberries, hulled and quartered

1 pint blackberries

½ cup sugar

1 teaspoon pure vanilla extract

Cake

10 large egg whites, at room temperature

1¼ teaspoons cream of tartar

¼ teaspoon table salt

¾ cup superfine sugar

1 teaspoon pure vanilla extract

1 teaspoon lemon zest

1 cup cake flour

1½ cups fresh blueberries

Light frozen whipped topping, thawed (see page 260)

Preheat the oven to 350°F.

To make the fruit, gently mix the blueberries, strawberries, blackberries, sugar, and vanilla in a bowl. Let the fruit sit for 3 to 4 hours at room temperature.

To make the cake, put the egg whites, cream of tartar, and salt in the bowl of a standing mixer fitted with the whisk attachment. Start blending the egg whites on low. As they begin to thicken, increase the speed to medium and continue whipping until soft peaks form. Add the superfine sugar, vanilla, and lemon zest and continue to whip until stiff peaks form. The egg whites should be shiny, but not dry.

Sift the flour over the egg whites. Using a rubber spatula, gently fold in the flour just until blended. Add the blueberries and fold in just until blended. Spoon the batter into an ungreased 10-inch angel food tube cake pan. Bake for 30 to 35 minutes, until a toothpick inserted into the center comes out clean. Remove the pan to a wire rack. Turn the pan upside down, but do not remove the cake. Let cool for 1 hour. Using a dinner knife, loosen the sides of the cake from the pan. Invert the cake onto a plate. Serve each slice of cake with ½ cup berry mixture and a dollop of whipped topping.

Grilled Fruit with Grand Marnier Whipped Topping

Grilling isn't just for burgers, steaks, and seafood. When I have a hankering for something sweet but it's too hot to bake, I make these grilled fruit skewers. Fruit cooked on the grill becomes something altogether different and wonderful with its sweet-smoky, caramelized flavors. Just cut, skewer, and grill the fruit. Top with some Grand Marnier whipped topping.

Makes 6 to 8 servings

Topping

1 8-ounce container Cool Whip whipped topping, thawed (see page 260)

2 tablespoons Grand Marnier

2 tablespoons (packed) light brown sugar

Grilled Fruit

⅔ cup (packed) light brown sugar

2 teaspoons ground cinnamon

Ground nutmeg

2 peaches, pitted and sliced into 4 to 6 pieces

2 plums, pitted and sliced into 4 to 6 pieces

1 pineapple, peeled, cored, and cut into 8 spears

1 quart strawberries, hulled

6 12-inch wooden skewers, soaked in water for 40 to 50 minutes

½ cup confectioners' sugar

To make the topping, put the whipped topping, Grand Marnier, and brown sugar in a bowl. Using a handheld electric mixer, whip the ingredients until combined, 1 to 2 minutes. Cover and refrigerate until ready to serve.

Preheat the grill to medium-high heat.

To make the grilled fruit, combine ⅓ cup of the brown sugar, 1 teaspoon of the cinnamon, and a dash of nutmeg in a bowl. Add the peaches and plums to the brown sugar mixture and toss well to combine. Let the fruit sit at room temperature for 30 minutes before grilling.

Combine the remaining ⅓ cup brown sugar, 1 teaspoon cinnamon, and another dash of nutmeg in a shallow dish. Roll the pineapple spears in the brown sugar mixture to coat on all sides. Put the pineapple spears on a platter and let them sit at room temperature for 20 to 30 minutes before grilling.

Thread 4 or 5 strawberries onto each skewer. Put the confectioners' sugar in a shallow dish. Roll the strawberry skewers in the confectioners' sugar to coat on all sides and put them on the platter with the pineapple spears. Let the skewers sit at room temperature for 15 to 20 minutes before grilling.

Put the pineapple spears, then the strawberries, and finally the peaches and plums on the grill in that order. Grill the fruit until brown, 3 to 4 minutes, on all sides. Serve with the Grand Marnier whipped topping.

Strawberry-Pineapple Frozen Yogurt

When summer temperatures soar, nothing hits the spot like an ice-cold, creamy treat. Since its introduction in the 1980s, frozen yogurt has become wildly popular. It seems as if there is a frozen yogurt shop on every corner. Frozen yogurt is easy to make and offers a great lower-calorie alternative to ice cream, yet still satisfies my sweet tooth. Strawberry and pineapple—two of my favorite fruits—work beautifully together in this combination.

Makes 6 to 8 servings

2 cups fresh strawberries, hulled and sliced

1½ cups ½-inch chunks fresh pineapple

3 tablespoons pineapple juice

¼ cup Truvía Natural Sweetener

1 14-ounce can coconut milk

3 cups full-fat vanilla Greek yogurt

Combine the strawberries, pineapple chunks, pineapple juice, and Truvía in a saucepan over medium heat. Cook, stirring occasionally, until the Truvía has dissolved. Pour the mixture into a blender and blend until smooth, about 30 seconds. Pour the mixture into a bowl and let cool for 10 minutes. Gradually whisk in the coconut milk, followed by the yogurt. Cover and chill the yogurt mixture in the refrigerator for 1 hour.

Pour the yogurt mixture into an ice cream maker. Churn until the yogurt is frozen, 25 to 30 minutes. Serve immediately, or transfer to a container and freeze for an additional 2 to 3 hours or overnight.

Fresh & Flavorful

When I stroll through my local farmer's market during the summer, my mind starts flying all over the place with ideas on how to use all those perfect vegetables, fruits, and herbs. The truth is that when vegetables are at their peak, you don't have to do much to them. Colorful tomatoes are simply layered in a stunning Heirloom Tomato Caprese with Balsamic Glaze. A Baked Vegetable Gratin uses the bounty of green zucchini, yellow squash, and plum tomatoes under a blanket of bread crumbs and Parmesan. Since peaches are my favorite summer fruit, I grill and pair them with some mozzarella on a bed of arugula.

During the winter, I see no reason to serve steamed broccoli, steamed potatoes, steamed whatever, when there are so many interesting ways to prepare vegetables. Roast broccoli with pine nuts and feta. Cook carrots in maple syrup and brown sugar and top with a sprinkle of chopped pecans. There's no excuse for a boring green salad when apples, Gorgonzola, and red onions can be tossed with pomegranate vinaigrette. Think of Butternut Squash Gratin or Cheesy Creamed Corn as vegetarian main dishes.

Finally, I have to honor my Southern roots with a recipe for collard greens with some smoky bacon and tangy cider vinegar. Now, that's something I can eat every day of the year.

Roasted Broccoli with Toasted Pine Nuts and Feta

Steamed broccoli is about as ordinary as it gets. When I want to dress it up a bit, I roast broccoli to bring out this vegetable's sweet, nutty flavor. But wait, I'm not done yet. I toss the broccoli with toasted pine nuts, crumbled feta, and just a sprinkling of cayenne for a little heat. All this results in the perfect broccoli makeover.

Makes 6 to 8 servings

¼ cup pine nuts or chopped walnuts

1 teaspoon canola oil

⅛ teaspoon cayenne

1⅛ teaspoons kosher salt

2 pounds broccoli, trimmed and cut into 2-inch spears

3 to 4 tablespoons extra-virgin olive oil

¾ teaspoon garlic powder

½ teaspoon freshly ground black pepper

1 cup (4 ounces) crumbled feta

Place a rack in the center of the oven. Preheat the oven to 350°F. Line a baking sheet with parchment paper.

Combine the pine nuts, canola oil, cayenne, and ⅛ teaspoon of the salt in a bowl, making sure that all of the pine nuts are coated. Transfer the pine nuts to the prepared baking sheet. Give the baking sheet a couple of good shakes to make sure the pine nuts are in a single layer. Bake for 3 to 5 minutes, until the pine nuts are golden brown. After removing the pine nuts from the oven, raise the oven temperature to 425°F. Pour the pine nuts into a bowl so the baking sheet can be used again for the broccoli.

Arrange the broccoli in a single layer on the baking sheet. Add the olive oil, garlic powder, the remaining 1 teaspoon salt, and the black pepper and toss to coat thoroughly. Bake for 10 to 15 minutes, giving the baking sheet a good shake so the broccoli doesn't stick. Transfer the broccoli to a bowl, toss with the feta, and garnish with the pine nuts before serving.

Stuffed Artichokes

When I go to Italian restaurants, I'm always thrilled to see stuffed artichokes on the menu. Here, I use large globe artichokes stuffed with bread crumbs, garlic, and plenty of cheese between the leaves. You pluck out and scrape each leaf along your teeth, dig out the stuffing, and then finally cut away the fuzzy "choke" to reach the heart. Serve stuffed artichokes as a first course at a dinner party. Be sure to encourage guests to use their fingers!

Makes 6 servings

6 large globe artichokes

1 lemon, cut in half

2 cups bread crumbs

1 cup (4 ounces) grated pecorino
    Romano cheese

1 teaspoon garlic salt

½ teaspoon freshly ground black pepper

½ teaspoon dried oregano

½ cup plus 2 tablespoons extra-virgin
    olive oil

1 lemon, cut into 6 wedges

Using a serrated knife, cut off the artichoke stems so they sit flat. Cut the top thirds off the artichokes, pull off the tough outer leaves, and trim the pointy leaves with kitchen shears. Using your hands, turn the artichokes upside down and press open the artichoke leaves to make room for the stuffing. Rinse the artichokes under running water to remove any dirt. Rub the cut leaves and bottoms with the lemon halves to keep the artichokes from turning dark. Set aside.

Mix together the bread crumbs, cheese, garlic salt, pepper, oregano, and 2 tablespoons of the olive oil in a bowl. Using your hands, push about ½ cup bread crumb mixture between the leaves of each artichoke. Put the artichokes in a Dutch oven—they should be upright and touch one another—and fill the pot with water halfway up the artichokes. Add 2 tablespoons of the olive oil to the water and drizzle 2 tablespoons olive oil over the artichokes. Cover and bring to a boil. Reduce the heat and simmer for 50 to 60 minutes, drizzling 1 to 2 tablespoons olive oil over the artichokes every 20 minutes and adding a little more water to the pot as necessary. There should always be 1 to 2 inches of water in the pot. The artichokes are done when a leaf can be easily pulled off. Serve the artichokes in shallow soup bowls with lemon wedges for squeezing over the tops.

Garlic Mashed Cauliflower and Potatoes

While garlic mashed potatoes make a great side dish, I find that they can sometimes be a bit too heavy with fish, chicken, or pork cutlets. For a lighter and fluffier take, I mash potatoes and garlic with some cooked cauliflower. You won't lose the flavor of the potatoes, but you will gain some nutritional value from the cauliflower, which is rich in much-needed fiber, folate, and vitamin C.

Makes 4 to 6 servings

2 pounds Yukon gold potatoes, peeled and quartered

4 garlic cloves, smashed

2 tablespoons plus 1 teaspoon kosher salt

1 quart chicken broth

1 head (2 pounds) of cauliflower, cored and cut into small florets

6 tablespoons (¾ stick) unsalted butter

1½ cups whole milk

1 5.2-ounce package garlic-herb Boursin, at room temperature

1½ teaspoons white pepper

Place the potatoes in a large pot and cover with water, 2 garlic cloves, and 2 tablespoons salt over high heat and bring to a boil. Reduce the heat to a simmer and cook until the potatoes are fork tender, 20 to 25 minutes. Drain the potatoes and garlic in a colander, then return them to the pot.

Pour the chicken broth into a second pot and bring to a boil. Add the cauliflower and the remaining 2 garlic cloves. Reduce the heat to a simmer and cook the cauliflower until fork tender, 10 to 12 minutes. Drain the cauliflower and garlic and add to the pot with the potatoes and garlic.

Put the butter and milk in the same pot that the cauliflower was cooked in. Melt the butter and heat the milk over medium-high heat, but do not boil. Add the warm milk and the garlic-herb cheese to the potatoes and cauliflower. Using a potato masher or handheld electric mixer, mash the ingredients until the mixture has a slightly chunky consistency. Don't overmix or the mixture will become gummy. Stir in the remaining 1 teaspoon salt and the white pepper and serve immediately.

Roasted Potatoes with Lemon and Herbs

For the last few years, I've been using more citrus, especially lemon, to add a perky flavor to my cooking. These potatoes are a perfect example. Lemon juice and zest add just the right amount of zing to this Greek-inspired potato dish. Serve it with roast chicken or grilled fish along with the Roasted Broccoli with Toasted Pine Nuts and Feta (page 224). You'll feel like you're having dinner right on the Mediterranean.

Makes 6 to 8 servings

1½ pounds small Red Bliss potatoes, quartered

1½ pounds fingerling potatoes, cut in half

¼ cup extra-virgin olive oil

2 teaspoons dried oregano

¾ teaspoon garlic powder

2 tablespoons fresh lemon juice

1 tablespoon kosher salt, plus more to taste

½ teaspoon coarsely ground black pepper, plus more to taste

4 tablespoons (½ stick) unsalted butter, melted

Zest of 1 lemon

2 tablespoons minced fresh oregano

2 tablespoons minced fresh parsley

2 tablespoons chopped fresh rosemary

Place a rack in the center of the oven. Preheat the oven to 450°F. Line a baking sheet with aluminum foil.

Put the Red Bliss potatoes, fingerling potatoes, olive oil, dried oregano, garlic powder, lemon juice, salt, and pepper in a bowl and toss well to coat. Arrange the potatoes in a single layer on the prepared baking sheet.

Roast the potatoes until they are fork tender on the inside and crispy on the outside, 25 to 30 minutes. Using a spatula, turn the potatoes halfway through cooking. While the potatoes are roasting, combine the melted butter with the lemon zest, fresh oregano, parsley, and rosemary. Remove the potatoes from the oven and transfer to a serving dish. Toss the potatoes with the herb-butter mixture and season with salt and pepper before serving.

Butternut Squash Gratin

Like sweet potatoes, butternut squash was served once a year at Mom's Thanksgiving dinner. The squash was cooked, puréed, and blended with other ingredients as a first-course soup. Now I enjoy this winter squash all year round in salads, risotto, or a creamy gratin. Thinly sliced squash—get out your mandoline—is layered with a cream and goat cheese sauce, then baked until ooey-gooey. Serve the gratin as a main course with the Apple, Gorgonzola, Red Onion, and Candied Walnut Salad with Pomegranate Vinaigrette (page 241) or as a side with roast beef, pork, or chicken.

Makes 6 to 8 servings

3 tablespoons unsalted butter

1 cup panko bread crumbs

3 medium butternut squash, peeled, cut in half, seeded, and cut into ⅛-inch slices

⅛ cup plus 2 tablespoons extra-virgin olive oil

1½ teaspoons kosher salt

½ teaspoon freshly ground black pepper

1 white onion, cut in half and very thinly sliced

2 cups heavy cream

⅛ teaspoon ground nutmeg

Leaves of 2 or 3 thyme sprigs, plus more for garnish (optional)

1 8-ounce container crème fraîche

4 ounces fresh goat cheese with herbs

½ cup (2 ounces) grated Parmigiano-Reggiano or grana Padano cheese

Preheat the oven to 375°F. Line 2 baking sheets with aluminum foil. Butter a 9 x 13-inch baking dish with 1 tablespoon of the butter.

Melt the remaining 2 tablespoons butter in a skillet over medium heat. Add the bread crumbs and cook, stirring frequently, until light brown, 4 to 5 minutes

Put the squash, ⅛ cup of the olive oil, the salt, and ¼ teaspoon of the pepper in a bowl. Toss well to coat the squash with the oil. Arrange the squash in a single layer on the baking sheets. Bake for 25 minutes, or until the squash is tender.

While the squash is baking, heat the remaining 2 tablespoons olive oil in a skillet over low heat. Add the onion and sauté, stirring occasionally, until caramelized, 25 to 30 minutes.

Combine the cream, nutmeg, the remaining ¼ teaspoon pepper, and the thyme in a saucepan over medium-high heat. Once the cream comes to a boil, reduce the heat and whisk in the crème fraîche, goat cheese, and ¼ cup of the Parmesan. Bring back to a boil and continue to stir until the cheese is melted and the sauce is smooth. Remove from the heat.

Combine the roasted squash, caramelized onion, and sauce in a large bowl and toss well. Pour the mixture into the prepared baking dish. Sprinkle with the bread crumbs, then with the remaining ¼ cup Parmesan. Cover with aluminum foil and bake for 15 minutes. Remove the foil and bake for an additional 15 minutes, or until bubbly. Let rest for 5 to 10 minutes before serving. Garnish with thyme leaves, if desired.

Collard Greens with Bacon and Vinegar

Because my dad adored collard greens so much, his mother made them every time we went to dinner at her house. Grandma Mimi cooked them with ham hocks or a leftover ham bone and cider vinegar, the traditional Southern way. I still prepare greens and vinegar, but I find it easier and quicker to use bacon than a ham bone.

Makes 4 to 5 servings

⅓ pound thick slab bacon, cut into ¼-inch-wide slices

1 large bunch of collard greens, stemmed, sliced, washed, and thoroughly dried

½ sweet onion, such as Vidalia or Walla Walla, thinly sliced

2 tablespoons extra-virgin olive oil, if necessary

½ teaspoon red pepper flakes

½ cup chicken broth

2 tablespoons cider vinegar, plus more for serving

Kosher salt and freshly ground black pepper

Hot sauce (optional)

Heat a large skillet over high heat. Add the bacon and cook for 2 to 3 minutes. Add the collard greens and onion and sauté for 4 to 5 minutes, adding the olive oil if there isn't enough bacon fat. Add the red pepper flakes and continue tossing until the greens are tender, 3 to 4 minutes. Add the chicken broth and vinegar. Reduce the heat, cover the skillet, and cook until tender, about 15 minutes. Season with salt and pepper. Serve immediately with hot sauce (if using) and vinegar on the side.

It's Easy Being Greens

Since collard, mustard, kale, spinach, and other dark, leafy greens are grown in sandy soil, it's important to clean them really well. Cut off an inch or two of the stems. Submerge the greens in a salad spinner filled with water and gently swish them around. Lift out the basket with the greens and set aside. Rinse out the spinner bowl well. Repeat with fresh water until no dirt is left on the bottom of the spinner. Thoroughly dry the greens in the clean salad spinner.

Cheesy Creamed Corn

My Grandma Burnzie had a huge vegetable garden and she spent much of August and September canning vegetables to feed her children and their families through the winter. She filled a big, old-fashioned pressure cooker with four quart-size Mason jars packed with green beans, squash, bell peppers, carrots, and more. I loved to go down to her basement and look at the hundreds of jars lining the shelves. Of all the vegetables Burnzie put up, my favorite was corn, which she used to make creamed corn. My spin on this dish is more of a casserole, with cheese and eggs holding it together. It's spoon-licking good.

Makes 6 to 8 servings

Vegetable oil spray

3 cups corn kernels from 4 to 5 ears corn, or canned and drained

1 14.5-ounce can creamed corn

3 large eggs, beaten

1 cup heavy cream

1 teaspoon kosher salt

3 tablespoons unsalted butter, melted

3 tablespoons all-purpose flour

2 tablespoons sugar

1 cup (4 ounces) grated pepper Jack

2 cups (8 ounces) shredded white sharp Cheddar

Preheat the oven to 350°F. Spray a 10 x 10-inch baking dish with vegetable oil spray.

Combine the corn kernels, creamed corn, eggs, cream, salt, butter, flour, sugar, pepper Jack, and Cheddar in a bowl. Pour into the prepared baking dish. Bake for 45 to 50 minutes, until set and brown on top. If the top is browning too quickly, cover the dish with aluminum foil for the last 10 minutes. Let rest for 5 to 10 minutes before serving.

Baked Vegetable Gratin FAN FAVORITE

When August rolls around, those squash plants seem to produce bushels of vegetables as soon as I turn my back. Even though I give bags of squash to my neighbors and make enough zucchini bread to start a bakery, I'm always looking for new ways to use my garden's bounty. I layer squash, tomatoes, onions, and some cheese in a baking dish and bake the gratin until the vegetables soften, the cheese melts, and the top becomes crispy. I love how the gratin smells while baking and bubbling away in the oven. The gratin goes well with anything from the grill—steaks, chicken, shrimp, and fish—or serve it as a vegetarian main course. This is a comforting dish you'll feel comfortable making again and again.

Makes 6 to 8 servings

¼ cup plus 2 tablespoons extra-virgin olive oil

2 medium onions, sliced ¼ inch thick

2 garlic cloves, thinly sliced

1½ cups panko bread crumbs

½ cup (2 ounces) finely shredded Asiago cheese

½ cup (2 ounces) grated Parmigiano-Reggiano

⅓ cup chopped fresh basil, plus more for garnish

1½ teaspoons dried oregano

1½ teaspoons kosher salt

1½ teaspoons freshly ground black pepper

½ cup vegetable broth

1 large yellow squash, cut into ¼-inch-thick rounds

10 plum tomatoes, cut into ¼-inch-thick rounds

1 large zucchini, cut into ¼-inch-thick rounds

Preheat the oven to 350°F.

Put 2 tablespoons of the olive oil in a skillet over low heat. Add the onions and sauté, stirring occasionally, until caramelized, 25 to 30 minutes. Add the garlic and sauté until fragrant, about 1 minute. Combine the bread crumbs, Asiago, Parmesan, basil, oregano, salt, and pepper in a bowl.

Pour the vegetable broth into a 9 x 13-inch baking dish. Layer the remaining ingredients in the baking dish in the following order: the yellow squash, ½ cup bread crumb mixture, half of the tomatoes, half of the onions, ½ cup bread crumb mixture, the zucchini, the remaining onions, ½ cup bread crumb mixture, the remaining tomatoes, and the remaining bread crumb mixture. Drizzle the remaining ¼ cup olive oil over the bread crumb mixture.

Cover the dish with aluminum foil and bake for about 1 hour, or until the vegetables are tender. Remove the foil and turn on the broiler. Broil until golden brown and crispy on top, 3 to 4 minutes. Let rest for 5 to 10 minutes and garnish with chopped basil before serving.

Individual Stuffed Eggplant Parmesan

Every month we celebrate a different food or cooking technique on *In the Kitchen with David*. Stuffed foods, such as chicken cordon bleu, peanut butter and jelly–filled cupcakes, and twice-stuffed potatoes, were a favorite theme. The possibilities are endless. In this preparation, I roast eggplants, scoop out the centers, and spoon in an eggplant-tomato-cheese filling. Then I sprinkle on bread crumbs and more cheese before baking them. Each guest is served boats that are cheesy, saucy, and *delizioso*.

Makes 6 servings

3 tablespoons extra-virgin olive oil

Eggplant Boats

6 medium (¾ to 1 pound each) eggplants, cut in half

1 teaspoon kosher salt

Tomato Sauce

2 tablespoons extra-virgin olive oil

1 medium Spanish onion, finely chopped

3 garlic cloves, minced

½ cup dry red wine

1 28-ounce can whole plum tomatoes with juices

1 14.5-ounce can crushed tomatoes with basil

2 teaspoons kosher salt

1 teaspoon dried oregano

½ teaspoon red pepper flakes

4 cups (1 pound) shredded mozzarella

¾ cup (3 ounces) grated Parmigiano-Reggiano, plus more for serving

⅓ cup Italian-seasoned bread crumbs

Preheat the oven to 350°F. Line a baking sheet with aluminum foil. Pour the olive oil onto the foil to coat evenly.

To make the eggplant boats, season the eggplant halves with the salt. Place the eggplant halves, cut side down, on the baking sheet in a single layer. Roast the eggplants until tender when pierced with a knife, 25 to 30 minutes.

To make the sauce, heat the olive oil in a saucepan over low heat. Add the onion and sauté until translucent, 5 to 6 minutes. Add the garlic and sauté until fragrant, about 1 minute. Add the red wine. Using a wooden spoon, scrape all the brown bits from the bottom of the pan. Reduce the wine until just 2 tablespoons remain. Add the plum tomatoes and the juices and cook, breaking up the tomatoes with a wooden spoon, for 5 to 6 minutes. Add the crushed tomatoes, salt, oregano, and red pepper flakes and stir until well combined. Bring the sauce to a boil. Reduce the heat and simmer the sauce for 20 to 30 minutes.

When the roasted eggplant halves are cool enough to handle, carefully scoop out the flesh, leaving a ¼-inch border on all sides. Put the eggplant flesh in a bowl and chop—don't mash—the insides into pieces and place them in a large bowl. Add 2 cups tomato sauce, 1½ cups of the mozzarella, and ½ cup of the Parmesan and combine well.

Pour half of the remaining tomato sauce into a baking dish large enough to hold the eggplant boats. Place the eggplant boats in the dish and divide the eggplant-tomato mixture among them. Sprinkle the remaining 2½ cups mozzarella on top. Mix the bread crumbs with the remaining ¼ cup Parmesan and sprinkle over the eggplant boats. *(The eggplant boats can be covered and refrigerated overnight. Bring them to room temperature before baking.)*

Bake for 30 to 35 minutes, until the cheese is melted and bubbly. If the cheese is becoming too brown, cover the boats with aluminum foil for the last 10 minutes. Remove the baking dish from the oven and let rest for 5 to 10 minutes. Serve each portion with the tomato sauce in the baking dish and Parmesan.

Loaded Green Bean Casserole

After turkey, I'll bet this is the second most popular dish at Thanksgiving tables. I'll also bet that most of us have been scolded by our mothers for picking the crispy onion rings off the top before dinner was served. While most people use the recipe from the soup can label, I decided to make this perennial favorite from scratch. If I was going to take the time to do that, then it had to be over the top. I tested and tasted this classic several times. It's creamy, rich, and has great texture. Tasting the results multiple times wasn't a problem. Trust me.

Makes 6 to 8 servings

1 tablespoon unsalted butter

2 tablespoons plus ¾ teaspoon kosher salt

1½ pounds green beans, trimmed and cut in half

2 tablespoons canola oil

10 ounces pancetta, chopped into ¼-inch cubes

8 ounces cremini mushrooms, sliced ¼ inch thick

1 cup finely chopped white onions

2 garlic cloves, minced

¼ cup all-purpose flour

2 cups whole milk, hot

3 cups heavy cream, hot

3½ cups French fried onions

½ teaspoon freshly ground black pepper

½ cup (2 ounces) grated Monterey Jack

½ cup (2 ounces) grated white extra-sharp Cheddar

Preheat the oven to 350°F. Butter a deep 10 x 10-inch baking dish.

Bring a large pot of water and 2 tablespoons of the salt to a boil. Fill a bowl with cold water and ice as described on page 215. Add the green beans to the boiling water and cook until tender but still crunchy, 3 to 4 minutes. Drain the beans in a colander and immediately plunge them into the bowl of ice water. When the beans are chilled, drain again.

Heat the canola oil in a large skillet over medium heat. Add the pancetta and sauté until lightly brown, 3 to 4 minutes. Using a slotted spoon, transfer the pancetta to a bowl. Add the mushrooms to the same skillet and sauté until lightly brown, 4 to 5 minutes. Using a slotted spoon, transfer the mushrooms to the bowl with the pancetta. Add the onions to the same skillet and sauté until soft, 4 to 5 minutes. Add the garlic and sauté until fragrant, about 1 minute. Discard all but ¼ cup fat from the skillet. Whisk in the flour and cook for 1 to 2 minutes. Whisk in the hot milk and cream and bring to a boil. Reduce the heat and simmer until thick, stirring occasionally, 4 to 5 minutes.

Combine the beans, the pancetta-mushroom mixture, 1½ cups of the French fried onions, the remaining ¾ teaspoon salt, the pepper, and the cream sauce in a bowl. Mix well and pour into the prepared baking dish. Sprinkle 1 cup of the French fried onions over the casserole. Top with the grated Monterey Jack and Cheddar and then finish with a layer of the remaining 1 cup French fried onions on top. Bake for 30 to 35 minutes, until the cheeses are melted and the sauce is bubbly.

Maple Brown Sugar–Glazed Carrots and Parsnips

While everyone is familiar with carrots, did you know that parsnips are also a root vegetable and close cousins? The parsnips are creamy in color and when cooked, they add a touch of a mellow flavor to other vegetables, such as carrots, potatoes, and winter squash. I serve carrots and parsnips (tell the kids they're white carrots) with a touch of maple syrup and plenty of toasted pecans.

Makes 6 to 8 servings

2 pounds carrots, cut into 1½-inch pieces

1 pound parsnips, peeled and cut into 1½-inch pieces

2 tablespoons extra-virgin olive oil

1 tablespoon kosher salt

½ teaspoon freshly ground black pepper

5⅓ tablespoons (⅓ cup) unsalted butter, cut into 6 or 7 pieces

¼ cup pure maple syrup

½ cup (packed) light brown sugar

Dash of ground nutmeg

½ cup pecans, chopped and toasted

1 tablespoon minced fresh parsley

Preheat the oven to 425°F. Line a baking sheet with aluminum foil.

Toss the carrots, parsnips, olive oil, salt, and pepper together in a bowl. Arrange the carrots and parsnips in a single layer on the prepared baking sheet. Roast until tender and the edges turn light brown, 20 to 25 minutes. After 15 minutes of roasting, give the pan a good shake to make sure the vegetables are cooking evenly and not sticking to the pan.

Fifteen minutes before the vegetables are done, melt the butter in a skillet over medium-high heat. Add the maple syrup, brown sugar, and nutmeg. Bring to a boil, stirring continuously, until the syrup becomes thicker. Reduce the heat to low and simmer for 5 to 10 minutes, until the syrup becomes a thick glaze. Add the roasted carrots and parsnips to the skillet, cook for 5 minutes, and toss to coat with the glaze. Transfer to a serving bowl and garnish with the toasted pecans and fresh parsley before serving immediately.

Apple, Gorgonzola, Red Onion, and Candied Walnut Salad with Pomegranate Vinaigrette

If you're like me, I'll bet you have a go-to green salad that you serve at just about every meal. Sometimes that gets kind of boring. When I found this assortment of ingredients in my pantry, I decided to create a different kind of salad, one with a variety of colors and textures. Crisp apples, tangy Gorgonzola, sweet red onions, crunchy walnuts, and a ruby-colored vinaigrette come together in one gorgeous salad. Pomegranate seeds are sold in the produce section of supermarkets and they make a bright garnish. This garden masterpiece is just the ticket when you're looking for a light first course before the herbed Turkey Breast with Roasted Vegetables (page 175) or Osso Buco (page 96), or at holiday meals.

Makes 6 servings

Vegetable oil spray

Candied Walnuts

2 cups walnut halves

2½ cups sugar

Vinaigrette

½ cup pomegranate juice

2 tablespoons chopped shallots

1 tablespoon honey

1 tablespoon Dijon mustard

2 teaspoons minced fresh parsley

½ teaspoon kosher salt

¼ teaspoon freshly ground black pepper

¾ cup extra-virgin olive oil

Salad

6 cups spring mix salad

1 medium red onion, thinly sliced

2 teaspoons kosher salt

1 teaspoon freshly ground black pepper

1 cup (4 ounces) crumbled Gorgonzola

1 Granny Smith apple, cored, peeled, and cut into ½-inch cubes

1 Gala or Fuji apple, cored, peeled, and cut into ½-inch cubes

1 teaspoon fresh lemon juice

½ cup pomegranate seeds

Preheat the oven to 300°F. Line a baking sheet with parchment paper and spray the parchment with vegetable oil spray.

To make the candied walnuts, combine the walnuts, sugar, and 1½ cups water in a saucepan. Bring to a boil over medium heat. Reduce the heat to low and simmer the walnuts for 10 to 12 minutes. Drain the water from the walnuts and then pour the walnuts onto the prepared baking sheet. Spread them out in a single layer. Bake for 12 to 14 minutes, until crisp. Once the walnuts are cool, break them into bite-size pieces, if necessary.

To make the vinaigrette, combine the pomegranate juice, shallots, honey, mustard, parsley, salt, and pepper in a food processor or blender. Blend for 20 to 30 seconds. With the machine running, gradually add the olive oil in a steady stream and blend until the oil is incorporated and the dressing is emulsified.

To make the salad, toss together the spring mix, red onion, salt, and pepper in a bowl. Divide the salad among six salad plates. Sprinkle on the Gorgonzola. Toss the apples and lemon juice together in a bowl to keep the apples from turning brown. Divide the apple pieces and the walnuts among the salads, drizzle on the dressing, and garnish with the pomegranate seeds.

Balsamic-Glazed Grilled Peaches with Mozzarella and Arugula

When I walk into a market or stop at a farm stand, I'm immediately drawn to the fresh peaches. Since their season is so short, I prepare them in as many ways as I can. Grilling fruit caramelizes it and brings out its sweet goodness. If you can't find peaches, try plums, mangos, nectarines, pineapples, or pears. A few tips for grilling fruit: Choose fresh fruit that is just ripe—not too firm, not too soft. Make sure the grate is clean; you don't want your peaches to taste like hamburgers.

Makes 4 servings

Balsamic Glaze

1 cup balsamic vinegar

3 tablespoons honey

1 tablespoon unsalted butter, at room temperature

Salad

1 large red onion, thinly sliced

2 tablespoons extra-virgin olive oil

¾ teaspoon kosher salt

¼ teaspoon freshly ground black pepper

2 medium peaches, pitted and cut into ½- or ¾-inch slices

2 tablespoons (¼ stick) unsalted butter, melted

4 cups arugula

½ pound fresh mozzarella, thinly sliced

Preheat the grill to medium-high heat.

To make the glaze, place the vinegar and honey in a saucepan over medium heat. Bring to a boil and then reduce the heat to low. Let the mixture simmer for 15 to 20 minutes, until reduced by half and thick enough to coat the back of a spoon. Whisk in the butter until incorporated. The glaze will thicken as it cools.

To make the salad, place the sliced red onion in a bowl and gently toss it with the olive oil and salt and pepper. Keep the onion slices intact for easy grilling. Brush the peach slices with the melted butter. Grill the peaches for 3 to 4 minutes per side and the onion for 2 to 3 minutes per side, until slightly softened.

Divide the arugula among four salad plates. Fan the mozzarella, peaches, and onion on the arugula. Drizzle 1 tablespoon balsamic glaze on each salad before serving.

Heirloom Tomato Caprese with Balsamic Glaze

Heirloom tomatoes come in such a dazzling rainbow of colors—lemon yellow, olive green, chocolate brown, soft pink, deep red, and eggplant purple—that I always buy way too many at my local farmer's market. Stunning to look at, these tomatoes are so good that they need nothing more than some mozzarella, red onions, and a drizzle of balsamic vinegar glaze. The secret to this presentation is to make sure that the tomatoes, mozzarella, and onions are top quality and evenly sliced for easy stacking. To me, these stacks say summer on a plate.

Makes 6 servings

1 cup balsamic vinegar

¼ cup (packed) light brown sugar

3 to 4 large heirloom tomatoes, cut into 18 ¼-inch rounds

2 medium red or Vidalia onions, cut into 18 ⅛-inch rounds

1 pound fresh mozzarella, cut into 18 ¼-inch rounds

12 large basil leaves, plus 6 small sprigs for garnish

2 tablespoons extra-virgin olive oil

⅛ teaspoon freshly ground black pepper

½ teaspoon kosher salt

Combine the vinegar and brown sugar in a saucepan over high heat. Stirring constantly, bring the mixture to a boil, then reduce the heat. Simmer the mixture until it is reduced by half and is thick enough to coat the back of a spoon, 20 to 30 minutes.

Put a slice of tomato on each of six salad plates. Top each with a slice of onion, a slice of mozzarella, and a large basil leaf. Repeat this layering 2 more times, ending with the mozzarella. Drizzle each stack with ½ teaspoon olive oil and add a sprinkle salt and pepper. Drizzle each stack with 2 teaspoons warm balsamic glaze and top with a basil sprig before serving.

Sweets & Treats

Desserts—God bless them. They come in creamy, crunchy, velvety, decadent, refreshing, satisfying, rich, and scrumptious shapes, styles, and flavors. If Mom served dessert after a meal, it was usually fruit. That's one of the many reasons I always loved going to visit my grandmothers. I knew I could count on them to have at least two homemade desserts after a satisfying dinner. Grandma Burnzie baked her signature coconut layer cake and a fruit pie, while Grandma Mimi could always be counted on for her blackberry cobbler and her popular lemon pound cake.

The sweets in this chapter put the crowning touch on and a comforting end to any meal. (Note that some of them require six hours or more of refrigerator or freezer time.) I love all desserts and would never turn down a bowl of Butter Almond Ice Cream with a couple of Oatmeal Lace Cookies with Chocolate Drizzle, a wedge of Apple-Walnut Rustic Tart, or a slice of Salted Caramel Chocolate Cake. If I had to choose just one category, give me a slice of pie—Mississippi Mud, Coconut Cream, or Key Lime—any day. Since pie is my favorite, I've spent some time watching how other people eat it. Some enjoy a slice layer by layer—first, a bit of the creamy topping, then a bite of the filling, finally a piece of the crust—and then start all over again. Personally, I like to push my fork down through the entire wedge and make sure I get a taste of everything in each bite. As one saying goes, "Life is short—eat dessert first." These are certainly words to live by. And I try.

Lemon Cheesecake Bars

A dose of lemon juice, lemon zest, and lemon curd gives this sweet confection just the right amount of pucker. A delicate, buttery crust is topped with a bit of tartness from the smooth filling and then finished with some whipped topping and a sprinkle of fine lemon zest. Plan ahead, because these bars need to be refrigerated overnight. One of my favorite ways to serve these treats is chilled right from the refrigerator, making them a refreshing summertime dessert.

Makes 15 to 20 large bars or 30 to 40 mini bars

Vegetable oil spray

Crust

2 cups all-purpose flour

⅛ teaspoon table salt

1 cup (2 sticks) unsalted butter, at room temperature

⅔ cup sugar

Filling

1 packet plus ¼ teaspoon unflavored gelatin

1½ tablespoons fresh lemon juice

½ cup sugar

1 cup boiling water

2 8-ounce packages cream cheese, at room temperature

2 tablespoons confectioners' sugar

2 tablespoons heavy cream

1½ tablespoons lemon zest

1 11-ounce jar lemon curd

Whipped topping, such as Reddi-wip

Finely chopped zest of 1 lemon

Preheat the oven to 350°F. Lightly spray a 9 x 13-inch baking pan with vegetable oil spray, then line the bottom and sides of the pan with parchment paper. Bring the parchment paper up the edges and just over the sides of the pan. This will make it easy for you to remove the bars and then easily cut them.

To make the crust, whisk together the flour and salt in a bowl. Cream the butter and sugar in the bowl of a standing mixer. On low speed, gradually add the flour mixture to the butter mixture until just combined. Put the dough into the prepared baking pan and, using your fingers, evenly press the dough into the bottom of the pan. Refrigerate for 10 minutes. Bake for 25 to 30 minutes, until the crust is light golden brown in color.

While the crust is baking, make the filling. Whisk together the gelatin, lemon juice, sugar, and boiling water in a bowl. Let rest for 5 to 10 minutes.

Combine the cream cheese, confectioners' sugar, cream, lemon zest, and ½ cup of the lemon curd in the bowl of a standing mixes on low speed. Gradually add the gelatin mixture to the mixer bowl, increasing the speed to medium to combine well.

Using the back of a spoon, evenly spread the remaining lemon curd onto the baked crust. Let rest for 5 minutes. Evenly spread the cream cheese mixture over the lemon curd in the baking pan. Cover the baking pan with plastic wrap and refrigerate overnight. Once the lemon bars are set, hold the sides of the parchment paper and lift it out of the baking pan. Cut into 15 to 20 large bars or 30 to 40 mini bars. To serve, top with a dollop of whipped topping and some grated lemon zest.

Peanut Butter Cup Cookies

Like all kids, I liked to press my face against the glass display case at the bakery, trying to decide which cookie I wanted. (Funny how the trays of sweets were always child high.) My choice was always a peanut butter cookie. These cookies are big, soft, and crazy good with that all-American combo of peanut butter *and* chocolate.

Makes 24

2½ cups all-purpose flour

1½ teaspoons baking soda

1 teaspoon baking powder

¼ teaspoon table salt

1 cup (2 sticks) unsalted butter, at room temperature

1½ cups (packed) light brown sugar

½ cup granulated sugar

1¼ cups creamy peanut butter

1 teaspoon pure vanilla extract

2 large eggs

2 8-ounce bags Reese's Minis, cut into quarters and frozen on a baking sheet

Whisk together the flour, baking soda, baking powder, and salt in a bowl.

Put the butter, brown sugar, granulated sugar, peanut butter, and vanilla in the bowl of a standing mixer. Start the mixer at low speed for 1 minute, then increase to medium, stopping the machine to scrape down the sides of the bowl once or twice. Mix until the ingredients are smooth and creamy. Add the eggs and mix until well combined. Reduce the speed to low and add ½ cup of the flour mixture at a time to the butter mixture, until all of the flour has been added. Remove the bowl from the machine and, using a wooden spoon or spatula, make sure all of the flour is well incorporated into the batter. Cover the bowl with plastic wrap and refrigerate for 2 hours.

Preheat the oven to 350°F. Line 2 baking sheets with parchment paper.

Roll a heaping tablespoon of cold dough into a 1½-inch ball. Repeat with the remaining dough and arrange the balls on the prepared baking sheets about 1½ inches apart. *(The cookies can be made ahead to this point and refrigerated for 5 days.)* Refrigerate for 30 minutes. Remove the cookies from the refrigerator and push a handful of frozen peanut butter cup pieces—4 to 6—into the top of each cookie, flattening each cookie slightly. Bake for 12 to 14 minutes, until the cookies are flat and lightly brown. Let the cookies cool on the baking sheets for 10 to 15 minutes, then transfer the cookies to wire racks to cool completely.

Oatmeal Lace Cookies with Chocolate Drizzle

Everybody loves a good oatmeal cookie—thick, soft, and plump with raisins. But you can also approach oatmeal cookies in a different way and elevate them to something more delicate and refined. These whisper-thin, dainty cookies with a drizzle of chocolate are just the ticket to serve with a pot of tea or coffee during an afternoon visit with friends.

Makes 18 cookies

¾ cup quick oats

¼ cup all-purpose flour

⅓ cup (packed) light brown sugar

6 tablespoons (¾ stick) unsalted butter, melted

2 tablespoons heavy cream

1½ tablespoons maple syrup

1 teaspoon pure vanilla extract

¼ teaspoon ground cinnamon

¼ teaspoon table salt

Pinch of ground nutmeg

3 ounces dark chocolate (60% cacao), broken into small pieces

Preheat the oven to 400°F. Line 3 baking sheets with parchment paper. If you have only 2 baking sheets, then bake the cookies in batches. Be sure the baking sheet is cool, not hot from the previous batch.

To make the cookies, put the oats in a food processor and pulse until coarsely chopped. Add the flour, brown sugar, butter, cream, maple syrup, vanilla, cinnamon, salt, and nutmeg and process until well combined. Drop 6 heaping teaspoonfuls of dough onto each baking sheet, 3 to 4 inches apart (6 cookies per baking sheet). The cookies will spread as they bake. Bake for 8 to 12 minutes, until the center is cooked through and the edges start to brown slightly. Let cool completely on the pan. Remove the cookies from the pan with a thin metal spatula.

Once the cookies are cool, put the chocolate pieces in a microwave-safe bowl and microwave on high for 30 to 40 seconds. Stir the chocolate and return to the microwave for another 30 to 40 seconds, until the chocolate is smooth and silky. The chocolate will harden as it sits, so use it immediately. Using a spoon, drizzle the chocolate over the cookies. Let the chocolate cool before serving.

Cherry Strudel

When I visited Germany during Oktoberfest, I was determined to eat lots of strudel. I couldn't believe how many varieties there were—apple, cherry, peach, plum, raspberry, and even sweet cheese—but I managed to try them all. Making strudel from scratch requires time, patience, and a big work surface topped with a tablecloth for gently stretching out the dough with the backs of your hands. When made this traditional way, the dough becomes so thin that you can actually read a newspaper through it. Instead of making strudel dough, I fill easy-to-use puff pastry with a cherry preserves and dried cherry filling and it's ready faster than you can say *danke*.

Makes 10 bars or 20 squares

1 cup cherry preserves

½ cup dried cherries

¼ cup sugar

¼ cup heavy cream

1 large egg

1 teaspoon pure vanilla extract

1 17.3-ounce package (2 sheets) puff pastry, thawed

1 tablespoon Sugar in the Raw

½ cup confectioners' sugar

1 to 1½ tablespoons whole milk

Preheat the oven to 425°F. Line a baking sheet with parchment paper.

Put the cherry preserves, dried cherries, sugar, 3 tablespoons of the cream, and the vanilla in a food processor and blend for 45 seconds to 1 minute. Whisk together the egg and the remaining 1 tablespoon cream to make an egg wash. Lay 1 sheet of puff pastry on a floured work surface. Using a rolling pin, roll the pastry into an 8 x 13-inch rectangle. Carefully transfer the rectangle to the prepared baking sheet. Lay the remaining sheet of puff pastry on a floured work surface. Using a knife, cut out eight to ten 1-inch diamond cutouts.

Spoon the cherry mixture onto the pastry on the baking sheet, leaving 1-inch borders at each end and 2-inch borders on both sides. Brush the edges of the pastry with the egg wash. Fold the long sides up and over the cherry mixture. The edges will overlap, so press lightly to seal. Press the shorter ends of the pastry together and tuck underneath slightly to seal. Brush the egg wash on one side of the diamond cutouts and place them decoratively on the strudel where it is sealed. Using a knife, cut 4- to 5½-inch slits down each side of the top of the strudel, slightly exposing the preserves. Brush the entire strudel with the egg wash and sprinkle on the Sugar in the Raw. Bake for 16 to 18 minutes, until the strudel is puffy and golden brown. Remove the sheet from the oven and place it on a wire rack to cool.

To make a glaze, whisk together the confectioners' sugar and milk until the sugar is dissolved, adding a few more drops of milk as necessary. Drizzle the glaze over the cooled strudel in a zigzag motion. Cut into bars or squares and serve.

Mimi's Blackberry Cobbler

Grandma Mimi had wild blackberry patches growing on her property. When the dark, purple berries came into season during the summer, she harvested the berries from the thorny bushes. With fruit bubbling and seeping out from under the crust, her blackberry cobbler was my dad's favorite dessert. Each portion came with a big scoop of vanilla ice cream, and I loved to watch the cold ice cream melt into the warm blackberry filling. Bring this bubbling cobbler to the table after dinner and watch everyone's eyes light up.

Makes 6 to 8 servings

Vegetable oil spray

Filling

6 cups blackberries

1¼ cups sugar

2 tablespoons honey

1 teaspoon pure vanilla extract

¼ cup cornstarch

Dough

2 large eggs

1 tablespoon whole milk

1⅓ cups all-purpose flour, plus more for dusting the work surface

⅓ cup sugar

¼ teaspoon baking powder

¼ teaspoon table salt

4 tablespoons (½ stick) cold butter, cut into 4 pieces

½ teaspoon pure vanilla extract

2 tablespoons Sugar in the Raw

Preheat the oven to 375°F. Spray a 2- or 3-quart round shallow baking dish with vegetable oil spray.

To make the fruit filling, combine the blackberries, sugar, honey, and vanilla in a saucepan and bring to a boil, stirring constantly. To make a slurry, whisk together the cornstarch with ¼ cup water until dissolved. Add the slurry to the filling and stir until the filling is thick. Remove from the heat and pour into the prepared baking dish.

To make the dough, whisk 1 of the eggs with the milk in a bowl to make an egg wash for the pastry crust. Combine the flour, sugar, baking powder, and salt in a food processor. Pulse for 4 to 5 seconds. Add the butter and pulse until the mixture has a coarse cornmeal texture and no bits of butter are visible. Add the remaining egg and the vanilla and pulse until a dough ball forms. If necessary, add a teaspoon or two of ice water to hold the dough together. On a floured work surface, roll out and trim the dough to fit the top of the baking dish. Place the dough on top of the filling and tuck in any ends. Cut ½-inch slits into the top of the crust. Brush the crust with the egg wash and then sprinkle the crust with the Sugar in the Raw. Bake for 35 to 40 minutes, until the fruit is bubbly and the crust is a nice golden brown color. Remove from the oven and let cool on a wire rack for 10 to 15 minutes. If desired, serve with vanilla ice cream.

Coconut Cream Pie

I've always felt that a good nickname for Coconut Cream Pie would be mile-high pie, because there are so many layers of textures and deliciousness. You get the creamy custard filling with mounds of airy whipped cream, but what makes this pie so special is the crowning touch of toasted, crunchy coconut. Give me this pie, a quart of milk, and thirty minutes. I'll do the rest. This pie needs to chill overnight.

Makes 8 servings

Crust

1 package Pillsbury Pie Crusts (2 crusts)

1 large egg

1 tablespoon unsweetened coconut milk

1 tablespoon sugar

Filling

⅔ cup sugar

⅓ cup cornstarch, sifted

⅛ teaspoon table salt

2 large eggs, beaten

4 large egg yolks

2 cups unsweetened coconut milk

1½ cups half-and-half

2 tablespoons (¼ stick) unsalted butter, cut into 3 or 4 pieces

1 teaspoon pure vanilla extract

1 cup sweetened flaked coconut, lightly toasted

Topping

1½ teaspoons unflavored gelatin

3 tablespoons cold water

1½ cups heavy cream

5 tablespoons confectioners' sugar

¾ teaspoon pure vanilla extract

About ⅓ cup sweetened flaked coconut, toasted

Preheat the oven to 425°F.

To make the crust, place the dough for 1 crust on a well-floured work surface. Whisk together the egg and coconut milk in a small bowl. Lightly brush the crust with the egg wash, then place the second crust on top. Using a rolling pin, roll the crusts together to form one 12- to 13-inch crust. Transfer the crust to a 9-inch pie plate. Fold under the overhanging dough and crimp the edges. Lightly brush the crust with the egg wash and sprinkle the sugar on the crimped edges. Line the crust with aluminum foil or parchment paper. Fill the foil with pie weights and bake the crust for

15 minutes. If the edges are becoming too brown, cover with aluminum foil, and bake for another 10 to 15 minutes. Remove from the oven and let cool on a wire rack.

To make the filling, mix together the sugar, cornstarch, and salt in a bowl. Whisk together the eggs and egg yolks in another bowl. Pour the coconut milk and half-and-half into a saucepan and heat to a simmer, but not boiling. Whisk in the cornstarch mixture until well combined.

Whisk ½ cup coconut milk mixture into the eggs. (Start with a small amount so you don't "scramble" the eggs.) Whisking continuously, slowly add the remaining coconut milk mixture. Return the egg–coconut milk mixture to the saucepan over medium heat and continue whisking constantly until the mixture thickens and starts to bubble. Pour the hot mixture through a fine-mesh strainer into a bowl for a smooth custard. Discard any lumps in the strainer. Whisk in the butter and vanilla until the mixture is combined and shiny. Stir in the flaked coconut. Pour the filling into the cooled piecrust and place a piece of plastic wrap directly on the filling so a skin doesn't form. Refrigerate the pie for a minimum of 6 hours or overnight.

To make the topping, stir together the gelatin and water in a microwave-safe bowl. Heat on high in 30-second intervals until the gelatin has dissolved. Let cool to room temperature. Put the cream in the bowl of a standing mixer with the whisk attachment. Whip the cream on medium for 1 minute, then increase the speed to high and whip until soft peaks form. Add the gelatin mixture to the cream while the mixer is running and continue beating. Add the confectioners' sugar and vanilla and beat until stiff peaks form. Spoon the whipped cream over the top of the pie and sprinkle on the toasted coconut.

Did Someone Say "Pie"?

Yes, my favorite dessert is pie. Yes, I like everything from a flaky, buttery, or graham cracker crust to a fruit or custardy filling to a whipped topping or another layer of crust. But I don't always have time to make everything from scratch. Why deprive myself when I can depend on the convenience of my grocery store? Feel free to use a prepared cookie crumb crust if time is short. I always keep a couple packages of frozen piecrust in my freezer. I can just roll out the dough, transfer it to a pie plate, fill with sliced peaches or apples, and top the fruit with another layer of dough. Sure, you can always substitute your favorite homemade piecrust, but by keeping these handy helpers in your fridge and freezer, you can enjoy a piece of pie faster than you can say "à la mode."

Key Lime Pie

My first taste of Key Lime Pie was on a trip to Key West, where practically every restaurant offers it on its menu. That was one tart, mouth-puckering dessert! Key limes are native to the Florida Keys, the string of islands atop coral reefs off the southern tip of Florida. The limes are smaller and more tart than common limes. Their skins and juice are pale yellow rather than lime green. Fresh Key limes are available in spring and autumn, but bottled Key lime juice can be purchased year-round.

Makes 8 servings

Crust

9 whole graham crackers

1 tablespoon (packed) light brown sugar

1 tablespoon granulated sugar

5 tablespoons butter, melted

Filling

1 14-ounce can sweetened condensed milk

4 large egg yolks

⅓ cup plus 1 tablespoon Key lime juice, fresh or bottled

1½ teaspoons Key lime zest (from 3 to 4 Key limes)

Topping

½ cup heavy cream

2 tablespoons confectioners' sugar

1 teaspoon pure vanilla extract

1 Key lime, cut into thin wedges

Preheat the oven to 350°F.

To make the crust, put the graham crackers, brown sugar, and granulated sugar in a food processor and process until fine. Add the melted butter and pulse just until combined. Pour the mixture into a 9-inch pie plate and press evenly on the bottom and up the sides of the plate. Bake for 8 to 10 minutes, until golden brown. Let the crust cool on a wire rack for 15 minutes while you make the filling.

To make the filling, whisk together the condensed milk, egg yolks, lime juice, and the lime zest in a bowl. Cover and let the filling sit at room temperature for 15 minutes. It will start to thicken.

Pour the filling into the crust, tilting the pie to make sure the filling is even. Bake for 15 to 20 minutes, until the pie is firm but still jiggles a bit in the center. Let the pie cool on a wire rack for 1 hour. Once the pie is completely cooled, cover loosely with plastic wrap and refrigerate until chilled and set, 3 to 4 hours.

To make the topping, put the cream, confectioners' sugar, and vanilla in the chilled bowl of a standing mixer with the whisk attachment. Beat on medium-low speed just until the cream is foamy, about 1 minute. Increase the speed to medium-high or high and whip the cream until stiff peaks form.

Serve each slice of pie with a big spoonful of the whipped cream and a Key lime wedge.

You're the Tops

Light, fluffy, and sweetened whipped cream is the icing on the cake ... or the pie ... or the milk shake, isn't it?

Heavy cream whips up best when the cream, the bowl, and the beaters or whisk attachment are as cold as possible, so chill everything in the refrigerator for a good thirty minutes. Pour the cream and any sugar or other flavoring into the bowl—I use a standing mixer with a whisk attachment. Beat on medium-low speed just until the cream is foamy, about 1 minute. Increase the speed to medium-high or high and whip the cream until soft, medium, or stiff peaks form. Soft peaks are a bit fluffy but don't hold their shape. Medium peaks first stand up but tip over. Stiff peaks stand up firmly and stay there. Overbeating whipped cream will turn it into butter. To make four to six hours ahead of time, pour the whipped cream into a fine-mesh strainer over a bowl and cover with plastic wrap before refrigerating. Discard the liquid in the bowl before using the whipped cream.

If you prefer, you can use an imitation whipped cream, such as Cool Whip, which has stabilizers to keep it from "weeping" or breaking apart. These products allow you to top desserts well ahead of time.

Peach Melba Icebox Pie

Does anything say summer more than this winning combination of peaches and raspberries? In an icebox pie, a longtime American classic, only the crust is baked, and the filling is chilled in the refrigerator, or icebox as it was called before there was electricity. A large block of ice was stored in the top of a big wooden box and the residual cold kept food chilled. Once the ice melted, the neighborhood iceman delivered another block. This pie needs to be frozen for at least eight hours or overnight.

Makes 8 servings

Crust

8 whole graham crackers, broken into
    pieces

1 cup sliced almonds, toasted

2 tablespoons sugar

5 tablespoons unsalted butter, melted

¼ cup seedless raspberry preserves,
    warmed

Filling

¾ cup sugar

5 medium fresh peaches, skins removed,
    pitted, and cut into ¼-inch cubes

5 ounces full-fat plain Greek yogurt

4 ounces whipped cream cheese

½ cup confectioners' sugar

1 teaspoon pure vanilla extract

1 8-ounce container frozen whipped
    topping, thawed (see page 260)

Peach slices and raspberries

Preheat the oven to 350°F.

    To make the crust, put the graham cracker pieces, almonds, and sugar into a food processor. Process until fine. Add the butter and process until smooth. Pour the mixture into a 9-inch pie plate and press evenly on the bottom and up the sides of the plate. Bake for 8 to 10 minutes, until golden brown. Let the crust cool on a wire rack for 30 minutes. Once cooled, use the back of a spoon to spread the warm raspberry preserves over the bottom of the crust.

    To make the filling, bring the sugar and ¼ cup water to a boil. Add the peach cubes, reduce the heat, and simmer until soft, but still holding their shape, 6 to 8 minutes. Drain the peaches and discard the liquid. Put the peach cubes into a bowl and refrigerate for 20 minutes.

Put the yogurt, cream cheese, confectioners' sugar, and vanilla in the bowl of a standing mixer. Blend the ingredients at medium speed until well combined, stopping the machine to scrape down the sides of the bowl as necessary. Stop the machine, add half of the whipped topping, and blend at medium speed until just combined. Using a spatula, fold in the chilled peaches and the remaining whipped topping. Spread the peach-yogurt mixture into the crust, leaving the edges of the graham cracker crust visible. Cover and freeze the pie for at least 8 hours or overnight.

Remove the pie from the freezer about 1 hour before serving. Garnish the center of the pie with peach slices and raspberries. For clean, even slices, dip a knife in warm water before slicing.

Mississippi Mud Pie

Oh boy. The first time I saw this on a menu, I had to order it. Nothing about this brownie in a pie plate makes me mad. If a slice of this warm, gooey, indulgent, rich, fudgy pie isn't enough, check out the garnishes—whipped cream, chocolate shavings, and chocolate chips. Dessert just doesn't get any better.

Makes 8 servings

4 ounces 60% bittersweet chocolate, chopped

1 ounce unsweetened chocolate, chopped

7 tablespoons unsalted butter

1 cup sugar

4 large eggs

1 teaspoon pure vanilla extract

¼ teaspoon table salt

⅔ cup all-purpose flour

¾ cup milk chocolate morsels

1 premade chocolate cookie piecrust (unbaked)

Whipped cream, chocolate shavings, and mini semisweet chocolate chips

Preheat the oven to 350°F.

    Melt the bittersweet chocolate, unsweetened chocolate, and butter together in the top of a double boiler over simmering water. Remove the pan from the heat. Put the sugar into a bowl and, using a spatula, add the melted chocolate mixture to the sugar and mix well. Mix in the eggs, one at a time, making sure each egg is well combined before adding the next one. Stir in the vanilla and salt. Mix in the flour, ¼ cup at a time, until well combined. Fold in the milk chocolate morsels. Pour the filling into the crust. Bake for 30 to 35 minutes, until a toothpick inserted into the center comes out almost clean. Let the pie cool completely on a wire rack. Garnish as desired with whipped cream, chocolate shavings, and mini chocolate chips.

White Chocolate Pumpkin Pie

Attention, pumpkin pie lovers! While pumpkin pie is a Thanksgiving holiday mainstay, get ready to enjoy a new twist on this American classic. The idea for this pie came to me while I was browsing around my local wine and spirits store and found a bottle of white chocolate liqueur. Since white chocolate is high on my list of foods I can't live without, I decided to combine this liqueur with a favorite holiday tradition. I hope this pie becomes as much of a new tradition in your house as it is in mine.

Makes 8 servings

Crust

30 small gingersnaps (about 1½ cups crumbs)

2 tablespoons granulated sugar

Pinch of table salt

5 tablespoons unsalted butter, melted

Filling

3 large eggs

1 15-ounce can pumpkin purée

½ cup heavy cream

½ cup (packed) light brown sugar

1 teaspoon ground cinnamon

½ teaspoon table salt

½ teaspoon ground ginger

⅛ teaspoon ground cloves

Topping

4 ounces white chocolate

1 cup heavy cream

3 tablespoons white chocolate liqueur

White chocolate shavings and finely crushed gingersnaps

Preheat the oven to 350°F.

To make the crust, put the gingersnaps, sugar, and salt in a food processor and process until the cookies are the consistency of sand. Add the melted butter and pulse 3 or 4 times. Pour the mixture into a 9-inch pie plate and press evenly on the bottom and up the sides of the plate. Bake for 3 to 4 minutes. Let the crust cool on a wire rack. Leave the oven on.

To make the filling, lightly whisk the eggs in a bowl. Add the pumpkin, cream, brown sugar, cinnamon, salt, ginger, and cloves and stir to combine. Pour the mixture into the prepared piecrust. Bake for 50 to 55 minutes, until a knife inserted into the filling comes out almost clean. If the edges are becoming too dark after 20 to 25 minutes, cover with aluminum foil. Let the pie cool completely on a wire rack.

To make the topping, melt the white chocolate in a saucepan. Put the cream and white chocolate liqueur in the bowl of a standing mixer with the whisk attachment. Beat on medium speed until soft peaks form. Put 2 tablespoons whipped cream into the saucepan with the melted white chocolate and mix well. Pour the white chocolate mixture in the saucepan into the bowl with the whipped cream and continue whipping until stiff peaks form.

Decorate the circumference of the pie with the whipped cream, reserving what is left over for the garnish. Sprinkle the white chocolate shavings and crushed gingersnaps in the center of the pie. Serve each slice with a hearty dollop of the remaining white chocolate whipped cream.

Blueberry–Cream Cheese Mini Pies

During the last few years, cupcakes and other mini desserts have become more and more popular. These two- or three-bite pastries filled with purple blueberries and sweet cream cheese are a cross between cupcakes and mini pies. They're perfect for brunch, bake sales, or an office birthday party. For a lunchtime surprise, wrap up a mini pie and put it in your kid's lunch box.

Makes 12

Vegetable oil spray

Crust

3 cups all-purpose flour

4½ tablespoons sugar

¼ teaspoon table salt

1 cup plus 2 tablespoons butter-flavored shortening, chilled

½ cup ice water

1 large egg

1 tablespoon heavy cream

Filling

⅔ cup plus 1⅓ cups fresh blueberries, plus more for garnish

2 8-ounce packages cream cheese, at room temperature

¾ cup confectioners' sugar

2 large eggs

1 teaspoon pure vanilla extract

Whipped cream (see page 260)

Preheat the oven to 425°F. Lightly spray a 12-cup muffin tin with vegetable oil spray.

To make the crust, whisk together the flour, sugar, and salt in a bowl. Add the shortening and, using a fork, blend until the mixture is like coarse meal. Using the fork, stir in the ice water and mix until the dough comes together. Using your hands, gather the dough into a ball and flatten slightly. Wrap in plastic wrap and refrigerate for 15 to 20 minutes. Make an egg wash by beating together the egg and cream.

Divide the dough into 12 parts. On a floured work surface, roll out 1 piece of dough to a 4-inch round and press it into a muffin cup. Cover the remaining dough with a towel so it doesn't dry out. Repeat with the rest of the dough. Place the dough cutouts in the prepared muffin cups and press the cutouts up the sides. With a knife, trim any excess dough from the edges. Prick the dough lightly with a fork.

Refrigerate for 20 minutes. Lightly brush the dough cups with the egg wash. Bake for 6 to 7 minutes, until lightly brown. Let the dough cups cool in the muffin tin on a wire rack. Reduce the oven heat to 350°F.

To make the filling, put ⅔ cup of the blueberries in a bowl and mash them with a fork. Put the cream cheese and confectioners' sugar in the bowl of a standing mixer with the whisk attachment. Beat on medium speed, scraping down the sides of the bowl as necessary, until smooth and creamy. Reduce the speed and add the eggs, one at a time, making sure that each egg is mixed well into the cream cheese mixture before adding the next one. Add the vanilla and beat until combined. Remove the bowl from the mixer and gently fold in the mashed blueberries and the remaining 1⅓ cups whole blueberries. Fill each baked shell to the top with the blueberry–cream cheese mixture, about ¼ cup. Bake for 20 to 25 minutes, until the top of the filling has set. Remove from the oven and let cool completely on a wire rack.

Garnish each mini pie with a dollop of whipped cream and a fresh blueberry.

Black Bottom Cupcakes

When I was in college and needed a study break, I walked to a convenience store near my UNC/Chapel Hill dorm and treated myself to a couple of chocolate cupcakes with cream filling and two mini cartons of milk. That memory inspired this recipe—rich chocolate cupcakes with a dollop of cream cheese batter on top. The cream cheese makes them extra rich so there's no need for frosting. When I eat these, I feel like I'm taking a study break all over again, but now I don't have to worry about any exams.

Makes 18

Cream Cheese Mixture

1 8-ounce package cream cheese, at room temperature

1 tablespoon sour cream

⅓ cup sugar

1 large egg

⅓ cup mini semisweet chocolate chips

Batter

⅓ cup unsweetened cocoa powder

1 cup all-purpose flour

1 teaspoon baking soda

¼ teaspoon table salt

1 cup sugar

1 teaspoon pure vanilla extract

¾ cup water

⅓ cup sour cream

4 tablespoons (½ stick) unsalted butter, melted

Preheat the oven to 350°F. Line 18 standard or 12 jumbo muffin cups with foil cupcake liners.

To make the cream cheese mixture, beat together the cream cheese, sour cream, sugar, and egg in the bowl of a standing mixer until smooth. Using a spatula, fold in the mini chips.

To make the batter, whisk together the cocoa, flour, baking soda, salt, and sugar in a bowl. Make a well in the center of the flour mixture and pour in the vanilla, water, sour cream, and melted butter. Using a fork, blend the wet ingredients into the dry ingredients.

Fill the muffin cups one-third full with the chocolate batter. Drop a heaping tablespoon cream cheese mixture on top of the chocolate batter. Bake for 25 to 30 minutes, until a cake tester inserted into the chocolate part of the cupcake comes out clean. Turn the cupcakes out onto a wire rack and let cool completely.

Apple-Walnut Rustic Tart

In France, this is called a "galette." In Italy, it's a crostata. I call it easy. Just roll out a premade piecrust and top it with an apple-raisin filling. Sprinkle on a walnut-crumb topping and bring the dough up over the filling for a free-form tart. Once baked, serve warm with a scoop of ice cream or some whipped cream. Remember, it's not supposed to look perfect, just rustic and delicious.

Makes 6 to 8 servings

Crumb Topping

½ cup coarsely chopped walnuts

¼ cup all-purpose flour

¼ cup (packed) light brown sugar

3 tablespoons unsalted butter, cut into small pieces

Tart

1 large egg

1 tablespoon whole milk

¼ cup plus 2 tablespoons granulated sugar

1 teaspoon ground cinnamon

2 Granny Smith apples, peeled, cored, and cut into ⅛-inch slices

2 Gala apples, peeled, cored, and cut into ⅛-inch slices

1 teaspoon fresh lemon juice

¾ cup golden raisins

⅓ cup (packed) light brown sugar

2 tablespoons all-purpose flour

⅛ teaspoon ground nutmeg

Pinch of ground cloves

1 package Pillsbury Pie Crusts (2 crusts)

Confectioners' sugar

Preheat the oven to 350°F. Line a baking sheet with parchment paper.

To make the crumb topping, put the walnuts, flour, brown sugar, and butter in a bowl. Using your fingers, blend the ingredients together until crumbly.

To make the tart, whisk together the egg and milk in a bowl to make an egg wash. Whisk together 2 tablespoons of the granulated sugar and ⅛ teaspoon of the cinnamon in another bowl. Combine the Granny Smith apples, Gala apples, the remaining ¼ cup granulated sugar, the lemon juice, raisins, brown sugar, flour, nutmeg, the remaining cinnamon, and cloves in a third bowl.

Dust a rolling pin and work surface lightly with flour. Cut one piecrust in half and combine it with the other crust to form a ball of dough. The remaining half of

the piecrust can be wrapped and stored in the fridge for up to a week, or frozen for use later. Roll the dough out to about ⅛-inch thickness to form a 12- to 14-inch circle. (The circle shouldn't be perfect.) Place the dough on the prepared baking sheet.

Using a slotted spoon, pile the apple filling into the center of the crust, leaving a 1½- to 2-inch border all around the edges. Fold the dough border over the edges, pressing together any edges that overlap and leaving an uneven circle in the middle. Using a pastry brush, brush the egg wash all over the dough, especially where the crust overlaps. Sprinkle the crust with the cinnamon sugar. Refrigerate the tart for 5 to 10 minutes. Sprinkle the crumb topping over the tart.

Bake the tart for 40 to 50 minutes, until the apples are soft and the tart is lightly brown. If the tart is browning too quickly, loosely cover it with aluminum foil during the last 10 minutes of baking. Let the tart cool for 5 to 10 minutes on a wire rack. Using a fine-mesh strainer, sprinkle some confectioners' sugar over the top. Serve warm with vanilla ice cream or whipped cream.

Snickers Candy Bar Cheesecake

Let me begin by giving you fair warning: This cheesecake is highly addictive and highly irresistible. Snickers, filled with nougat, caramel, and peanuts and enrobed in milk chocolate, is one of the world's most popular candy bars. What if I could put all that chewy, nutty, chocolaty candy bar goodness into and on top of a creamy cheesecake? I did, and you will not believe how incredible this dessert is. The cheesecake should be made six hours or more in advance, but it's definitely worth the wait.

Makes 10 to 12 servings

Vegetable oil spray

Crust

2 9-ounce boxes thin chocolate wafer cookies

3 tablespoons sugar

10 tablespoons (1¼ sticks) unsalted butter, melted

Filling

5 ounces soft caramel candies

2 tablespoons heavy cream

5 ounces mini Snickers bars, frozen and cut into small chunks

½ cup coarsely chopped roasted and salted peanuts

4 8-ounce packages cream cheese, at room temperature

1¼ cups sugar

4 large eggs, at room temperature

1½ teaspoons pure vanilla extract

¼ cup chocolate chips, melted

Decoration

1½ cups whipped topping (see page 260)

6 ounces mini Snickers, frozen and cut into small chunks

2 ounces soft caramels, melted with 2 teaspoons heavy cream

⅛ cup semisweet chocolate chips, melted

Preheat the oven to 350°F. Line the bottom of a 9-inch springform pan with parchment paper. Lightly spray the inside with vegetable oil spray. Wrap the outside tightly with 2 sheets of heavy-duty aluminum foil so the batter doesn't leak.

 To make the crust, put the cookies and sugar in a food processor. Process until finely chopped. Add the melted butter and process until well combined. Spoon the mixture into the prepared pan and press evenly on the bottom and up the sides of

the pan. Bake for 3 to 4 minutes. Let cool for 20 minutes on a wire rack. Keep the oven on.

To make the filling, put the caramels and cream in a microwave-safe bowl. Microwave on high for 1 minute. Stir until the caramels are melted. Pour the caramel sauce on top of the crust. Sprinkle the chopped Snickers over the caramel, followed by the chopped peanuts.

Put the cream cheese and sugar in the bowl of a standing mixer with the whisk attachment. Beat at medium speed until the mixture is creamy. Increase the speed to high and whip for 1 more minute. Reduce the speed to medium and add the eggs, one at a time, making sure that each egg is mixed well into the cream cheese mixture before adding the next one. Stop the machine to scrape down the sides of the bowl as necessary. Add the vanilla and mix for 30 more seconds. Transfer 1 cup of the cream cheese mixture to another bowl. Add the melted chocolate to the cup of cream cheese mixture and stir until well combined.

Pour the plain cheesecake mixture into the springform pan, allowing ¼ inch of crust to show. Using a tablespoon, evenly distribute 6 or 7 dollops of the chocolate cheesecake mixture over the top of the cheesecake. Using a wooden skewer or toothpick, gently swirl the chocolate through the plain cheesecake for a marbleized look.

Place a roasting pan large enough to hold the springform pan in the oven. Put the springform pan in the roasting pan and then add enough boiling water to come halfway up the sides of the cake pan. Bake for 45 to 50 minutes, until the cheesecake is set when jiggled. Do not open the oven while the cake is baking. When the cake is done, turn the oven off and let the cheesecake sit in the water in the oven for 1 hour. Again, do not open the oven. Remove the cheesecake from the roasting pan and let cool completely on a wire rack. Cover and refrigerate for at least 6 hours before removing the springform ring and decorating the cheesecake.

To decorate, spread the whipped topping over the top of the cheesecake, leaving about a ¼-inch border on all sides. Sprinkle the chopped Snickers on the whipped topping. Drizzle the caramel mixture and the melted chocolate over the top of the cake.

Salted Caramel Chocolate Cake

This is the best chocolate cake I have ever put in my mouth. Each bite is so moist, it's almost impossible to keep on your fork. Everything about this cake is decadent and divine—two layers of rich chocolate cake are separated by and frosted with a chocolate and cream ganache. Bits of toffee candy are pressed into the sides, and the top is drizzled with a sauce made of caramel and sea salt. A toothpick is used to feather the caramel and make a decorative design. Make this cake for a special birthday, anniversary, gathering, party, and celebration . . . oh, just make it!

Makes 12 servings

Vegetable cooking spray

Cake

2 cups all-purpose flour, plus more for dusting the cake pan

2 cups sugar

¾ cup Hershey's Special Dark Cocoa

2 teaspoons baking powder

1½ teaspoons baking soda

1 teaspoon table salt

1 teaspoon instant coffee granules

1 cup whole milk

½ cup canola oil

2 large eggs

2 teaspoons pure vanilla extract

1 cup boiling water

Chocolate Ganache

1 pound bittersweet chocolate (60% cacao), chopped into small pieces

½ teaspoon instant coffee granules

1⅓ cups plus 1 tablespoon heavy cream

2 cups Heath Bits 'O Brickle Toffee Bits

2 ounces soft caramels

1 teaspoon sea salt

Preheat the oven to 350°F. Spray two 9-inch round cake pans with vegetable oil spray and flour lightly.

To make the cake, whisk together by hand the flour, sugar, cocoa, baking powder, baking soda, salt, and instant coffee in the bowl of a standing mixer. Add the milk, canola oil, eggs, and vanilla to the flour mixture and mix together on medium speed until well combined. Reduce the speed and carefully add the water to the cake batter. Increase the speed to high and beat for about 1 more minute.

Divide the cake batter between the prepared pans. Bake for 35 to 45 minutes,

until a cake tester inserted into the center comes out clean. Transfer to a wire rack and let cool completely. Carefully remove the cakes from the pans. To level a cake layer that is higher in the middle than at the circumference, put the cake on a flat surface with the round side up and, using a sharp serrated knife, gently saw through it to cut off the center mound. Place 1 cake layer, cut side down, on a slightly raised work surface or cake-decorating stand.

To make the ganache, put the chopped chocolate and instant coffee in a bowl. Heat 1⅓ cups of the cream in a saucepan over medium heat, but do not boil. Pour the hot cream over the chocolate and coffee, whisking constantly until all of the chocolate has melted and the ganache is smooth. Remove ½ cup ganache to another bowl and refrigerate. Spread ¾ to 1 cup ganache on the top of the first cake layer. Sprinkle with ½ cup of the toffee bits. Let set for 3 to 4 minutes. Place the second cake layer over the first layer, cut side down. Pour the remaining ganache over the top layer, making sure to spread it over the top and evenly down the sides of the cake.

To decorate the cake, press the remaining 1½ cups toffee bits around the sides of the cake. Put the caramels and the remaining 1 tablespoon cream in a microwave-safe bowl and microwave on high for 1 minute. Add the sea salt and stir until the caramels are melted and well combined with the cream. Using a small spoon, drizzle 4 or 5 evenly spaced lines across the top of the cake. Take a toothpick and, perpendicular to the lines, drag it across the lines to create a feathering effect on the top of the cake.

Sarah's Apricot Cake `FAN FAVORITE`

Sometimes the best recipes are born out of shortcuts. My mom, Sarah, often personalized boxed cake mixes by adding her own ingredients and creative toppings, such as apricot nectar and Greek yogurt. Whenever she baked this cake, I could smell it all over the house. Knowing how much I loved this cake, Mom always cut me an extra-generous slice.

Makes 10 to 12 servings

Vegetable oil spray

Cake

1 16-ounce box pound cake mix

¼ cup canola oil

¾ cup apricot nectar

⅓ cup apricot jam or preserves

⅓ cup nonfat Greek yogurt

2 large eggs

Sauce

1½ pounds fresh peaches, peeled and sliced, or frozen sliced peaches, thawed

1½ cups apricot nectar

⅓ cup plus 2 tablespoons sugar

Put one rack in the middle of the oven. Preheat the oven to 350°F. Lightly spray a 12-cup Bundt pan with vegetable oil spray.

To make the cake, put the cake mix, canola oil, and apricot nectar into the bowl of a standing mixer. Mix on medium-low speed until the ingredients are well blended. Stop the machine and scrape down the sides of the bowl. Add the apricot jam and yogurt and mix on low speed to combine. Add the eggs and mix until blended.

Evenly spread the batter into the prepared pan. Bake for 40 to 50 minutes, until a tester inserted into the cake comes out clean. Let the cake cool completely on a wire rack. When the cake is completely cool, invert it onto a serving plate and remove from the pan.

To make the sauce, combine the peaches, apricot nectar, and sugar in a saucepan over medium heat. Cook until the liquid has evaporated, 10 to 15 minutes. Remove from the heat and let cool for 30 minutes.

Place the sauce mixture in a food processor and process until smooth. Pour some of the peach sauce over each slice before serving.

Butter Almond Ice Cream

We all scream for ice cream! I can vividly remember one particular day when my dad and I stopped at a dairy store to buy some ice cream. I was offered a taste of sweet, smooth, nutty butter almond ice cream, and after that, it was the only flavor I ever let Dad buy. When he came home with a brown paper bag holding a half gallon of ice cream, I knew it was my lucky day. Although hard to find in ice cream shops and supermarkets, butter almond remains my favorite, which is why I created this recipe.

Makes 6 to 8 servings

5 tablespoons unsalted butter

1 cup sliced almonds, skin on and coarsely chopped

3½ cups heavy cream

1 14-ounce can sweetened condensed milk

3 large egg yolks

1 teaspoon pure vanilla extract

½ teaspoon pure almond extract

Melt 2 tablespoons of the butter in a skillet over medium heat. Add the almonds and sauté until the almonds are fragrant, 2 to 3 minutes. Pour the almonds into a bowl so they will cool quickly.

Put 1 cup of the heavy cream, the condensed milk, and the remaining 3 tablespoons butter in a saucepan and bring to a boil. Remove from the heat. Put the egg yolks in a bowl. Gradually pour the hot cream mixture into the egg yolks, whisking constantly until well blended.

Return the cream-egg mixture to the saucepan and cook, stirring constantly, over medium heat, until the custard coats the back of a spoon. Remove from the heat and pour into a large bowl. Whisk in the remaining 2½ cups cream, the vanilla, and almond extract. Put the bowl with the custard into a larger bowl filled with ice to cool down the custard quickly.

Pour the custard into an ice cream maker's freezer bowl and freeze according to the manufacturer's instructions. Add the buttered almonds to the machine and churn for another 5 minutes. Serve immediately, or if you prefer a denser ice cream, transfer the ice cream to a plastic container and freeze for 2 to 3 hours. *The ice cream will keep in the freezer for 3 days.*

Comfort & Joy

I love everything about Christmas. Rediscovering favorite ornaments every year when decorating a fresh evergreen tree with its woodsy smell. Setting the dinner table with my finest china, glassware, and silver on top of a freshly pressed tablecloth and napkins. Decorating the house with evergreens, candles, and wreaths.

When it comes to Christmas dinner, I want to encourage you to pull out all the stops. Here's a holiday menu that you and your family will be talking about for years to come. Greet guests with a mug of warm cider for the kids and a Hot Apple Cider Cocktail for the adults. Everyone can help themselves to the lobster dip on crostini. Once cooked, the standing rib roast is tented with aluminum foil to rest before it's carved, freeing up the oven for the Sweet Potato Biscuits and the Loaded Baked Potato Casserole. The Green Beans with Almonds and Dried Cherries just need to be combined and heated in a skillet. A separate table looks like a Christmas wonderland with Chocolate Sugar Cookies, Chocolate-Champagne Truffles, Easy Gingerbread Cookies, and Peppermint Holiday Cake. Once I make the mushroom gravy, the candles are lit, the wine is poured, and everyone is called to the table.

Christmas is a time to stop and remember our blessings and to entertain with a meal that says, "You mean the world to me."

Lobster Dip Crostini

While you're bustling about and putting the finishing touches on your Christmas meal, offer this rich lobster dip as an hors d'oeuvre to your hungry guests.

Makes 2 to 2½ cups

Lobster Dip

1 tablespoon unsalted butter

½ cup finely chopped yellow onion

1 8-ounce package cream cheese, at room temperature

4 ounces (½ cup) crème fraîche

1½ tablespoons prepared horseradish

1 teaspoon fresh lemon juice

½ teaspoon kosher salt, plus more to taste

7 ounces cooked lobster meat, chopped (see Note)

2 tablespoons minced fresh parsley

Crostini

1 baguette, sliced diagonally into ½-inch pieces

4 tablespoons (½ stick) unsalted butter, melted

Freshly ground black pepper

Preheat the oven to 375°F.

To make the lobster dip, melt the butter in a skillet over medium heat. Add the onion and sauté until translucent, 5 to 6 minutes. Whisk together the cream cheese, crème fraîche, horseradish, lemon juice, and salt in a bowl. Fold in the cooked onion, the lobster meat, and parsley until combined. Cover and refrigerate until ready to serve. *(The dip can be made 1 day in advance.)*

To make the crostini, brush both sides of the bread slices with the melted butter. Arrange the bread on a baking sheet. Season with salt and pepper. Bake the bread for 10 to 12 minutes, turning the slices after 6 or 7 minutes, until light golden brown. Serve the lobster dip with the crostini.

Note: If you can't find cooked lobster meat in the freezer section of the grocery store, three 4-ounce lobster tails can be substituted. Drop the lobster tails into a pot of boiling water and cook for 1 minute per ounce. Plunge the lobster tails into a bowl of ice water to stop the cooking. Once they are cool enough to handle, remove the shells and cut the lobster meat into ½-inch pieces. Seven ounces of lump crabmeat or cooked, chopped shrimp can be used as well.

Hot Apple Cider Cocktail

When I was wine shopping for the holidays, I was intrigued to find apple pie liqueur on one of the shelves. Hmmm, bet I can create a holiday cocktail with that, I thought. I played around, adding some fresh apple cider and brandy to the liqueur, until I had just the right balance for this drink. I offer this cocktail to guests when they arrive at my door. What a lovely way to kick off a holiday celebration.

Makes 8 to 10 servings

½ gallon apple cider

4 to 5 cinnamon sticks, plus more for garnish

1 cup brandy

1 cup Travis Hasse's Apple Pie Liqueur

3 tablespoons sugar

½ teaspoon ground cinnamon, plus more for garnish

Whipped cream

Heat the cider and cinnamon sticks in a saucepan or slow cooker until simmering and fragrant, 30 to 40 minutes. Stir in the brandy and apple pie liqueur and simmer for 5 to 10 minutes.

Mix together the sugar and ground cinnamon on a small plate. Put a few tablespoons hot cider on another plate. Quickly dip the rims of heatproof glasses or other mugs in the cider, then into the sugar-cinnamon mixture. Fill the mugs three-quarters full with the cider mixture. Garnish each mug with whipped cream, a dash of ground cinnamon, and a cinnamon stick.

Green Beans with Almonds and Dried Cherries

Green beans were the one vegetable my mother never had to negotiate with me to eat. A festive way to dress them up is with toasted almonds and dried cherries for a pop of both sweet and tart flavors at the same time. To make this vegetable holiday-special, use *haricots verts,* a French term that refers to the small, thin, tender green beans that are half the size of other beans. Most grocery and big box stores now carry them. If you can't find them, regular string beans work just fine. The cooked beans, the shallot mixture, cherries, and toasted almonds can be prepared three to four hours ahead of time and assembled just before serving.

Makes 8 servings

2 tablespoons plus ½ teaspoon kosher salt

2 pounds haricots verts

1 tablespoon plus 2 tablespoons unsalted butter

1 tablespoon extra-virgin olive oil

¼ cup minced shallots

2 garlic cloves, minced

½ cup dried cherries

¾ cup sliced almonds, toasted

¼ teaspoon freshly ground black pepper

Bring a large pot of water and 2 tablespoons of the salt to a boil. Fill a bowl with cold water and ice as described on page 215. Add the beans to the boiling water, stir, and bring the water back to a boil. Reduce the heat and simmer the beans for 2 to 3 minutes. Immediately drain the beans in a colander and then put them in the bowl with the ice water. As soon as they're cool, drain the beans.

Heat 1 tablespoon butter and the olive oil in a skillet large enough to hold the beans, over medium-high heat. Add the shallots and garlic and sauté for 1 to 2 minutes, stirring constantly, until fragrant. Transfer the mixture to a bowl.

Just before serving, melt the 2 tablespoons butter in the same skillet over medium-high heat. Add the beans to the pan and sauté for 3 to 4 minutes, tossing frequently. Add the dried cherries, ½ cup of the almonds, and the shallot-garlic mixture and toss to distribute evenly with the beans. Toss with the remaining ½ teaspoon salt and the pepper. Transfer the beans to a serving bowl and garnish with the remaining ¼ cup almonds before serving.

Loaded Baked Potato Casserole

What's better than a loaded baked potato? Why, a loaded baked potato *casserole,* of course. Everything I love—mashed potatoes, sour cream, butter, bacon, and Cheddar—is here in one delectable dish. I swear I could swan-dive into this and be very happy. It would be a shame to enjoy this just once a year. Make it for a family-reunion dinner, Sunday supper, or other celebration. You don't need a special reason just a craving for loaded baked potatoes.

Makes 6 to 8 servings

8 tablespoons (1 stick) unsalted butter, cut into 6 pieces, plus 1 tablespoon for the pan

3 pounds Yukon gold potatoes, peeled and quartered

4 tablespoons kosher salt

5 garlic cloves

12 center-cut bacon slices

½ cup heavy cream

½ cup buttermilk

½ teaspoon white pepper

½ cup sour cream

½ cup (2 ounces) shredded yellow extra-sharp Cheddar cheese

½ cup (2 ounces) shredded white extra-sharp Cheddar cheese

2 tablespoons minced fresh chives

Lightly butter a 9 x 13-inch baking dish.

Place the potatoes, salt, and the garlic in a large pot and cover with water. Bring to a boil over high heat. Reduce the heat to a simmer and cook the potatoes until they are fork tender, 20 to 25 minutes. Drain the potatoes and garlic in a colander and return to the pot.

While the potatoes are cooking, arrange the bacon slices—no overlapping—on a baking sheet lined with aluminum foil. Put the bacon in a cold oven and turn the oven on to 400°F. Bake until crisp, 10 to 15 minutes. When the bacon is cool enough to handle, chop it into small bits. Reserve 2 tablespoons bacon fat. Reduce the oven temperature to 350°F.

Put the remaining 6 pieces of butter, the cream, and buttermilk in a saucepan. Cook over low heat, stirring occasionally to make sure the butter is melting, for 5 to 10 minutes. Once the butter is melted, remove the saucepan from the heat and cover to keep warm until the potatoes are cooked and drained.

Using a potato masher, mash the potatoes and garlic with half of the cream mixture. Once the liquid is absorbed, add the remaining cream mixture to the potatoes and mash well. Add the pepper, the remaining 1 teaspoon salt, the sour cream, bacon bits (except for ¼ cup reserved "bits"), ¼ cup of the yellow Cheddar, and ¼ cup of the white Cheddar and mix well. Taste and season with salt, if needed. Spoon the mashed potatoes into the prepared casserole dish. Brush the mashed potatoes with the reserved bacon fat. Top with the remaining ¼ cup bacon bits, the remaining ¼ cup yellow Cheddar, and the remaining ¼ cup white Cheddar. Cover with aluminum foil. Bake for 20 minutes. Remove the foil and bake for another 10 to 15 minutes, until the cheeses are melted and bubbly. Sprinkle on the chives during the last 5 minutes of baking. Let the casserole rest for 5 to 10 minutes before serving.

Standing Rib Roast

The main dish for holiday dinner is usually a huge ham, but if you want to really wow your guests, then a standing rib roast is the way to go. What sets this one apart is the rub that forms a great crust on the outside and infuses the meat with a deep, herb flavor. With any luck, you'll have a few leftover slices for sandwiches the next day.

Makes 6 to 8 servings

Rub

3 garlic cloves, minced

¼ cup Dijon mustard

3 tablespoons finely chopped fresh rosemary

2½ tablespoons kosher salt

2½ tablespoons freshly ground black pepper

Roast

4 cups sliced white onions

2 carrots, cut into 2-inch pieces

2 to 3 celery stalks, cut into 2-inch pieces

8 ounces cremini mushrooms, caps and stems divided, caps thinly sliced

3 tablespoons plus 2 tablespoons extra-virgin olive oil

3 tablespoons kosher salt

1½ tablespoons plus 2 teaspoons freshly ground black pepper

2 cups full-bodied red wine, such as Cabernet Sauvignon

2 cups beef broth

1 6- to 8-pound (3 to 5 ribs) standing rib roast of beef, trimmed and tied

1 tablespoon cornstarch

3 tablespoons unsalted butter, cut into 3 or 4 pieces

Preheat the oven to 425°F.

To make the rub, combine the garlic, mustard, rosemary, salt, and pepper in a bowl.

To make the roast, scatter the onions, carrots, celery, and mushroom stems in the bottom of a roasting pan and toss them with 3 tablespoons of olive oil, 1 tablespoon of the salt, and 2 teaspoons of the pepper. Stir 1 cup of the red wine and 1 cup of the beef broth into the roasting pan. Place a rack in the pan and put the roast on top. Season the sides and the bottom of the roast with the remaining 2 tablespoons salt and 1½ tablespoons pepper. Evenly spread the rub only on the top of the roast. Roast for 20 minutes. Reduce the heat to 350°F. Cook the roast, basting with the pan juices every 30 minutes, until an instant-read thermometer inserted into the thickest part reaches 130°F, 1½ to 2 hours. Remove the roast from the oven, transfer to a cutting board, tent with aluminum foil, and let it rest for 20 to 25 minutes while preparing the mushroom caps and gravy.

Heat the remaining 2 tablespoons of olive oil in a skillet over high heat. Add the sliced mushroom caps and sauté until they are soft and lightly brown, 4 to 5 minutes. Set aside.

Using a slotted spoon, remove and discard the vegetables from the roasting pan, leaving any liquid in the pan. Place the roasting pan on the stovetop over high heat. Add the remaining 1 cup red wine and, using a wooden spoon, scrape all the brown bits from the bottom of the pan. Lower the heat and simmer until the liquid has reduced slightly. Add ¾ cup of the beef broth and stir well. To make a slurry, dissolve the cornstarch into the remaining ¼ cup beef broth. Stir the slurry into the roasting pan to thicken the gravy. Stir in the mushroom caps and coat well. Reduce the heat and add the butter, one piece at a time, letting each piece melt before adding the next one. Just before serving, slice the meat between the bones and serve with the mushroom gravy.

Sweet Potato Biscuits with Maple-Cinnamon Butter

Any big family meal calls for homemade bread, but the holidays call for something extra special. Since these biscuits are made with sweet potatoes, they're a bit denser than traditional biscuits. Sweet, yet savory, these are tender and moist and will fill your house with warm, seasonal aromas as they bake. Roll the maple-cinnamon butter into logs and slice, or put the flavored butter into a decorating bag and pipe out little stars to round out the holiday theme.

Makes 14 to 16

Vegetable oil spray

Maple-Cinnamon Butter

8 tablespoons (1 stick) unsalted butter, at room temperature

½ teaspoon ground cinnamon

¼ teaspoon pure vanilla extract

1½ tablespoons pure maple syrup

¼ teaspoon ground nutmeg

Biscuits

2 medium (about 2 cups) sweet potatoes, cooked, mashed, and chilled

2 cups buttermilk

4 cups all-purpose flour

⅓ cup sugar

2 tablespoons baking powder

½ teaspoon baking soda

1 teaspoon table salt

2 teaspoons ground cinnamon

½ teaspoon ground nutmeg

⅛ teaspoon ground cloves

¾ cup (1½ sticks) cold unsalted butter, cut into 12 pieces

Preheat the oven to 450°F. Lightly spray three 9-inch round cake pans with vegetable oil spray.

To make the maple-cinnamon butter, place the butter, cinnamon, vanilla, maple syrup, and nutmeg in a food processor. Process until well mixed. For an extra-special touch, using a decorating bag fitted with a star tip, pipe the butter into individual serving pieces on a piece of parchment paper. Refrigerate or freeze until ready to serve with the warm biscuits. *(The butter can be made ahead of time and frozen for up to 1 month—just like a compound butter.)*

To make the biscuits, mix the cold mashed sweet potatoes with 1 cup of the buttermilk until well combined. Whisk together the flour, sugar, baking powder, baking soda, salt, cinnamon, nutmeg, and cloves in a bowl. Using two knives or a pastry cutter, cut the butter pieces into the flour mixture and blend until the mixture resembles coarse meal. Add the sweet potato mixture and all but 1 tablespoon of the remaining 1 cup buttermilk. Mix until the dough is just combined, moist, and shaggy.

Scrape the dough onto a well-floured surface. Lightly flour your hands and gently push the dough into a ½-inch-thick round. Fold the dough into thirds like an envelope and, using your hands, press the dough into a 1-inch-thick round. Do not overwork the dough. Using a 3-inch biscuit cutter, press down without twisting and cut out as many biscuits as possible. Gather the remaining dough and press out to a 1-inch thickness and cut out additional biscuits. Place the biscuits in the prepared pans, fitting them snuggly next to one another. Brush the tops of the biscuits with the remaining 1 tablespoon buttermilk. Bake for 12 to 16 minutes. Serve warm with the maple-cinnamon butter.

Easy Gingerbread Cookies FAN FAVORITE

Gingerbread cookies are as synonymous with Christmas as Santa Claus. They are typically rolled and cut with cookie cutters, but my version calls for a bit of a shortcut. Roll the dough into balls and dip them in sugar before baking. The hardest part is putting them aside and not eating them warm from the oven. I've been baking these gingerbread cookies with my niece and nephew on Christmas Eve since they were toddlers. Now that they're older, baking these comforting, gingery cookies is a family tradition we still look forward to every year.

Makes 40 to 42 cookies

2½ cups all-purpose flour

1 teaspoon baking soda

1¾ teaspoons ground ginger

½ teaspoon ground cinnamon

¼ teaspoon ground cloves

8 tablespoons (1 stick) unsalted butter, softened

1 cup sugar, plus more for rolling the dough in

1 large egg

¼ cup molasses

1 teaspoon fresh lemon juice

Preheat the oven to 325°F. Line two baking sheets with parchment paper.

Sift the flour, baking soda, ginger, cinnamon, and cloves into a bowl.

Combine the butter and sugar in the bowl of a standing mixer and beat until creamy and light. Add the egg, molasses, and lemon juice. Mix to combine. Add the flour mixture and mix on low speed until a soft dough forms. Be careful not to overmix.

Shape the dough into 1-inch balls. Roll the balls in sugar and place them 2 inches apart on the prepared baking sheets. Bake for 18 to 20 minutes, until the cookies are just firm to the touch. Transfer the cookies to wire racks to cool.

Variation: To make cut-out gingerbread cookies, use ½ teaspoon baking soda, 6 tablespoons (¾ stick) unsalted butter, 1¼ cups sugar, and ¼ cup plus 1 tablespoon molasses. Prepare the dough as directed and chill for 2 hours. Roll out on a floured surface to a ¼-inch thickness, cut with a cookie cutter, and bake the cookies at 350°F for 12 to 15 minutes.

Chocolate Sugar Cookies

Sugar cookies are a classic Christmas tradition. But why not take a little creative license and make chocolate sugar cookies? This soft, chocolaty, sugary dough is given a double dose of flavor with the addition of chocolate chunks. Oh, be sure to leave several of these cookies and a cup of hot cocoa for Santa and his reindeer.

Makes 30 cookies

1¼ cups all-purpose flour

½ cup granulated sugar

½ cup (packed) light brown sugar

⅓ cup unsweetened cocoa powder

½ teaspoon baking soda

¼ teaspoon baking powder

¼ teaspoon table salt

8 tablespoons (1 stick) cold unsalted butter, cut into 5 pieces

1 large egg

1 large egg yolk

½ teaspoon pure vanilla extract

⅛ to ¼ cup ice water

1 11.5-ounce bag Nestlé Toll House Semi-Sweet Chocolate Chunks

2 tablespoons confectioners' sugar

Preheat the oven to 375°F. Line two baking sheets with parchment paper.

Combine the flour, granulated sugar, brown sugar, cocoa, baking soda, baking powder, and salt in a food processor and pulse just until mixed. Add the butter and pulse until the mixture resembles coarse meal. Add the egg, egg yolk, and vanilla. With the machine running, pour in the ice water, adding just enough water to help the dough come together. Remove the dough and shape it into a ball.

Pinch off a heaping tablespoon of dough and using your palms, roll it into a ball. Place the ball on a prepared baking sheet and continue with the remaining dough, placing the balls 1½ inches apart. Using your thumb, lightly press the center of each ball to make a slight indentation. Bake for 8 to 10 minutes. Remove the baking sheets from the oven to wire racks and gently push 4 or 5 chocolate chunks into the tops of each cookie. Let the cookies cool for 10 minutes. Using a spatula, transfer the cookies to the wire racks and let cool for 10 to 15 minutes. Dust the cookies with confectioners' sugar before serving.

Chocolate-Champagne Truffles FAN FAVORITE

Nothing says comfort like fine chocolate. And nothing says elegant like Champagne. When you combine them in these indulgent truffles, you get the creamiest, smoothest, most velvety candy you can imagine. End with these at a dinner party or a holiday meal, or give a box to someone special on birthdays or anniversaries.

Makes 32 truffles

10 ounces semisweet chocolate, coarsely chopped

¾ cup heavy cream

1 tablespoon sugar

⅛ cup Champagne

1 pound semisweet chocolate chips

Edible gold leaves (optional)

Line a baking sheet with parchment paper.

Place the chopped semisweet chocolate in a medium bowl. Set aside.

Combine the cream and sugar in a saucepan and bring the mixture to a boil over medium-high heat, stirring occasionally. Immediately pour the hot cream mixture over the chopped chocolate. Let it sit for 1 minute, then gently whisk until the chocolate has melted. Pour the Champagne into the chocolate mixture and whisk gently until incorporated. Cover with plastic wrap and refrigerate for 4 to 5 hours, or overnight.

Using a small ice cream scoop, scoop the chilled mixture into balls onto the prepared baking sheet. Refrigerate the truffles for 2 hours. Place all but ½ cup chocolate chips in a heat-safe bowl. Set aside.

Bring 3 to 4 cups water to a boil in a saucepan. Turn off the heat and place the bowl with the chocolate chips on top of the saucepan. Let it sit for 3 to 5 minutes. Lightly whisk the chocolate chips until melted. Remove the bowl from the saucepan, add the reserved ½ cup chocolate chips, and whisk until completely melted.

Dip the truffles into the melted chocolate and place them on a baking sheet lined with a new piece of parchment paper. Let the truffles sit until the chocolate has completely hardened. Serve immediately or cover and refrigerate for 2 days.

Peppermint Holiday Cake

As a little boy I loved peppermint candy canes. I remember how they turned my lips and tongue bright red. This festive holiday layer cake includes peppermint in every bite—peppermint extract in the batter, peppermint candies between the layers (be sure to grind them finely), and peppermint candy canes pressed into the frosting around the cake. The whole package is tied with a ribbon. To save time during the busy holiday season, I use a cake mix and white chocolate pudding mix. Cool Whip is used on this peppermint cake, but if you prefer real whipped cream, then by all means, go right ahead.

The possibilities for decorating this cake are endless. You can stencil stars on top with decorating sugar, arrange marzipan holly leaves and berries around the cake, or use red and green gumdrops. No matter how you dress up this cake, it's a gorgeous addition to any holiday table.

Makes 12 servings

Vegetable oil spray

Cake

1 18.25-ounce box white cake mix

1 3.6-ounce box white chocolate pudding mix

⅓ cup canola oil

1 cup whole milk

4 large eggs, at room temperature

¼ teaspoon peppermint extract

Frosting

1 11.5-ounce container whipped cream cheese

2 cups confectioners' sugar

1 to 2 drops peppermint extract

12 ounces Cool Whip whipped topping

Finely ground candy canes or Andes Peppermint Crunch Baking Chips

30 to 40 candy canes

1 24- to 30-inch piece red ribbon

Preheat the oven to 325°F. Spray two 9-inch round cake pans with vegetable oil spray and lightly flour the pans.

To make the cake, whisk together the cake mix and pudding mix in the bowl of a standing mixer with the paddle attachment until well blended. Add the canola oil, milk, eggs, and peppermint extract. Starting at low speed, mix for 20 to 30 seconds, until the ingredients are just blended together. Stop the machine and, using a spatula, scrape down the sides of the bowl, then raise the speed to medium and mix for 2 minutes, or until well blended. Do not overmix the batter. Evenly divide the batter between the cake pans. Bake for 30 to 40 minutes, until a cake tester inserted into both layers comes out clean. Remove from the oven and let cool in the pans on a wire rack for 10 to 15 minutes. Turn the layers out onto a wire rack and let cool completely before frosting.

To make the frosting, put the cream cheese, confectioners' sugar, and peppermint extract in the bowl of a standing mixer with the whisk attachment. Starting at low speed, mix for 1 minute. Stop the machine and use a spatula to scrape down the sides of the bowl. Raise the speed to medium-high and mix until the frosting is smooth and creamy, 1 to 2 minutes. Using a spatula, gently fold in the whipped topping. Cover and refrigerate the frosting while the cake is baking and cooling.

To decorate the cake, place one layer on a cake stand and frost the top of the cake. Sprinkle the crushed candy canes over the frosting. Top with the second layer and frost the top and sides of the cake. *(Refrigerate the cake for up to 2 days.)* One or two hours before serving, gently press the candy canes into the frosting on the sides of the cake. Tie the ribbon around the cake, but be sure to remove it before slicing.

Acknowledgments

Much gratitude goes to my family, especially my mother, Sarah. You continue to encourage me to dream big dreams and cook wonderful food. You are a special treasure in my life.

My close friends and loved ones, you are the family I have chosen for myself: Jimmy D'Angelo—your support, compassion, and encouragement is a priceless gift to me. Thanks so much. Cosmo, Dewey, Mr. Raleighs, Tara, Gail, Ed, John, Kevin, Doreen, Cheryl, Michael, Lenny, Mary Beth, Jill, Jane (Honey), and Will.

My *In the Kitchen with David* team, Jonathan Dowdell, Mary DeAngelis, Lori Leone, Amy Lucas, Wes Weisser, Tovi T. Taylor, Jennifer Leonard, Heather Leff, Tara Cahill, Kaitlin Lord, Colleen Duffey, Gabe Steiner, Mariann Shumbo, Beth Mann, Barbara Eckenrode, John Soppick, and Rachel Knorr, our show and this book are both possible because of each of you.

Nancy Swisher, you are always there for me—keeping me on schedule, organizing my work-life, and always quick with a hug and a smile. I adore you.

My cookbook project manager, Priscilla Millard, you made this effort work from beginning to end. What a blessing to have you on this journey.

Harriet Bell, my friend and my wordsmith, we have formed an unshakeable bond and I am better because I know you!

Photographer Ben Fink, your amazing talent to see what others don't brings my food to life.

Many thanks to my editor and friend Pam Cannon. You and your team at Ballantine Books have made this project a truly wonderful experience.

To culinary team leader Ruth Herdan, you have an unmatched ability to read my culinary mind and make magic in the kitchen. Additional thanks go to the other members of our culinary team: Andrea Schwob, Stephen Delaney, Lynn Willis, Scott Hebert, John Burwell, Michele Pilone, Jess Amandola, Kerry Matner, John Wolferth, Harley Blaisdell, and Sarah Zeller-Anello.

To Peter Browne and Joe Pascavage, my creative team, you both brought such talent and joy to this project. Your vision for this book shines on every page.

To Maria McCool, Kim Green, and Toi Sweeney, thanks for making my wardrobe come together so perfectly.

To Adrienne Bearden, thanks for your makeup wizardry. You are my angel.

To our production team and kitchen staff: John Thalheimer, Sherry Soldan, Laura Glas, James Davignon, Timothy Kimmel, and Paula Bower; you all made this project run without a hitch.

To Noreen and David Geibel and Kathleen and Bill Penney, thank you for allowing us to use your beautiful homes as a backdrop for our cookbook photos.

To our QVC management team: Mike George, Claire Watts, Doug Rose, Mary Campbell, Karen Fonner, Jack Comstock, Ken O'Brien, Michelle Barbacane, Sue Atherholt, Heather McNicholl, and Tara Hunter; your support is invaluable to me.

To our QVC cookbook buying team: Christina Pennypacker and Andrea Alfonso; it is a true joy to partner with you and to share our mutual love of cookbooks with Foodies everywhere.

To Ree Drummond, for your friendship and support. Thank you for writing the foreword to my book. We are culinary kindred spirits!

Finally, to all the Foodies who watch *In the Kitchen with David* each week. You are the reason I do what I do at QVC. Your excitement for our show is contagious and keeps me motivated and inspired every day!

Index

almond(s):
    Butter Almond Ice Cream, 281
    Green Beans with Almonds and Dried
        Cherries, 280
Angel Food Cake with Berries, 216–217
appetizers, 3–30
    Bacon Cheese Straws, 8–10
    Beef and Bean Tostadas, 27–28
    Buffalo Chicken Dip, 4
    Chicken Cheesesteak Egg Rolls, 20–21
    Coconut Shrimp with Spicy Mango
        Dipping Sauce, 22–24
    French Onion Soup Dumplings, 17–19
    Garlic-Curry Hummus and Sweet Potato
        Chips, 7
    Mac 'n' Cheese Bites, 12–14
    Mini Crab Cakes with Old Bay Mayonnaise,
        25–26
    Potato Pierogies with Sour Cream–Chive
        Sauce, 15–16
    Sausage Party Bites with Mustard Sauce, 30
    Smoked Salmon Crostini with Avocado
        Cream, 29
    Spinach-Feta Cups, 11
    Warm Bacon–Cheese Dip, 5–6
Apple Butter, Dutch Baby with, 38–39
apple(s):
    Apple-Cinnamon Muffins with Caramel
        Sauce, 59–60
    Apple, Gorgonzola, Red Onion, and
        Candied Walnut Salad with Pomegranate
        Vinaigrette, 240–242
    Apple, Pear, and Fig Chutney, 130
    Apple-Walnut Rustic Tart, 270–273

Brunch Panini with Apple-Cranberry
    Chutney, 50–51
Dutch Baby with Apple Butter, 38–39
Hot Apple Cider Cocktail, 285
Pork Chops with Sauerkraut, Apples, and
    Potatoes, 128
apricot(s):
    Sarah's Apricot Cake, 280
Artichokes, Stuffed, 225
Asiago Croutons, 111
Asian Pulled Pork, 98–99
asparagus:
    Bacon-Wrapped Asparagus Bundles, 156
avocado:
    Avocado Cream, Smoked Salmon Crostini
        with, 29
    Avocado Salsa, Steak Tacos with Chipotle
        Slaw and, 189–191

bacon:
    Wrapped Asparagus Bundles, 156
    Breakfast Poppers with Grits and Bacon,
        62–63
    Cheese Straws, 8–10
    Collard Greens with Bacon and Vinegar,
        230
    defined, 43
    Smoked Gouda, Bacon, and Pea Risotto,
        86–87
    Spiced Bacon Skewers, 42–43
    Warm Bacon–Cheese Dip, 5–6
Baked Perciatelli with Mini Meatballs, 162–163
Baked Shrimp and Feta, 183
Baked Vegetable Gratin, 232–234

About the Author

DAVID VENABLE, QVC's Resident Foodie, joined the network as a program host in 1993 and has since helped establish and build the multimedia retailer's gourmet food business. His hit show, *In the Kitchen with David,*® offers a unique interactive viewership experience and features the latest in gourmet foods, cookware, and kitchen gadgets. Since the launch of his first cookbook, Venable has appeared on national broadcast programs including *Today, The Chew,* and *The Rachael Ray Show,* among others. His recipes have appeared in *People, The Huffington Post,* and many other publications nationwide. Venable regularly blogs with his "foodies" on QVC.com and connects with them on Facebook, Twitter, Pinterest, and Instagram. Prior to joining QVC, Venable was an anchor/reporter for WOAY-TV in Oak Hill, West Virginia, and CBS affiliate WTAJ-TV in Altoona, Pennsylvania. He earned his bachelor's degree from the University of North Carolina, Chapel Hill, and currently lives in Pennsylvania.

Facebook.com/DavidVenableQVC

@DavidVenableQVC

About the Type

This book was set in Archer, a slab serif digital typeface designed in 2001 by Hoefler & Frere-Johns. The face is unique for combining the geometric structure of twentieth-century European slab-serifs but imbuing the face with a domestic, liess strident tone of voice.